Reagan and Thatcher's Special Relationship

Edinburgh Studies in Anglo-American Relations

Series Editors: Steve Marsh and Alan P. Dobson

Published and forthcoming titles

The Anglo-American Relationship
Steve Marsh and Alan P. Dobson

The Arsenal of Democracy: Aircraft Supply and the Anglo-American Alliance, 1938–1942
Gavin J. Bailey

Post-War Planning on the Periphery: Anglo-American Economic Diplomacy in South America, 1939–1945
Thomas C. Mills

Best Friends, Former Enemies: The Anglo-American Special Relationship and German Reunification
Luca Ratti

Reagan and Thatcher's Special Relationship: Latin America and Anglo-American Relations
Sally-Ann Treharne

Tacit Alliance: Franklin Roosevelt and the Anglo-American 'Special Relationship' before Churchill, 1933–1940
Tony McCulloch

The Politics of Diplomacy: U.S. Presidents and the Northern Ireland Conflict, 1967–1998
James Cooper

Jimmy Carter and the Anglo-American 'Special Relationship'
Thomas K. Robb

The Congo Crisis: Anglo-American Relations and the United Nations, 1960–1964
Alanna O'Malley

www.euppublishing.com/series/esar

Reagan and Thatcher's Special Relationship

Latin America and Anglo-American Relations

Sally-Ann Treharne

EDINBURGH
University Press

© Sally-Ann Treharne, 2015, 2026
Photos are reproduced courtesy Ronald Reagan Library

Edinburgh University Press Ltd
13 Infirmary Street, Edinburgh, EH1 1LT
www.euppublishing.com

First published in hardback by Edinburgh University Press 2015

Typeset in 11/14 Sabon by
Servis Filmsetting Ltd, Stockport, Cheshire

A CIP record for this book is available from the British Library

ISBN 978 0 7486 8606 3 (hardback)
ISBN 978 1 3995 7076 3 (paperback)
ISBN 978 0 7486 8607 0 (webready PDF)
ISBN 978 0 7486 8609 4 (epub)

The right of Sally-Ann Treharne to be identified as author of this work has
been asserted in accordance with the Copyright, Designs and Patents Act 1988
and the Copyright and Related Rights Regulations 2003 (SI No. 2498).

Contents

Figures

Acknowledgements

There are a number of people who are owed obvious debts of gratitude for their help in making this book possible. I would like to thank the interviewees who so generously gave their time to speak with me on all aspects of the Reagan–Thatcher relationship. Sincere thanks to Lords Geoffrey Howe, Michael Heseltine, Peter Carrington, Neil Kinnock, Charles Powell, Cecil Parkinson and Timothy Bell; Sirs Bernard Ingham, John Nott and Adrian Beamish; and Baroness Gloria Hooper. Thanks are also due to the personal assistants who juggled hectic House of Lords schedules on a number of occasions to accommodate me. I am indebted to Dr Mervyn O'Driscoll in University College Cork (UCC), who, as my mentor during my PhD and beyond, has consistently provided invaluable advice, constructive criticism and encouragement. His insightful comments have greatly improved this work. I would like to thank my PhD examiners, Professors David Ryan and John Dumbrell, for their valued suggestions on how to improve upon my original doctoral dissertation. Many thanks also to the School of History, UCC, which provided much appreciated encouragement and funding through various travel grants that enabled me to undertake important research trips to the US and the UK throughout the PhD process. The Irish Research Council deserves particular thanks for the financial support I received as an Irish Research Council Government of Ireland Postdoctoral Fellow in UCC. This funding allowed me to conduct additional research trips to gain access to the most recently released declassified documents in the US and the UK. I would like to thank the staff in the Ronald Reagan Presidential Library in Simi Valley, California, for their help during my research visits, in particular, senior archivist, Shelly Williams. Andrew Riley, curator of the Thatcher Papers in the Churchill Archives Centre, Cambridge, deserves particular thanks for his time and help during my trips to the archives. Thanks also to Christopher Collins in the Margaret Thatcher Foundation. The foundation is an invaluable resource to students and those interested in contemporary British history. I am also grateful to the staff in the National Archives in Kew, Surrey, for their assistance during my visits there. In addition, I would like to thank the staff at Edinburgh University Press for their help and guidance during the writing process, in particular, Dr Steve Marsh, Professor Alan P. Dobson, Nicola Ramsey and Michelle Houston. A special word of thanks is due to those who took the time to read draft chapters and offer their thoughts on how to strengthen the book, in particular, Jocelyn Treharne. The completion of this book owes much of its credit to my family, whose unwavering support and encouragement has helped me in innumerable ways during the last few years. Finally, my greatest debt of gratitude is to my husband, Kennedy Stevens, and my mother, Sally Treharne. It is with heartfelt appreciation that I dedicate this book to them.

Acronyms and Abbreviations

BDF	Belize Defence Force
CAB	Cabinet Office Records (TNA)
CADC	Central American Defence Council
CAP	Common Agricultural Policy
CARICOM	Caribbean Community
CBERA	Caribbean Basin Economic Recovery Act
CBI	Caribbean Basin Initiative
CC	Central Committee
CIA	Central Intelligence Agency
CINCLANT	Commander in Chief Atlantic
Cmnd.	Command Paper
CND	Campaign for Nuclear Disarmament
CO	Country File (RL)
CPPG	Crisis Pre-Planning Group
CSC	Chile Solidarity Campaign
CTBT	Comprehensive Test Ban Treaty
DEFE	Ministry of Defence Records (TNA)
DOD	Department of Defense
DOP	Defence and Overseas Policy Committee
EEC	European Economic Community
EGP	Ejército Guerrillero de los Pobres (Guerrilla Army of the Poor, Guatemala)
EMU	European Monetary Union
EPS	Ejército Popular Sandinista (Sandinista People's Army, Nicaragua)
ERDF	European Regional Development Fund
ESAC	Ejército Secreto Anti-Comunista (Secret Anti-Communist Army, Guatemala)

FAO	Frente Amplio de Oposición (Broad Opposition Front, Nicaragua)
FAR	Fuerzas Armadas Rebeldes (Rebel Armed Forces, Guatemala)
FCO	Foreign and Commonwealth Office and/or Foreign and Commonwealth Office and predecessors records (TNA)
FDN	Fuerza Democrática Nicaragüense (Nicaraguan Democratic Force)
FMLN	Frente Farabundo Martí para la Liberación Nacional (National Liberation Front, El Salvador)
FMS	Foreign Military Sales
FO	records created and inherited by the Foreign Office (TNA)
FSLN	Frente Sandinista de Liberación Nacional (Sandinista National Liberation Front, Nicaragua)
FY	fiscal year
GCHQ	Government Communications Headquarters
GOB	Government of Belize
GOG	Government of Guatemala
GRN	Junta del Gobierno de Reconstrucción Nacional (Provisional Government of National Reconstruction, Nicaragua)
HCPP	House of Commons Parliamentary Papers
HMG	Her Majesty's Government
HMNZS	Her Majesty's New Zealand Ship
HMSO	Her Majesty's Stationery Office
ICJ	International Court of Justice
IMF	International Monetary Fund
ITT	International Telephone and Telegraph Corporation
JCS	Joint Chiefs of Staff
JIC	Joint Intelligence Committee
KMS	Keenie Meenie Services
MDN	Movimiento Democrático Nicaragüense (Nicaraguan Democratic Movement)
Memcon.	memorandum of conversation
MEP	Member of the European Parliament

MI5	British Security Service
MI6	British Secret Intelligence Service
MLN	Movimiento de Liberación Nacional (National Liberation Movement, Guatemala)
MNF	multinational force
MOD	Ministry of Defence
MOU	memorandum of understanding
MP	Member of Parliament
MPU	Movimiento Pueblo Unido (United People's Movement, Nicaragua)
NARA	National Archives and Records Administration
NATO	North Atlantic Treaty Organisation
NBCCA	National Bipartisan Commission on Central America
NEO	non-combatant evacuation operation
NGO	non-governmental organisation
NJM	New Jewel Movement (Grenada)
NSA	National Security Agency
NSC	National Security Council
NSDD	National Security Decision Directive
NSDM	National Security Decision Memorandum
NSPG	National Security Planning Group
OAS	Organisation of American States
OD	Cabinet Defence and Overseas Policy Committee and/or records created or inherited by the Department of Technical Cooperation and of successive Overseas Development Bodies (TNA)
ODSA	South Atlantic sub-committee of the Overseas and Defence Policy Committee of the Cabinet
OECS	Organisation of Eastern Caribbean States
OPEC	Organisation of Petroleum Exporting Countries
ORPA	Organización Revolucionaria del Pueblo en Armas (Revolutionary Organisation of the People in Arms, Guatemala)
PACs	Patrullas de Autodefensa Civil (Civilian Self-Defence Patrols, Guatemala)
PLO	Palestine Liberation Organisation
PM	Prime Minister

PREM	Prime Minister's Office records (TNA)
PRG	People's Revolutionary Government (Grenada)
PUP	People's United Party (Belize)
RAF	Royal Air Force
RIG	Restricted Interagency Group
RL	Ronald Reagan Presidential Library
RMC	Revolutionary Military Council (Grenada)
RR	Ronald Reagan
RSS	Regional Security System
SALT	Strategic Arms Limitation Talks
SAS	Special Air Service
SIGINT	signal and satellite intelligence
Sitrep.	Situation report
SLBM	submarine-launched ballistic missile
Telno.	telegram number
TESONs	troops trained in jungle and night-time operations
THCR	Baroness Thatcher papers
TNA	the National Archives (UK)
TOW	tube-launched, optically tracked, wire-guided, antitank missiles
UDEL	Unión Democrática de Liberación (Democratic Union of Liberation, Nicaragua)
UN	United Nations
UNGA	United Nations General Assembly
UNSC	United Nations Security Council
UNSCR	United Nations Security Council Resolution
UP	Unidad Popular (Popular Party, Chile)
UPITN	United Press International Television News
URNG	Unidad Revolucionaria Nacional Guatemalteca (Guatemalan National Revolutionary Unit)
USG	United States Government
USSR	Union of Soviet Socialist Republics
WHORM	White House Office of Records Management Files (RL)

Introduction

Individuals and relations between leaders play a role in international politics. The broadly parallel leaderships of President Ronald W. Reagan and Prime Minister Margaret Thatcher saw a revival of the Anglo-American 'Special Relationship' in the 1980s. The quality and intensity of their personal rapport is frequently assumed to have played a role in this. Deepening Cold War tensions and a strong anti-communist rhetoric also played important roles in drawing the two leaders closer. A commonality of many critical interests, along with cultural, linguistic, political and filial ties, underpinned their growing attachment and friendship. In addition, pre-existing intelligence cooperation, defence and nuclear interdependence (most would say British dependence on the US) helped to forge strong links between both countries.[1] The closeness of the Anglo-American relationship during the period and its apparent personification in the rapport between the two leaders approached only the quality and intensity of the relationships seen between Churchill and Roosevelt, Macmillan and Eisenhower, and Macmillan and Kennedy.[2] As always, since the Second World War, a wide asymmetry in objective power characterised the Anglo-American pairing. Indeed, the imbalance by the 1980s was cavernous by comparison to earlier decades. Like their predecessors, Reagan and Thatcher faced powerful critics of the Special Relationship within their governments and societies.

The pair first met on 9 April 1975 when Reagan was in London to address the Pilgrim Society at the Savoy Hotel. Having recently retired as Governor of California, Reagan had set his sights firmly on the 1976 US Republican presidential nomination, and he was keen to establish close political ties in Britain. Reagan was refused a meeting with the then Labour Prime Minister Harold Wilson and was therefore keen to meet with the recently elected Leader of the Opposition Margaret Thatcher. Thatcher, too, was eager to meet Reagan, a man of whom her husband Denis had spoken highly following an address Reagan had given to the Institute of Directors in London a few years earlier in 1969. Denis is said to have forecast to his wife that Reagan would 'go a long way'.[3] Thatcher read the speech with interest, and was inspired to read many of his subsequent speeches and fortnightly addresses to the people of California which were sent to her by Reagan's Press Secretary. In fact, she 'agreed with them all'.[4] A clearly enthusiastic Thatcher finally met with Reagan in her rooms in the House of Commons in 1975, and the pair immediately found that they had a strong political and personal rapport. The meeting was a resounding success and went well beyond the forty-five minutes allocated; it lasted an hour and a half. Thatcher later wrote of that meeting: 'I was immediately won over by his charm, sense of humour and directness.'[5] Reagan, too, was seemingly captivated by Thatcher: 'I liked her immediately – she was warm, feminine, gracious, and intelligent.'[6] Reagan wrote to Thatcher shortly after their first meeting: 'please know that you have an enthusiastic supporter out here in the "colonies"'.[7] The pair met again in London in November 1978 and, despite Reagan having lost the 1976 Republican nomination, Thatcher was delighted to meet with the charismatic and engaging future contender for the 1980 presidential race. Both spoke animatedly about a host of issues, including their foreign policy interests. Reagan's foreign policy adviser and future National Security Advisor Richard V. Allen, who accompanied him on the meeting, later recalled that this meeting started a 'beautiful intellectual romance'.[8] These meetings marked the beginning of the close personal relationship that was to become the linchpin of Anglo-American relations throughout the 1980s.

Following the gradual retreat of the US from international affairs after the Vietnam War and the ongoing decline of British influence in line with Britain's withdrawal 'east of Suez' in the 1970s, both leaders recognised the importance of possessing an influential transatlantic ally.[9] Such an ally, it was hoped, would champion one another's ideals in the international community, and would also lend credibility to two leaders who perhaps were considered as eccentricities. Thatcher was the first female Prime Minister of the UK and Reagan was a former actor turned President.[10] The Reagan administration gravitated towards Britain, a country with whom the US had had a long-standing relationship, particularly since the Second World War. Indeed, a strong European ally was of signal importance during a period of renewed European integration and development. Thatcher's developing image as the so-called 'Iron Lady' was greatly admired by Reagan and he was happy to have such a staunch ally.[11] For her part, the Prime Minister was predisposed to the President based upon their previous meetings, and she was keen to cultivate improved Anglo-American relations. A strong US ally would help her to counter domestic and international critics, particularly those in Europe who despaired of an uncompromising Prime Minister (Thatcher was, at the time, embroiled in a bitter dispute over British contributions to the European Economic Community (EEC) budget).[12]

Thatcher had been in power for over a year when it was announced that Reagan had won the US presidential election on 4 November 1980.[13] She was determined to be the first major foreign leader to visit the new President. This would help her to develop close bilateral ties and fortify her status at home, in the US and in the wider international community. Thus, Britain's Ambassador to the US, Nicholas Henderson, was assigned the task of soliciting an invitation for a prime ministerial visit to Washington. In early December, Henderson approached Reagan's then campaign Chief of Staff, and soon to be Counsellor to the President, Edwin 'Ed' Meese III, regarding a visit by Thatcher following Reagan's inauguration on 21 January 1981. Meese enthusiastically supported the idea and an invitation was issued to Thatcher shortly afterwards.[14] Thatcher was overjoyed and capitalised on her good fortune by laying the groundwork for closer Anglo-American relations. She was quick to congratulate her friend on the day of his inauguration. In a letter to Reagan that was to mark the beginning of their voluminous correspondence throughout their terms in office and beyond Thatcher wrote:

> Your inauguration is a symbol of hope for the Alliance and you can depend on our confidence and support as we work together to meet the challenges of the 1980s. I look forward to renewing our friendship when we meet in Washington next month, and to consolidating the close relationship between our two countries.[15]

The pair spoke warmly on the telephone the following day, with the President stating: 'I look forward to working with you now and maintaining and emphasising this relationship that we have between our two countries.' To which Thatcher responded: 'That is very kind of you and we are looking forward to it too. Indeed, I think somehow the whole of Britain is. You know they recognise that we have to keep absolutely close together.'[16] Reagan developed his leitmotif of a Special Relationship between the US and the UK in his letter to Thatcher on 2 February:

> we share a very special concern for democracy and liberty. That is the essence of the special relationship between our two countries, and it is similarly an excellent basis for inaugurating an extended period of cooperation and close consultation between your government and my administration.[17]

Thatcher's much anticipated visit to Washington from 26 to 28 February was greeted with great ceremony and press coverage in the US and the UK. The Special Relationship was on show for all to see. Upon her arrival on the White House south lawn, Thatcher's commitment to the Anglo-American alliance was manifest as she stated: 'The message that I have brought across the Atlantic, is that we in Britain stand with you. America's successes will be our successes. Your problems will be our problems, and when you look for friends we will be there.'[18] In a State Dinner toast honouring the Prime Minister on 26 February, Reagan waxed lyrical about his friend: 'it's widely known that I share many of your ideals and beliefs . . . My admiration for you was reinforced during today's productive meeting. I believe, however, that our relationship goes beyond cordiality and shared ideals.'[19] Thatcher was accompanied on the visit by her husband and her daughter, Carol, which helped to consolidate a more intimate and friendly

Figure 1 Thatcher's first visit. The President and Prime Minister on the South Lawn during her arrival ceremony, 26 February 1981

relationship between the two leaders and their respective families. The visit was a personal and political success for both leaders, and the Reagan administration saw it as transcending the 'traditional context of US–UK bilateral relations'.[20] In its aftermath, written correspondence became more informal in nature as they referred to each other as 'Ron' and 'Margaret'. The Prime Minister preferred to use 'Yours ever, Margaret' when ending her letters to Reagan, whereas the President preferred 'Warm regards, Ron'. This type of warmth was rarely, if ever, displayed in Reagan's and Thatcher's correspondence with other world leaders during their terms in office. The pair found that they enjoyed a comfortable friendship, which would allow them to pursue the bonds of close personal and political diplomacy.

Figure 2 Walking along the cross hall at the White House State Dinner with Nancy Reagan and Denis Thatcher, 26 February 1981

Following this visit, the Special Relationship became an integral component of both leaders' wider international foreign policy objectives. In the UK, the importance of this relationship was evident among the inner circle of the Thatcher Cabinet and among her close friends and confidants. The Prime Minister's former Private Secretary Charles Powell describes the relationship as 'a marriage made in heaven . . . both clicked from the very beginning and were thus delighted when they found themselves in office coterminously'.[21] Powell suggests that the relationship was 'very close, personal and ideological', and that it 'has not really been repeated since. It was unique.' He believes that the Prime Minister's 'number one objective was a strong relationship with the United States. She believed profoundly that was what British foreign policy should be based on.'[22]

Thatcher's former Chief Press Secretary Bernard Ingham suggests that they were 'political soul mates', but argues that the relationship was subject to Thatcher's 'spartan view of friendship' based upon the view that: 'She saw her role as giving support, but on the basis of the frankest rapport.' Ingham also speaks of a loyalty between both leaders: 'The relationship was defined by a close unity of political philosophy, Margaret Thatcher's fierce integrity and reliability as an ally and Ronald Reagan's recognition of her candid alliance.' He believes that the Special Relationship was significant:

> not merely for personal reasons but also for her policy success and her standing in the world, not merely in the USA. I believe it was of substantial strategic benefit to the UK . . . I think Reagan found considerable benefit for the USA in having in this somewhat turbulent woman such a thinking, straight ally.[23]

Thatcher's former Chancellor of the Exchequer and Secretary of State for Foreign and Commonwealth Affairs (later Deputy Prime Minister) Geoffrey Howe recalls that Thatcher 'never pulled her punches' when dealing with Reagan, but he acknowledges some reticence by the Prime Minister when dealing with her American counterpart: 'She never wanted to stray overboard. She never thought that she was commanding officer. She was just as persuasive as she could be. And the fact that it was a personal relationship between the two of them . . . was very important.'[24] Former Chairman of the Conservative Party and Secretary of State for Trade and Industry Cecil Parkinson, presents a slightly different picture of the dynamics of the Reagan–Thatcher relationship, as he argues that Thatcher 'never saw herself as a sort of cheerleader' for Reagan.[25] The UK's former Secretary of State for Trade and Industry and Secretary of State for Defence John Nott, suggests that the Special Relationship was 'of great benefit to us [the UK]. More importantly, I think that personal relationship was of critical importance to the ending of the Cold War.'[26]

However, not all of the expanding and rich literature on Anglo-American relations during the 1980s holds similar views regarding the concept of a Special Relationship between Thatcher and Reagan. While some argue that there was a distinct personal rapport between the two leaders, others believe this to be a popular myth. For example, Geoffrey Smith is unequivocal in his estimation of a close friendship between the pair that helped to ease subsequent dealings between them. So, too, is Robert M. Hendershot, who refers to an 'iconic' friendship between both leaders. Kathleen Burk suggests that the pair had a 'great personal affection for each other'.[27] According to Christopher Hitchens, however, the Reagan–Thatcher relationship was 'clientelistic', whereas Richard Aldous suggests that Thatcher's ability to keep the Anglo-American relationship on an even keel in the 1980s was to a significant degree institutional, not personal. He contends that it was a testament to the strength of the pre-existing Atlantic Alliance.[28] Others point to both leaders', in particular Thatcher's, foreign policy motivations as a guiding force in cultivating close bilateral relations at the time. As David Reynolds suggests, for Thatcher, the Special Relationship was the 'axiom' of foreign policy.[29] More generally, aspects of their economic and political relationship have been explored in a host of memoirs and biographies.[30] In fact, emphasis is often placed on the similarity of both leaders' economic views and their methods of policy-making, referred to as Thatcherism and Reaganomics. Their respective roles in the nuclear arms environment and the East–West Cold War are also the subject of extensive academic debate.[31] While all these are important considerations when examining the Reagan–Thatcher relationship, much remains to be done with regard to the role of personal diplomacy in the cultivation of improved bilateral relations in the 1980s. By untangling some of the personal diplomacy between Thatcher and Reagan, this book will provide a new perspective on Anglo-American relations. By examining the evolution of such diplomacy over this period of time, it will demonstrate that the Special Relationship between both leaders frequently helped to overcome obstacles which threatened to overwhelm a reinvigoration of close bilateral ties. To a significant degree, this book will show how these obstacles ultimately strengthened the political and personal bond between two contentious figures in contemporary history.

Moreover, there is little written on the effects of the Latin American region upon the development of Anglo-American relations during the 1980s.[32] There has been a relative neglect of the region as a factor in the Reagan–Thatcher relationship. This book will argue that the Special Relationship was unequivocally manifest in Latin American affairs during this time. The region certainly caused episodes of tension and mistrust between both leaders and their respective governments. But, more importantly, it highlighted an ongoing commitment to a renewal in close Anglo-American relations by Reagan and Thatcher. This broaches the central rationale for this book: it seeks to redress significantly this neglect by looking at the case studies of the Falklands War, the US invasion of Grenada, the Anglo-Guatemalan dispute over Belize and US involvement in Nicaragua.

By and large, there was an asymmetry of interests between the US and the UK in Latin America. This was an area of sizeable importance to the domestic and foreign policy objectives of the Reagan administration, where the US sought to roll-back the perceived communist threat in a region that it saw as its own 'back yard'. This involvement was justified under the auspices of what later became known as the Reagan Doctrine.[33] In order to deter the Soviet Union and Cuba from gaining a foothold in this politically fragile region, the US was, at times, prepared to embark on unilateral action that was often of dubious legality and covert in its nature. This action sometimes clashed with its supposed commitment to the Anglo-American relationship. In contrast, the UK wanted to distance itself from the region by promoting decolonisation and self-government whilst simultaneously maintaining a strong influence upon its former imperial conquests. These differing foreign policy objectives threatened to test the Special Relationship as it operated under Reagan and Thatcher.

By examining these four specific case studies, this book will place the bilateral Anglo-American relationship in the context of both countries' individual interests in the Latin American region. Therefore, it will provide a regionally focused approach to the study of transatlantic relations under Reagan and Thatcher. And, by exploring how challenges emanating from the Latin American and South Atlantic region had potentially far-reaching negative consequences for the Special Relationship, it will reveal that the personal diplomacy of Reagan and Thatcher prevented and tempered disputes between their administrations from deleteriously affecting the wider Anglo-American relationship. In doing so, this book will provide a reappraisal of the much-debated role of the two leaders in the Special Relationship. It will redress the relative lack of historical insight and detail on the intergovernmental deliberations and consultation (at times, lack thereof) during the course of important Latin American crises.

This book draws much of its information from the extensive analysis of a wide variety of primary sources, including recently released government documents from British and American archives, namely, the Ronald Reagan Presidential Library (RL) in Simi Valley, California, and the UK National Archives (TNA) in Kew, Surrey.[34] Other sources of primary material have also been used, such as the Margaret Thatcher Foundation official website, the House of Commons Parliamentary Papers (HCPP) and the Churchill Archives Centre in Cambridge.[35] However, it is arguably the inclusion of excerpts from interviews that I conducted with key figures in British politics during the 1980s, members of the Foreign and Commonwealth Office (FCO) and close friends and confidants of Thatcher that allow this book to elucidate a strong British perspective on the importance of the Reagan–Thatcher Special Relationship. As such, this book does not purport to explicate corresponding American views on the relationship. In fact, the interview materials are intended to help explore the hitherto tightly guarded insights of key British protagonists with regard to the impact of these Latin American crises on Anglo-American relations. Moreover, they will reveal the enduring importance of the Reagan–Thatcher relationship in British circles across the political divide. These interviewees include the previously mentioned Lords Howe, Parkinson and Powell, and Sir Bernard Ingham and Sir John Nott. The book will also include excerpts from interviews with former Leader of the Opposition Lord Neil Kinnock; former Secretary of State for Foreign and Commonwealth Affairs Lord Peter Carrington; former Secretary of State for Defence Lord Michael Heseltine; former Government Whip in the House of Lords Baroness Gloria Hooper; former managing director of Saatchi & Saatchi Lord Timothy Bell; and former diplomat and head of the Falklands Department in the FCO Sir Adrian Beamish.[36]

In terms of structure, the book will briefly assess the temper of general Anglo-American relations and US–UK relations with

Latin America during the 1970s. This will help to frame the importance of the Reagan–Thatcher relationship (with an emphasis on the Latin American region) within a renewal in transatlantic ties during the last remaining years of the Cold War. It will subsequently assess the operation of the Special Relationship through the detailed examination of the four Latin American case studies in broad chronological order. This book will demonstrate that the fortitude of both leaders' commitment to reinvigorated and improved Anglo-American relations surmounted these obstacles and buttressed a political and personal relationship that has continued to catch the popular imagination.

Notes

1. The commonality of interests that underpinned the development of close Anglo-American relations are the subject of a large and growing literature across several disciplines, including history, political science and international relations theory. A sample of some of the major works include: Alex Danchev, *On Specialness: Essays in Anglo-American Relations* (Basingstoke: Macmillan, 1998); John Dumbrell, *A Special Relationship: Anglo-American Relations from the Cold War to Iraq*, 2nd edn (Basingstoke: Palgrave Macmillan, 2006); John Baylis (ed.), *Anglo-American Relations since 1939: The Enduring Alliance* (Manchester: Manchester University Press, 1997); Kathleen Burk, *Old World, New World: The Story of Britain and America* (London: Little, Brown, 2009); David Dimbleby and David Reynolds, *An Ocean Apart: The Relationship between Britain and America in the Twentieth Century* (New York: Vintage Books, 1989); Alan P. Dobson, *Anglo-American Relations in the Twentieth Century: Of Friendship, Conflict and the Rise and Decline of Superpowers* (London: Routledge, 1995); Alan P. Dobson, *The Politics of the Anglo-American Economic Special Relationship, 1940–1987* (Brighton: Wheatsheaf, 1988). Intelligence cooperation, along with military and nuclear interdependence, intrinsically linked the US and the UK from the postwar period onwards. This relationship was cultivated through the signature of many defence and nuclear agreements (some of which will be detailed in Chapter 1). This enabled the UK to secure its ongoing defence capabilities and to counter any potential Soviet aggression throughout the Cold

War period. It also provided the US with a valuable ally within the North Atlantic Treaty Organisation (NATO), and afforded it access to key British military bases. For more on the development of the Anglo-American intelligence and nuclear defence relationship from 1945 until the 1980s, see Dumbrell, *A Special Relationship*, pp. 160–83. More generally, see John Baylis, *Anglo-American Defence Relations, 1939–1984: The Special Relationship* (London: Macmillan, 1984); Steve Marsh, 'The Anglo-American defence relationship', in Alan P. Dobson and Steve Marsh (eds), *Anglo-American Relations: Contemporary Perspectives* (Abingdon: Routledge, 2013), pp. 179–206; Richard J. Aldrich, *GCHQ: The Uncensored Story of Britain's Most Secret Intelligence Agency* (London: HarperPress, 2010).

2. The personal diplomacy that existed under these leaders has been explored in many noteworthy works, including: David Reynolds, *From World War to Cold War: Churchill, Roosevelt and the International History of the 1940s* (Oxford: Oxford University Press, 2007); Klaus Larres, *Churchill's Cold War: The Politics of Personal Diplomacy* (New Haven, CT: Yale University Press, 2002); E. Bruce Geelhoed, *Eisenhower, Macmillan and Allied Unity, 1957–1961* (Basingstoke: Palgrave Macmillan, 2003); Nigel Ashton, *Kennedy, Macmillan and the Cold War: The Irony of Interdependence* (Basingstoke: Palgrave Macmillan, 2002); David Brandon Shields, *Kennedy and Macmillan: Cold War Politics* (Lanham, MD: University Press of America, 2006).

3. Margaret Thatcher, *The Path to Power* (London: HarperCollins, 1995), p. 372; interview with Bernard Ingham, 25 May 2010. Denis Thatcher would later refer to his wife's relationship with Reagan as a 'mutual admiration society'. See Carol Thatcher, *Below the Parapet: The Biography of Denis Thatcher* (Bath: Chivers Press, 1997), p. 338.

4. Thatcher, *Path to Power*, p. 372.

5. *Ibid.*, p. 372.

6. Ronald Reagan, *An American Life* (New York: Simon & Schuster, 1990), p. 204.

7. Churchill Archives Centre, the Papers of Baroness Thatcher (THCR), THCR 6/4/1/7, Reagan to Thatcher, 30 April 1975.

8. Transcript of interview with Richard V. Allen, 28 May 2002, p. 31, Ronald Reagan Oral History Project, the Miller Center, University of Virginia, available at: www.millercenter.org/president/reagan/oralhistory/richard-allen, accessed 13 December 2013.

9. In January 1968, Harold Wilson announced Britain's withdrawal from its military bases in the Persian Gulf or 'East of Suez'. The impact of this withdrawal is examined in Saki Dockrill, *Britain's Retreat from East of Suez: The Choice between Europe and the World? 1945–1968* (London: Palgrave Macmillan, 2002); William Roger Louis, *Ends of British Imperialism: The Scramble for Empire, Suez and Decolonization* (London: I. B. Tauris, 2006); Jeffrey Pickering, *Britain's Withdrawal from East of Suez: The Politics of Retrenchment* (New York: St. Martin's Press, 1998).
10. The argument that Reagan and Thatcher were drawn to each other as former political outcasts is often put forward when examining the origins of their relationship. Both future leaders were initially overlooked by their party as possible leaders of their respective countries. See Geoffrey Smith, *Reagan and Thatcher* (London: Bodley Head, 1990), p. 3.
11. This moniker was given to Thatcher by the Soviet *Red Star* magazine in 1976.
12. The view that Thatcher was motivated to build a strong relationship with the US in order to mitigate her isolation in Europe to some extent has also been put forward in Richard Aldous, *Reagan and Thatcher: The Difficult Relationship* (London: Hutchinson, 2012), p. 39. It has also been suggested that Thatcher's relationship with Reagan proved to be critical in raising her standing among world leaders at the time. See Anthony Seldon and Daniel Collings, *Britain under Thatcher* (Harlow: Longman, 2000), p. 73.
13. Reagan defeated the incumbent Democrat President Jimmy Carter in a landslide election, achieving 50.7 per cent of the popular vote and 489 electoral votes in comparison to Carter's 41 per cent of the popular vote and 49 electoral votes. The third independent presidential candidate, John B. Anderson, achieved a mere 6.6 per cent of the popular vote.
14. Nicholas Henderson, *Mandarin: The Diaries of Nicholas Henderson, 1969–1982* (London: Weidenfeld & Nicolson, 1994), p. 374.
15. Thatcher to Reagan, 20 January 1981, file: United Kingdom Prime Minister (PM) Thatcher Cables (1/4), box 34, Executive Secretariat National Security Council (NSC) Head of State File Records, Ronald Reagan Library.
16. Churchill Archives Centre, THCR 3/1/12 (1), file: 81/6–81/9, Memorandum of conversation (Memcon) of Reagan–Thatcher discussion, 21 January 1981.
17. Reagan to Thatcher, 2 February 1981, file: Thatcher Visit

(02/26/1981–02/28/1981) (3/4), box 90318, James M. Rentschler Files, Ronald Reagan Library.

18. Smith, *Reagan and Thatcher*, p. 46.
19. Reagan toast at state dinner, 26 February 1981, file: Country File (CO) 167 024000–024499, WHORM Subject Files, Ronald Reagan Library.
20. Allen to Reagan, n.d., file: Thatcher Visit (02/26/1981–02/28/1981) (4/4), box 90318, WHORM Subject Files, Ronald Reagan Library.
21. Interview with Charles Powell, 29 June 2010.
22. *Ibid.*
23. Interview with Bernard Ingham.
24. Interview with Geoffrey Howe, 13 December 2010.
25. Interview with Cecil Parkinson, 6 April 2011.
26. Interview with John Nott, 6 June 2011.
27. Smith, *Reagan and Thatcher*, p. 265; Robert M. Hendershot, '"Affection is the cement which binds us": understanding the cultural sinews of the Anglo-American special relationship', in Alan P. Dobson and Steve Marsh (eds), *Anglo-American Relations: Contemporary Perspectives* (Abingdon: Routledge, 2013), p. 71; Burk, *Old World, New World*, p. 630.
28. Christopher Hitchens, *Blood, Class and Empire: The Enduring Anglo-American Relationship*, 2nd edn (London: Atlantic Books, 2006), p. xxii; Aldous, *Reagan and Thatcher*, p. 7.
29. David Reynolds, 'Rethinking Anglo-American relations', *International Affairs*, 65(1) (Winter 1988–9): 89–111, at p. 89.
30. Some of the most notable include: Margaret Thatcher, *The Downing Street Years* (New York: HarperCollins, 1993); Charles Moore, *Margaret Thatcher: The Authorized Biography, vol. 1: Not For Turning* (London: Penguin, 2014); James Cooper, *Margaret Thatcher and Ronald Reagan: A Very Political Special Relationship* (Basingstoke: Palgrave Macmillan, 2012); Nicholas Wapshott, *Ronald Reagan and Margaret Thatcher: A Political Marriage* (New York: Sentinel, 2007); John Campbell, *Margaret Thatcher, vol. 2: The Iron Lady* (London: Jonathan Cape, 2003); Edmund Morris, *Dutch: A Memoir of Ronald Reagan* (New York: Modern Library, 1990); Jonathan Aiken, *Margaret Thatcher: Power and Personality* (London: Bloomsbury, 2013); Nile Gardiner and Stephen Thompson, *Margaret Thatcher on Leadership: Lessons for American Conservatives Today* (Washington, DC: Regnery Publishing, 2013); John Patrick Diggins, *Ronald Reagan: Fate, Freedom, and the Making of History* (New York: W. W. Norton, 2007).

31. For more on the similarities between Reagan's and Thatcher's economic policies, see Joel Krieger, *Reagan, Thatcher and the Politics of Decline* (Cambridge: Polity Press, 1986).

    Reaganomics, also known as supply-side economics, were the economic policies promoted by the Reagan administration. Reagan advocated four principal economic objectives, i.e.: to cut taxes; to reduce the size of the government; to control inflation; and to deregulate the economy in his 'Program for Economic Recovery'. For more on Reaganomics, see William A. Niskanen, *Reaganomics: An Insider's Account of the Policies and the People* (Oxford: Oxford University Press, 1988). Thatcherism is the term commonly used to refer to Thatcher's social and economic policies during her premiership. It is similar to Reaganomics in that it refers to supply-side economics, reductions in taxation and inflation. It also promoted the privatisation of public industry. For more on Thatcherism, see Dennis Kavanagh, *Thatcherism and British Politics: The End of Consensus?* (Oxford: Oxford University Press, 1987); Eric J. Evans, *Thatcher and Thatcherism*, 2nd edn (London: Routledge, 2004). For a useful discourse on both leaders' perceived role in ending the Cold War and their individual relationships with the Soviet premier, Mikhail Gorbachev, see Jack F. Matlock, Jr, *Reagan and Gorbachev: How the Cold War Ended* (New York: Random House, 2004); Mikhail Gorbachev, *Memoirs* (New York: Doubleday, 1996); John O'Sullivan, *The President, the Pope, and the Prime Minister: Three Who Changed the World* (Washington, DC: Regnery Publishing, 2006).

32. A noteworthy exception is Louise Richardson, *When Allies Differ: Anglo-American Relations during the Suez and Falklands Crises* (Basingstoke: Macmillan, 1996). William D. Rogers suggested that while it is relevant to inquire how the Special Relationship was manifest in Latin American affairs in the first five years of the Reagan presidency, the answer was 'not very'. See William D. Rogers, 'The "Unspecial Relationship" in Latin America', in William Roger Louis and Hedley Bull (eds), *The 'Special Relationship': Anglo-American Relations since 1945* (Oxford: Clarendon Press, 1986), p. 341. This book refutes Rogers' assertion. For various essays on the importance of the Latin American region to the Thatcher government and on the UK's support of the US in the region, see Latin America Bureau, *The Thatcher Years: Britain and Latin America* (London: Latin America Bureau, 1988); Victor Bulmer-Thomas (ed.), *Britain and Latin America: A Changing Relationship*

(Cambridge: Cambridge University Press, 1989). Works written on Anglo-American relations with Latin America during the interwar and postwar periods have primarily focused on the importance of economic diplomacy. For more information, see Thomas C. Mills, *Post-War Planning on the Periphery: Anglo-American Economic Diplomacy in South America, 1939–1945* (Edinburgh: Edinburgh University Press, 2012); Rory Miller, *Britain and Latin America in the Nineteenth and Twentieth Centuries* (London: Longman, 1993). For the purposes of this book the Latin American region is termed as the area covering Central and South America, including the countries of Belize and Grenada and the Falkland Islands. As the islands have been claimed by Argentina as Argentinian territory, and it refers to the islands as 'Las Islas Malvinas', they fall within the area of Latin America. Both Belize and Grenada are former British possessions and, as such, British interests remained in the region. These countries are part of what is commonly referred to as Central America. It can be argued that, to all intents and purposes, Central America is an inherent part of Latin America in terms of its culture and imperial origins as part of the Spanish Empire.

33. The term 'back yard' has frequently been associated with US influence in the Latin American region. A large literature exists exploring this concept; some of the most notable include: William M. LeoGrande, *Our Own Backyard: The US in Central America, 1977–1992* (Chapel Hill, NC: University of North Carolina Press, 1998); Grace Livingstone, *America's Backyard: The United States and Latin America from the Monroe Doctrine to the War on Terror* (London: Zed Books, 2009); Greg Grandin, *Empire's Workshop: Latin America, the United States and the Rise of the New Imperialism* (New York: Metropolitan Owl Books, 2007). The Reagan Doctrine was a strategy implemented by the Reagan administration to address the issue of Soviet-backed governments in Asia, Africa and Latin America. It provided for overt and covert aid to resistance movements to roll-back the perceived communist threat. For more information on the Reagan Doctrine, see James M. Scott, *Deciding to Intervene: The Reagan Doctrine and American Foreign Policy* (Durham, NC: Duke University Press, 1996); Walter F. Hahn (ed.), *Central America and the Reagan Doctrine* (Lanham, MD: University Press of America, 1987); Mark P. Lagon, *The Reagan Doctrine: Sources of American Conduct in the Cold War's Last Chapter* (Westport, CT: Praeger, 1994).

34. The Reagan Library houses over 50 million pages of presidential

documents. The facility is administered by the National Archives and Records Administration (NARA) in the US and it is the primary depository of documents pertaining to the Reagan presidency. This book uses a host of primary documents accessed on a number of research visits to the Reagan Library. It also uses a number of primary documents accessed in the TNA during similar research trips, including documents released in 2014 and 2013 (see chapter introductions for identification of the most recently released TNA file series).

35. The Margaret Thatcher Foundation consented to the inclusion of a number of items of Thatcher copyright material, 'Copyright estate of Lady Thatcher, drawn from www.margaretthatcher.org'.

36. Biographical information on the interviewees can be found in the Appendix.

1   The 1970s: A Decline in Anglo-American Specialness and US–UK Relations with Latin America

Anglo-American relations could not be termed as particularly 'special' during the 1970s. This was a decade of overall decline in the Special Relationship. The relationship ebbed and flowed and experienced moments of improved cooperation and development, but these were largely overshadowed by diverging political and economic interests, growing US isolationism and a decline in British influence in world affairs.[1] It can come as no surprise that the Latin American region held little importance to wider Anglo-American relations at this time. In fact, the region was marginalised by both the US and the UK governments in the 1970s as various domestic issues came to the fore. There was one exception, and that was Chile; US–UK relations with Chile were predicated upon a desire to closely monitor the regime of General Augusto Pinochet Ugarte.

This chapter will examine the tone of Anglo-American relations in the 1970s as a benchmark from which to appreciate the importance of the subsequent Reagan–Thatcher relationship. It will also briefly examine relations between Thatcher and Carter from 1979 to 1981 as a period of indifferent quality in bilateral relations. By assessing the general temper of US–UK relations during the 1970s, the chapter will highlight the often competing concerns of both countries and their impact on the evolution of Anglo-American relations. Secondly, the chapter will examine the central thrust of US–UK relations with Latin America during this time with a particular emphasis on both countries' relations with Chile. In doing so, it will help to contextualise the significance of the book's forthcoming Latin American case studies and their impacts, both positive and otherwise, upon the Anglo-American Special Relationship throughout the 1980s.

A decline in Anglo-American specialness

Anglo-American relations during the 1970s did not enjoy the same elevated status as they did under the previous leaderships of Churchill and Roosevelt, Macmillan and Eisenhower or Macmillan and Kennedy. President Richard M. Nixon was initially inclined to look favourably upon the concept of a Special Relationship with the UK. His British counterpart, Prime Minister Harold Wilson, was not entirely helpful and Anglo-American relations failed to experience any significant renewal. Wilson's call for a general election in the UK resulted in the surprise victory by Wilson's long-standing rival, the Conservative Edward Heath, on 18 June 1970. For his part, Heath was apathetic towards Anglo-American relations as he had economic, trade union and unemployment issues to contend with at home and was determined to take Britain into the EEC. Notwithstanding this, Nixon tried unsuccessfully to improve US–UK relations. In a letter to the new Prime Minister on 7 July 1970, Nixon wrote of the 'uniquely harmonious partnership' that existed between both countries.[2] This marked the first of numerous attempts by Nixon to forge closer diplomatic ties. However, the concept of a Special Relationship was not an easy one for Heath. In a speech during a visit to Washington in December 1970, Heath stated that he 'did not favour the suggestion of a "special relationship" between our two countries ... I believe in a natural relationship, the result of our common history and institutions, which nobody could take away from us.'[3] Former National Security Advisor and US Secretary of State Henry Kissinger, later wrote that Heath dealt with the US with an 'unsentimentality quite at variance with the special relationship'.[4] Donald Cameron Watt similarly suggests that Heath was unimpressed with Nixon's courtship of him.[5]

Indeed, Heath was sceptical of Britain's past obsession with the US and he was ambivalent in his approach to transatlantic relations. The Prime Minister was more concerned with cultivating

Britain's European ties as he concentrated his efforts on British entry into the EEC and on dealing with the overarching issues of the European Monetary Union (EMU) and the European Regional Development Fund (ERDF).[6] Across the Atlantic in the US, Nixon was preoccupied with floating the dollar against other currencies in 1971, the infamous Watergate scandal of 1972, Vietnamising the war in South Vietnam and ongoing Strategic Arms Limitation Talks (SALT) negotiations with the Soviet Union.[7] Heath's refusal to allow the US to use British bases to transport American supplies to Israel during the Yom Kippur War of October 1973 did little to improve relations. This was considered a slight against the US by its supposed partner and a snub against Kissinger's 'Year of Europe'.[8] The war highlighted differences in Anglo-American policies towards the Middle East and was an unwelcome reminder of the Suez debacle of 1956.[9] The strain in Anglo-American relations did not go unnoticed, with former Prime Minister and then Foreign Secretary Alec Douglas-Home declaring in late 1973 that Britain should combine its European policy 'with the preservation of a fruitful Anglo-American and transatlantic relationship'.[10]

Despite the accession of two new leaders in 1974, Prime Minister Harold Wilson in March and President Gerald R. Ford in August, Anglo-American relations continued to stagnate. The UK continued to focus on Europe, in particular, the renegotiation of British contributions to the EEC budget and, within that, the Common Agricultural Policy (CAP). As a result, Wilson's government failed to achieve any tangible improvements in transatlantic relations. There was limited Anglo-American cooperation following the signing of a US–UK memorandum of understanding (MOU) on 24 September 1975 regarding the production and procurement of defence equipment. The MOU set out a number of provisions designed to provide a long-term equitable balance in defence trade between the two countries. It effectively extended Anglo-American cooperation in research and development and procurement in a bid to improve both countries' strategic defence capabilities and the broader aims of NATO rationalisation/standardisation.[11]

When Prime Minister James Callaghan came to power in the UK in April 1976 Anglo-American relations saw a marginal improvement. Callaghan was more Eurosceptic and was therefore more open to cordial relations with the US. He believed that the Atlantic Alliance should be strengthened as the British leaning towards the EEC in recent years had weakened the bonds of the Special Relationship. Callaghan's convictions had little time to reap any noteworthy benefits as bilateral relations suffered a blow in June 1976 when the UK approached the US Federal Reserve along with various other banks for a line of credit in order to support a weakened sterling. The US agreed to extend the credit on condition that if Britain was unable to repay the credit it would ask the International Monetary Fund (IMF) for a loan to cover the costs.[12] Britain was outraged as it negatively impacted an already weakened pound in a period of significant British economic difficulty: it effectively broke the 'social contract' between the government and the unions, namely, that in return for wage constraints the government would spend on health, education and welfare. The IMF loans conditionally limited the public borrowing right and undermined the government's ability to keep its side of the bargain. The British economy began to spiral downwards and unofficial or 'wildcat' strikes erupted throughout the country.[13]

A change in administration in the US in January 1977 saw President Jimmy Carter come to power, and with him a return to closer US–UK relations. Improved Anglo-American relations were also facilitated by a cordial relationship between US Secretary of State Cyrus Vance and British Foreign Secretary David Owen.[14] The cultivation of close relations between high-ranking British and American officials was a vital component in diplomatic relations, particularly when governments had competing concerns. While the Callaghan government did not necessarily agree with all Carter's foreign policies, Owen later termed the US foreign policy agenda at the time as 'radical' and 'ill-thought-out', the UK was keen to engage in close consultation and dialogue with the US.[15] Moreover, Carter and Callaghan enjoyed a relative concordance in views on a host of subjects, including Anglo-American defence relations, the Middle East and the Soviet Union. Callaghan was the driving force behind improved relations, and later stated that he 'cultivated' Carter in that he turned to him for support on issues of 'mutual concern'.[16] Callaghan's desire to cultivate the US President was illustrated during a state visit to Washington in March 1977 when the Prime Minister spoke of the ease, intimacy and the common feeling that Britons and Americans shared.[17]

A noticeable symmetry in Anglo-American views towards the Middle East was evident in January 1978, when Callaghan met the Egyptian President Anwar El Sadat in Cairo in a bid to facilitate a framework for peace in the Middle East. During the meeting, Callaghan relayed Carter's views to Sadat, which helped to spur progress in ongoing negotiations between the US, Egypt and Israel.[18] A further area of cooperation between the US and the UK was evident in late November 1978 when efforts were made to discuss a renewal of the 1958 US–UK Nuclear Defence Bilateral Agreement. In addition, the US–UK defence relationship was augmented in February 1979 with US–UK meetings to discuss the US procurement of British AV8B Harriers and Rapier aircraft.[19] Callaghan's request to upgrade the UK's Trident missile system was also agreed in principle. However, domestic and international factors soon began to overshadow any notable improvements in bilateral relations.

The 'Winter of Discontent' (1978/9), plagued Callaghan's government as the UK was beset by a host of problems, including a weakened economy, struggling currency and widespread trades union strikes. This, coupled with Labour's minority standing in the House of Commons, resulted in a decidedly unpopular government. Strong divisions in the Cabinet ultimately resulted in a vote of no confidence in the Prime Minister by a vote of 311 to 310 on 28 March 1979.[20] This vote of no confidence was followed shortly thereafter by a general election, which saw Margaret Thatcher come to power as the first female Prime Minister of the UK on 4 May 1979. Thatcher's success came as a complete surprise to many; not least the Prime Minister herself. In fact, Thatcher had not been expected to win the Conservative Party leadership contest in February 1975. Cecil Parkinson confirms this view: 'Nobody really, except for a few devotees thought she could win.'[21] Peter Carrington laughingly suggests that 'everybody was astonished including her'.[22] Thatcher's success was to have a profound impact on the cultivation of closer Anglo-American relations.

Meanwhile, deepening Cold War tensions, the Iran Hostage Crisis, SALT negotiations and the Soviet invasion of Afghanistan in December 1979 dominated the international political environment. Nevertheless, there were some improvements in bilateral relations under Carter and Thatcher. The new Prime Minister visited Washington in mid-December 1979 to discuss issues of joint concern, which resulted in a joint communiqué detailing both countries' agreement on 'the importance of maintaining a credible British strategic deterrent and US/UK strategic cooperation'.[23] Thatcher and Carter continued to maintain regular but formal contact on a variety of issues, including SALT, East–West relations and a Comprehensive Test Ban Treaty (CTBT). A stand-out achievement, in particular for the British, was made on 14 July 1980 when a US–UK agreement was signed ensuring the British acquisition of Trident C4 submarine-launched ballistic missiles (SLBMs) at the remarkably low cost of £1 billion along with a mere 5 per cent contribution to the American research and development costs.[24] This deal was considered a great success by Thatcher as it ensured the longevity of the British strategic defence system and also reasserted the US commitment to the defence of Western Europe and its key British ally therein. In return for the British purchase of Trident C4, the US was granted the right to expand its military base on the British-owned island of Diego Garcia in the Indian Ocean.

The pair also maintained regular contact over the internal situation in Poland in 1980. Carter wrote to Thatcher on 7 October 1980 stating:

It is vital that we maintain close and frank collaboration with regard both to our assessment of what is taking place and to the measures we might undertake to achieve our common aim of deterring Soviet intervention and supporting trends towards internal liberalization in Poland.[25]

Before leaving office in January 1981, Carter again wrote to Thatcher: 'I believe the Alliance has achieved an important degree of unity in responding to adversity – in no small measure because of your leadership.'[26] This relationship, although closer than that of previous administrations, lacked the warmth and familiarity that was evident between Thatcher and Reagan. As Carrington argues: 'Carter and Margaret Thatcher were not going to be great friends and weren't. They were always very polite but they had nothing in common at all.'[27] It is true that while Thatcher admired Carter as a man of 'obvious sincerity' she was under-whelmed by him. She later wrote in her memoirs that Carter had an 'unsure handle on economics' and had 'no large vision' for America's future.[28] Carter was slightly more magnanimous in his recollection of the Prime Minister: 'Margaret Thatcher is a tough lady, highly opinionated, strong-willed, cannot admit that she doesn't know something.'[29] This was a far cry from Thatcher's and Reagan's subsequent commendations of one another. Notwithstanding such lacklustre remarks, the Thatcher–Carter relationship highlighted a desire, by Thatcher in particular, to improve Anglo-American diplomatic relations towards the end of the 1970s. Their relationship helped to maintain some of the core elements underlying US–UK relations, such as nuclear inter-dependence and the sharing of intelligence. But it was the close working and personal relationship between Reagan and Thatcher in the 1980s that would ultimately restore bilateral relations.

US–UK relations with Latin America

Latin America remained on the periphery of US–UK interests during the tenures of the various US presidents and UK prime ministers in the 1970s. A move towards economic liberalisation in the region during the 1970s did little to encourage stronger economic and trading attachments by either country. Undeterred, Latin America looked towards Europe to promote trade and investment, whilst moving away from the traditional US economic tutelage of the postwar period. However, economic stagnation along with substantial growth in population rates and regional political crises made progress difficult to achieve. For its part, the UK afforded the region marginal attention as wider international and domestic concerns were prioritised, in particular, Britain's orientation towards the EEC (with the notable exceptions of the

Falkland Islands and Belize, which were the subject of intermittent negotiations between the UK and the governments of Argentina and Guatemala, respectively. See Chapters 2 and 4).[30] British banks engaged in some lending to the region in the 1970s, but the rate of lending did not reflect growing British–Latin American trade links. An increase in British awareness towards the region was evident on 26 January 1972 when the House of Lords met to debate opportunities for closer ties between the UK and Latin America. This debate was followed by a government-sponsored seminar on UK–Latin American commercial and diplomatic relations at Lancaster House, London, 16–17 May 1972.[31]

The Organisation of Petroleum Exporting Countries (OPEC) oil crisis in 1973 hindered any meaningful improvements in trade links with the region as the UK focused its attention on cultivating trade with European markets. Latin America, therefore, became increasing marginalised in importance to the British. Neil Kinnock suggests that there was a lack of political, democratic and diplomatic engagement between the UK and Latin America, and this showed in terms of Britain's trade profile with the region.[32] In fact, the importance of Latin America's trade profile was significantly reduced in line with a decline in British exports to the region.[33] Latin America's importance was negligible in wider British politics. For example, when the UK's new Permanent Under-Secretary in the FCO, Sir Michael Palliser, visited the region on a three-week tour in 1976, it left little lasting impression on him. Palliser was decidedly indifferent in his recollection of his visit as he recalled upon his return to the UK: 'Each country in the area is different from its neighbours.'[34] Nonetheless, Latin America attracted some attention in the late 1970s as awareness grew in the UK over the deteriorating socioeconomic conditions in the region; a number of non-governmental organisations (NGOs), such as the London-based Latin America Bureau, were thereafter established.[35]

In the US, successive presidents viewed the region primarily in terms of its leftist leanings, the growth of nationalism and mounting human rights violations. However, the global spread of stagflation in the 1970s influenced US policy and there was a corresponding gradual US economic retreat from Latin America.

Direct US foreign investment in the region fell steadily, in particular, following the oil crises of 1973 and 1979. By 1980, total direct US foreign investment in Latin America had fallen in percentage terms to a mere 18 per cent in comparison to 26 per cent in 1960.[36] This US disengagement with Latin America was in line with US economic protectionist measures and a general reappraisal of US foreign policy following the end of the Vietnam War, after which the US was reluctant to assume such a strong role in the hemisphere.[37] However, the US continued to maintain a strong interest in the political orientation of various Latin American governments and monitored events closely as they unfolded in countries such as Argentina, Nicaragua and El Salvador. Nicaragua, in particular, was considered of great strategic importance due to its central geographical location in the region, its tumultuous political leadership and possible development as a Marxist client of the Soviet Union (the declining political environment in Nicaragua in the 1970s will be examined in greater detail in Chapter 5). Nonetheless, this was the era of détente and the US was engaged in extensive negotiations with the Soviet Union, which took precedence over events in Latin America. Furthermore, with Carter's inauguration, the US sought to normalise its relations with Latin America in the hope of addressing rising human rights violations.[38] Given the differences in US–UK policies towards Latin America in the 1970s, the case of Chile was an anomaly and as such, requires more extensive analysis from an Anglo-American perspective.

Chile

In the 1970s Chile was a volatile country that elicited strong British and American interest. Following the inauguration of the Socialist President Salvador Allende Gossens (head of the Unidad Popular (UP, or Popular Party) on 4 November 1970, the US sought ways in which to establish a more US-friendly, democratic government in Chile. The development of close ties with North Korea and China along with Allende's plans to nationalise many Chilean industries, including the banking and transport sectors, mining, chemical and textile industries, were unacceptable to the US. Allende's plans for agrarian reform were equally as troubling. Nixon was determined to undermine the Allende government and signed National Security Decision Memorandum (NSDM) 93: 'Policy towards Chile', on 9 November 1970. The NSDM stated that US posture would be 'correct but cool' towards Chile. More importantly, the US would seek to maximise financial pressure on the Allende government. It stated that the US wanted 'no new bilateral economic aid commitments to be undertaken with the Government of Chile'. Existing commitments would be fulfilled, but could be 'reduced, delayed, or terminated'.[39] This type of US economic policy towards Chile was later referred to by Allende as the 'invisible blockade'.[40]

The US had many economic interests in Chile in 1970, in particular, the International Telephone and Telegraph Corporation (ITT). Thus, the US was prepared, in concert with the ITT, to try to destabilise the Allende government. As a result, the US looked for compensation for Allende's proposed nationalisation plans.[41] Allende's collectivisation and nationalisation plans caused many problems within his government as officials were divided on how, or indeed if, the plans should proceed. Allende became increasingly isolated within his own government. Notwithstanding such internal divisions, the Allende government extended its influence in Latin America in November 1970 through the resumption of diplomatic ties with Cuba. In doing so, Chile effectively flouted the isolation of Cuba by the Organisation of American States (OAS), which had been in place since January 1962.[42] Such actions reinforced US views that Allende was a communist, and the Nixon administration began to look at ways in which to help the opposition to overthrow him.

A programme of economic and political destabilisation followed, and this, coupled with a growing polarisation within the Chilean government, resulted in a new government coming to power in Chile. On 11 September 1973 a bloody US-backed coup d'état saw Allende killed along with countless others, and the Commander-in-Chief of the Chilean Army, General Augusto Pinochet Ugarte, come to power as the ruling head of the military junta of Chile. The Nixon administration denied any participation in the coup, but the extent of US involvement was revealed a year later during a briefing by Central Intelligence Agency (CIA) Director William E. Colby before the House Armed Services Committee. It was revealed that US$8 million had been spent by the Nixon administration on covert operations in Chile; the details of which were released to various domestic newspapers. The new US President, Gerald R. Ford, had little option but to confirm the financial assistance provided, but he strongly denied US involvement in the coup itself.[43]

The new ruling junta in Chile consisted of Pinochet, General Gustavo Leigh (head of the Air Force), Admiral José Merino (head of the Navy) and General César Mendoza (head of the National Police Force).[44] Under the junta's rule Chile was seen by the US as increasingly repressive. The junta divided Chile into thirteen regions with each region assigned a military administrator, and military officials were appointed to run the country's universities.[45] Those suspected of leftist political orientation were dealt with in a harsh and uncompromising manner. The junta embarked on a devastating campaign against Chilean society in order to neutralise all opposition to the government. Thousands of people were tortured and murdered, trade unions were banned and all opposition parties eradicated. Countless Chileans fled into exile.[46] Poverty was rife in the country and unemployment rates soared.

Although the junta claimed it was anti-communist, the US continued to assert Chile's communist connections throughout Latin America and the wider international community. The junta's failure to reverse Allende's nationalisation plans remained a point of contention for the US. In a bid to open Chile's markets to global trade, the junta implemented numerous economic reforms, including the privatisation of many state-controlled industries. The junta was influenced by a group of economists who had studied in the US, otherwise known as the 'Chicago Boys', who devised a plan for Chilean economic recovery.[47] Despite such moves in favour of a free-market economy, relations continued to stagnate between the US and Chile.

The UK, for its part, had enjoyed 'cordial but distant' relations with the country under Allende, but it began to reassess its ties with Chile under the military junta.[48] The British public openly denounced the coup and the oppressive tactics used by the junta. As a result, the Chile Solidarity Campaign (CSC) was established in the UK in September 1973 along with the Chile Campaign for Human Rights. Both organisations had broad popular support within the British public and highlighted the extent of frustration in the UK at ongoing atrocities in Chile at the time.[49] The CSC campaigned vigorously to highlight the mounting human rights issues and pressured the British government to apply sanctions against Chile. Similar solidarity groups were established in the US, but none were as vocal as the British. Nevertheless, the British government under Heath maintained a cautious stance towards the new junta. This was largely inspired by outstanding British commitments to Chile, particularly in the area of defence contracts. For example, in December 1973 there were three major defence contracts outstanding between Chile and British contractors: the December 1969 agreement to supply two Leander frigates and two Oberon submarines to Chile (these were to be delivered at various points throughout 1974); the supply of eight refurbished aircraft to Chile; and the refit of two Chilean destroyers by British contractors.[50]

The British were also mindful of the extent of outstanding Chilean debts to the UK, which were in the process of being renegotiated. Chile had already defaulted on payments of a loan previously extended by the British, and had debts amounting to a considerable £25 million.[51] The UK did not want to risk these renegotiations and thus the British government continued its defence trade with Chile. To that end, the FCO continued to approve licences for the export of arms/explosives to Chile with the result that, up to March 1974, the FCO approved licences for: 112 aeroplane tyres; nine Avon aero engines; various spares for Seacat guided missiles, mining detonators and relays. The FCO refused, however, the Chilean request for export licences for a £300,000-order of automatic rifles and machine guns.[52] The Wilson government continued to maintain diplomatic relations with Chile after the ruling military junta officially appointed Pinochet as President of Chile on 17 December 1974.

Allegations continued to abound regarding human rights

violations in Chile, and Anglo-Chilean diplomatic relations deteriorated in December 1975 following the arrest and torture of a British national, Dr Sheila Cassidy, by the Chilean secret police. The public outcry in the UK was overwhelming. The CSC made numerous public demands on the government to address the escalating human rights situation in Chile. The British media mirrored calls for a strong government response. The Wilson government was effectively forced to suspend all diplomatic relations with the Pinochet government. It subsequently cancelled all future British arms sales to Chile.[53] However, the UK retained pre-existing contracts with Chile and, following the Cassidy case, the UK came under increasing domestic pressure to cancel all arms sales including those pending delivery to Chile. This would bring British policy towards Chile more in line with the US. In response to the human rights situation in Chile, Congress had previously enacted the Kennedy Amendment (named after Democrat Senator Edward 'Ted' Kennedy who proposed the act) in 1974, which effectively suspended all US security assistance and weapons sales to Chile.[54]

The UK's new Prime Minister James Callaghan addressed the Cabinet on the issue of arms sales to Chile on 17 June 1976. Callaghan informed the Cabinet that, by law, the UK was obliged to honour its existing contracts with Chile. The Prime Minister referred to 'inescapable existing contracts' for warships and spares to be delivered to Chile.[55] Regarding the question of two submarines yet to be delivered to Chile, Callaghan argued that as Chile was up to date on the repayments for the first submarine, the contract would be honoured. However, it had been decided by the Defence and Overseas Policy Committee (DOP) that because Chile was late with a payment for the second Hyatt submarine, the UK would inform Chile that unless it made the necessary payments, the UK would take steps to ensure that the Hyatt 'did not acquire legal immunity as a warship'. Callaghan advised that despite the general feeling that all arms sales should be halted after the Cassidy case, this could not be justified in domestic or international law. Furthermore, the DOP saw no alternative other than to supply Chile with ammunition and missiles under existing contracts 'distasteful though it would be to do so'.[56]

Meanwhile, the Ford administration continued its efforts

to address human rights violations in Latin America, including Chile. Congress extended the Kennedy Amendment in July 1976 through the International Security Assistance and Arms Export Control Act, which prohibited US weapons transfers to any country seen to be involved in prolonged human rights violations.[57] The UK began to reassess its policy towards Chile in December 1976. In a letter from the head of the FCO's Latin America Department, Hugh Carless, to the Minister of State at the FCO, Ted Rowlands, it was acknowledged that Germany and France were taking a more 'pragmatic' approach to Chile than the UK at the time. It was also suggested that the new Carter administration in the US 'may perhaps harden its attitudes' towards Chile.[58] The French and German approach was based upon the belief that future EEC policy towards Chile should be set in proportion to a global policy on human rights.[59] Inspired by this, the UK discussed how its policy towards Chile could be modified in 'minor ways' during a meeting between Rowlands and various Latin America Department staff members on 29 December 1976. Rowlands favoured, in principle, the idea of a visit by a senior British official to Santiago to discuss issues such as progress in human and democratic rights. However, he remained reluctant to appoint a new Ambassador to Chile.[60]

The US began to re-emphasise its focus on the deteriorating human rights issue in Latin America in the latter half of the 1970s, and the Carter administration continued to closely monitor events as they unfolded in Chile. The US was dissatisfied with the Chilean response to the murder of a former Chilean politician and economist, Orlando Letelier, who was assassinated by Chilean secret services in Washington DC in September 1976. The Letelier case remained a source of contention in US–Chilean relations and did little to improve bilateral relations. Nonetheless, the US resumed a limited amount of aid to Chile in May 1978 when the Department of Agriculture extended official credit of US\$39 million to Chile on semi-concessionary terms. This marked a softening in US resolve towards Chile. These funds were offered for the purchase of wheat and breeding cattle supplies from US producers. According to the head of the FCO's South America Department (later Assistant Under-Secretary in the FCO), John B.

Ure, the Carter administration's attitude towards Chile continued to be subject to 'internal disputes'. It was hoped in British circles that any new attempt to approach the US about policy towards Chile would be more effective when Assistant Secretary of State for Latin American Affairs Terence A. Todman, who was considered a 'well-known "dove" on Chile', stepped down from office in July 1978.[61] The UK evidently wanted more in-depth consultations with the US at this time regarding British and American policy towards Chile.

There is a dichotomy evident in British views towards Chile towards the end of the 1970s. On the one hand, it looked towards senior level Anglo-Chilean consultations; on the other, it sought to convince the US of the need to put more pressure on the Pinochet regime. According to more correspondence from the FCO's South America Department at the time, it was felt that the UK should 'seek to "undermine Pinochet", and "stiffen up the State Department" … this is the time when we and the Americans should be doing everything we can to maximise the pressure on Pinochet'.[62] This correspondence suggests a general dissatisfaction within British circles regarding the stance that the US had applied to Chile in the latter half of the 1970s. The UK was pleased when the US stated that it would pursue the Letelier case further with Chile, as it was hoped that the US could be 'encouraged to make the maximum political running with this ball at the moment'. The UK also encouraged a more aggressive US stance on Chile as it believed that anything that helped to unseat Pinochet would be in the best interests of Chilean democracy and its own long-term interests with Chile.[63] The US, however, refused to engage in activities that would oust Pinochet as it believed that it was possible that the Chilean armed forces would try to oust Pinochet within the next year (Pinochet remained as President in Chile until 11 March 1990).[64] Furthermore, the US believed that if Pinochet was removed from power there would be no quick return to civilian rule.[65]

Despite such US reluctance, the British embassy in Washington remained in close contact with US officials regarding Chile. During a meeting between Rowlands and new US Assistant Secretary of State for Inter-American Affairs Viron P. Vaky in New York on

28 September 1978, Chile was discussed at length. Vaky suggested that with the exception of the Letelier case, Chile seemed to be moving towards democratisation. Rowlands stated that the UK had decided not to deal with the current regime in Chile, but to encourage contacts with the democratic opposition. Vaky responded that it was US policy in general to use 'both the carrot and the stick', and recommended that pressure should be 'maintained for now'.[66] This exchange highlighted a partial divergence in Anglo-American attitudes towards Chile in the late 1970s. Notwithstanding these diverging views, both the US and the UK continued to monitor Pinochet closely.

With the advent of the Thatcher government, Anglo-Chilean relations improved significantly. Britain restored full export credit guarantees for UK business with Chile in June 1979 and full diplomatic relations were reinstated in January 1980. The UK's arms embargo against Chile was lifted in July 1980.[67] The following month, Cecil Parkinson, then Minister of State at the Department of Trade and Industry, made a controversial visit to Chile and Argentina. This signified a British attempt to support Chile's and Argentina's efforts to liberalise their economies, privatise their industries and reduce barriers to trade.[68] Parkinson contends: 'We weren't supporting Pinochet and Videla [President of Argentina], we were supporting Martínez de Hoz [Argentina's Minister of the Economy] and the Chicago-school economists in Chile.'[69] This visit, combined with the restoration of full diplomatic relations, marked the beginning of a period of more harmonious Anglo-Chilean relations. The US, too, adopted a more harmonious stance on Chile following Reagan's inauguration in 1981 as it sought to improve US–Chilean relations through quiet diplomacy.

On a broader scale, the US became more militant in its view towards Latin America, as is evident in its application of the Reagan Doctrine throughout the 1980s. The Thatcher government was, for the most part, happy to support the US in its quest to topple communism and promote liberal democracy in the region. This was a cause that Thatcher held dear as she later explained: 'Communism recognised no limits except those posed by the power of its enemies.'[70] Indeed, Thatcher's Britain was to become increasingly aware of, and involved in, Latin America. Moreover, during the Reagan–Thatcher epoch the region became of signal importance to the development of the Special Relationship. And yet, Anglo-American relations were not impervious to challenges emanating from Latin America. Diverging foreign policy objectives coupled with a US propensity for unilateralism in the region resulted in a host of crises that threatened to undermine improved Anglo-American relations under Reagan and Thatcher. The first of which came in the thorny guise of the Falklands War.

Notes

1. The contraction of British power and influence in the late 1960s to early 1970s in particular, saw the UK become increasingly reliant upon the US for its security and defence capabilities. As a result, the UK's role as a powerful ally to the US during the 1970s was limited, for the most part, to its participation in NATO and its burgeoning role in the EEC. For more information on the UK's decline in importance to the US during this time, see David Reynolds, 'A "special relationship"? America, Britain and the international order since the Second World War', *International Affairs*, 62(1) (Winter 1985/6): 1–20, at pp. 13–16.
2. Catherine Hynes, *The Year that Never Was: Heath, the Nixon Administration and the Year of Europe* (Dublin: University College Dublin Press, 2009), p. 12.
3. Edward Heath, *The Course of My Life: My Autobiography* (London: Hodder & Stoughton, 1998), p. 472.
4. Henry Kissinger, *Years of Upheaval* (London: Weidenfeld & Nicolson, 1982), p. 147.
5. Donald Cameron Watt, *Succeeding John Bull: America in Britain's Place, 1900–1975* (Cambridge: Cambridge University Press, 1984), p. 155.
6. For a more comprehensive account of the Heath government, see Stuart Ball and Anthony Seldon (eds), *The Heath Government, 1970–1974: A Reappraisal*, revised edn (Abingdon: Routledge, 2013). More generally, see Philip Ziegler, *Edward Heath: The Authorised Biography* (London: HarperPress, 2010); John Campbell, *Edward Heath: A Biography* (London: Pimlico, 1994).
7. For more on the Nixon presidency, see Richard Nixon, *RN: The Memoirs of Richard Nixon*, revised edn (New York: Simon &

Schuster, 2013); Richard Reeves, *President Nixon: Alone in the White House* (New York: Simon & Schuster, 2007).

8. David Watt, 'Perceptions of the United States in Europe, 1945–83', in Lawrence D. Freedman (ed.), *The Troubled Alliance: Atlantic Relations in the 1980s* (New York: St. Martin's Press, 1983), p. 39. Kissinger announced 1973 to be the 'Year of Europe' at an Associated Press luncheon on 23 April 1973. This was in a bid to improve US relations with Europe, which had declined in recent years. The Nixon administration encouraged closer cooperation by reasserting the traditional shared interests and values between the US and Europe. For more information, see Keith Hamilton and Patrick Salmon (eds), *The Year of Europe: America, Europe and the Energy Crisis, 1972–74: Documents on British Policy Overseas, Series III, vol. 4*, 2nd edn (Abingdon: Routledge, 2012); Alistair Horne, *Kissinger's Year: 1973* (London: Weidenfeld & Nicolson, 2009).

9. Anglo-American relations were strained in 1956 when US diplomatic and financial pressure forced the UK to withdraw from a joint operation with France and Israel in response to Egypt's nationalisation of the Suez Canal.

10. TNA, PREM 15/2089, FCO paper 'The Year of Europe: The Impact of Transatlantic and Anglo-American Relations; An Analytical Account', February–July 1973.

11. TNA, DEFE 13/1152, document on procurement of defence equipment, 24 September 1975, p. 4.

12. Burk, *Old World, New World*, p. 627.

13. For more on the British economy during this time, including the IMF crisis, see Richard Coopey and Nicholas Woodward (eds), *Britain in the 1970s: The Troubled Economy* (London: UCL Press, 1996); Kevin Hickson, *The IMF Crisis of 1976 and British Politics* (London: I. B. Tauris, 2005). More generally, see James Callaghan, *Time and Chance*, revised edn (London: Politico's, 2006).

14. Geir Lundestad, *The United States and Western Europe since 1945: From 'Empire' by Invitation to Transatlantic Drift* (Oxford: Oxford University Press, 2005), p. 203.

15. David Owen, *Time to Declare* (London: Michael Joseph, 1991), p. 260.

16. Kenneth O. Morgan, *Callaghan: A Life* (Oxford: Oxford University Press, 1997), p. 589.

17. Remarks made by Callaghan at a dinner honouring him in Washington, 10 March 1977.

18. For more on the Carter administration's involvement in the search for a Middle Eastern settlement see John Dumbrell, *American Foreign Policy: Carter to Clinton* (Basingstoke: Macmillan, 1997), pp. 28–31. More generally, see Jimmy Carter, *White House Diary* (New York: Farrar, Straus & Giroux, 2010); Cyrus Vance, *Hard Choices: Critical Years in America's Foreign Policy* (New York: Simon & Schuster, 1983); Zbigniew Brzezinski, *Power and Principle: Memoirs of the National Security Advisor, 1977–1981* (New York: Farrar, Straus & Giroux, 1983).

19. TNA, DEFE 13/1281, Information on sale of AV8B and Rapier, 21 February 1979.

20. Roy Hattersley, 'The party's over', *The Guardian*, 22 March 2009.

21. Interview with Cecil Parkinson.

22. Interview with Peter Carrington, 30 January 2013.

23. Lawrence D. Freedman, *Britain and Nuclear Weapons* (Basingstoke: Macmillan, 1980), p. 67.

24. David Fairhall, '£5 Billion Trident Deal', *The Guardian*, 16 July 1980.

25. TNA, PREM 19/331, Carter to Thatcher, 7 October 1980, p. 1.

26. Churchill Archives Centre, THCR 3/1/12 (1), file: 81/6–81/9, Carter to Thatcher, 13 January 1981.

27. Interview with Peter Carrington.

28. Thatcher, *Downing Street Years*, pp. 68–9.

29. Jimmy Carter, *Keeping Faith: Memoirs of a President* (New York: Bantam, 1982), p. 119.

30. David Atkinson, 'Trade, aid and investment since 1950', in Victor Bulmer-Thomas (ed.), *Britain and Latin America: A Changing Relationship* (Cambridge: Cambridge University Press, 1989), p. 106.

31. House of Lords debate, Latin America and the United Kingdom, 26 January 1972, available at: www.hansard.millbanksystems. com/lords/1972/jan/26/latin-america-and-the-united-kingdom, accessed 13 May 2014; Robert Graham, 'British policy towards Latin America', in Victor Bulmer-Thomas (ed.), *Britain and Latin America: A Changing Relationship* (Cambridge: Cambridge University Press, 1989), p. 59.

32. Interview with Neil Kinnock, 29 January 2013.

33. Graham, 'British policy towards Latin America', p. 52.

34. *Ibid.*

35. Louise Fawcett and Eduardo Posada-Carbó, *Britain and Latin*

America: Hope in a Time of Change? (London: Institute of Latin American Studies, 1996), p. 6.

36. Kevin J. Middlebrook and Carlos Rico, 'The United States and Latin America in the 1980s: change, complexity, and contending perspectives', in Kevin J. Middlebrook and Carlos Rico (eds), *The United States and Latin America in the 1980s* (Pittsburgh, PA: University of Pittsburgh Press, 1988), p. 30; Riordan Roett, 'The debt crisis and economic development in Latin America', in Jonathan Hartlyn *et al.* (eds), *The United States and Latin America in the 1990s: Beyond the Cold War* (Chapel Hill, NC: University of North Carolina Press, 1992), p. 134.

37. Roland H. Ebel *et al.*, *Political Culture and Foreign Policy in Latin America: Case Studies from the Circum-Caribbean* (Albany, NY: State University of New York Press, 1991), p. 70.

38. Lars Schoultz, *Beneath the United States: A History of US Policy Toward Latin America* (Cambridge, MA: Harvard University Press, 2009), p. 362; Thomas M. Leonard, *Central America and the United States: The Search for Stability* (Athens, GA: University of Georgia Press, 1991), p. 167.

39. NSDM 93: 'Policy towards Chile', 9 November 1970, Richard Nixon Library, available at: www.nixonlibrary.gov/virtuallibrary/documents/nsdm/nsdm-93, accessed 13 April 2013.

40. Allende referred to the invisible financial and economic blockade exercised by the US against Chile in a speech before the United Nations (UN) in December 1972.

41. David R. Mares and Francisco Rojas Aravena, *The United States and Chile: Coming in from the Cold* (New York: Routledge, 2001), p. 11; Tanya Harmer, *Allende's Chile and the Inter-American Cold War* (Chapel Hill, NC: University of North Carolina Press, 2011), p. 110.

42. Harmer, *Allende's Chile*, p. 2.

43. Marc Falcoff, *Small Countries, Large Issues: Studies in US–Latin American Asymmetries* (Washington, DC: American Enterprise Institute for Public Research, 1984), pp. 67–8. For more information on the extent of US involvement in the coup, see Peter Kornbluh, *The Pinochet File: A Declassified Dossier on Atrocity and Accountability* (New York: New Press, 2004).

44. Andy Beckett, *Pinochet in Piccadilly: Britain and Chile's Hidden History* (London: Faber & Faber, 2002), p. 137.

45. Diana Childress, *Augusto Pinochet's Chile* (Minneapolis, MN: Twenty-First Century Books, 2009), pp. 59–60.

46. Michael D. Wilkinson, 'The Chile Solidarity Campaign and British government policy towards Chile, 1973–1990', *European Review of Latin American and Caribbean Studies (Revista Europea de Estudios Latinoamericanos y del Caribe)* No. 52 (June 1992): 57–74, at p. 57.
47. The 'Chicago Boys' were a group of Chilean economists who studied in the University of Chicago (as part of an exchange programme) under renowned economists Milton Friedman and Arnold Harberger between 1955 and 1964. They promoted free-market economics and put together a plan for Chilean economic recovery in late 1972. For more information on the 'Chicago Boys' school of economics in Chile, see Juan Gabriel Valdés, *Pinochet's Economists: The Chicago School in Chile* (Cambridge: Cambridge University Press, 1995).
48. Salvatore Bizzaro, *Historical Dictionary of Chile*, 3rd edn (Lanham, MD: Scarecrow Press, 2005), p. 749
49. Wilkinson, 'Chile Solidarity Campaign', p. 57.
50. TNA, FCO 7/2432, memo regarding defence equipment for Chile, n.d.
51. TNA, PREM 16/13, memo on Chile debt negotiations, 14 June 1974.
52. *Ibid.*, memo on UK defence sales, March 1974.
53. Jon Barnes, 'Birds of a feather: Britain and Chile', in Latin America Bureau, *The Thatcher Years: Britain and Latin America* (London: Latin America Bureau, 1988), p. 54.
54. For more information on the Kennedy Amendment, see Robert A. Pastor, *Congress and the Politics of US Foreign Economic Policy* (Berkeley, CA: University of California Press, 1982), pp. 308–9; Paul E. Sigmund, *The Overthrow of Allende and the Politics of Chile, 1964–1976* (Pittsburgh, PA: University of Pittsburgh Press, 1977), p. 260.
55. TNA, FCO 7/3084, extract from Cabinet minutes, 17 June 1976.
56. *Ibid.*
57. Kornbluh, *Pinochet File*, p. 10.
58. TNA, FCO 7/3084, Carless to Rowlands, 20 December 1976.
59. *Ibid.* FCO background notes on Chile, n.d., p. 4.
60. *Ibid.* Record of Minister of State meeting with Latin America Department officials, 29 December 1976.
61. TNA, FCO 7/3487, Ure letter regarding US relations with Chile, 19 July 1978.
62. *Ibid.* Ure letter regarding US relations with Chile, 25 July 1978.

63. *Ibid.* Ure letter regarding relations with Chile, 28 July 1978, p. 1.
64. *Ibid.* J. P. Millington to Ure, 6 September 1978.
65. *Ibid.* A. J. Sindall to Rowlands, 19 September 1978.
66. *Ibid.* Memcon. of Rowlands–Vaky meeting, 28 September 1978.
67. Barnes, 'Birds of a feather', p. 55.
68. Cecil Parkinson, *Right at the Centre: An Autobiography* (London: Weidenfeld & Nicolson, 1992), p. 165.
69. Interview with Cecil Parkinson.
70. Margaret Thatcher, *Statecraft: Strategies for a Changing World* (London: HarperCollins, 2002), p. 15.

2 The Special Relationship and the Falklands War

The Falklands War between Britain and Argentina from April to June 1982 was an emotive political and ideological issue for the UK and its Prime Minister, who fought tirelessly to safeguard the Falkland islanders' right to self-determination. The war represented a considerable financial and moral commitment by the British to the Falkland Islands and their 1,800 inhabitants in a time of significant economic uncertainty in the UK. Notwithstanding this, Britain's hegemony and influence over the islands was reasserted in the face of perceived Argentine aggression. Britain's victory was considered a great success in the UK given the strategic difficulties involved in orchestrating a war in a wind-swept archipelago nearly 8,000 miles from the British mainland, but a mere 400 miles from Argentina. Moreover, it helped to secure Thatcher's re-election the following year and was a source of national pride for the jubilant British public.[1]

The war also had a significant impact upon the development of the Special Relationship under the guidance of Reagan and Thatcher and their subordinates. It was a test of US commitment to its ally, the UK. The US had traditionally viewed the South Atlantic region as peripheral in terms of hemispheric importance. It was sceptical of British colonial aspirations and was initially reluctant to actively support the UK. Britain's assumption of unqualified American support during the war was quickly disproved. The Reagan administration's initial declaration of neutrality led to scepticism within Parliament about the US commitment to the so-called Special Relationship and a distrust of its subsequent mediation efforts. In Argentina this neutrality was seen as evidence of US deference to its recently improved bilateral relationship with Washington. American neutrality was later withdrawn much to the delight of the Thatcher government, as it enabled the US to provide valuable material support to the UK (some intelligence support was provided by the US before the end of diplomatic neutrality, see section on US Material Support, below). However, the mediation process that preceded the US declaration of support for the British was not always satisfactory to either the US or the UK, and there were numerous instances of Anglo-American tension. These tensions invariably strained the development of transatlantic relations.

This chapter is not intended as a definitive study of the many battles and operations that constituted the Falklands War. Rather, it will analyse the notable strain the war put on Anglo-American relations. In this way, it provides a new and detailed assessment of the diplomatic wrangling that went on behind the scenes between US and UK officials both prior to and during the war itself. In doing so, it uses a host of recently released primary documents from British and American archival sources (including documents released by the TNA in December 2012, such as the PREM 19/624, PREM 19/633 and PREM 19/652 file series, and the PREM 19/959 and PREM 19/1152 file series released in August 2013). It will briefly examine British and Argentine claims to the Falkland Islands and the negotiations that preceded the war in order to understand the diplomatic and legal complexities involved. These and other considerations fed into the US reluctance to formally support its British ally. The chapter is distinctive from extant literature in that it examines British readings, that is, former key British officials, of US-sponsored mediation efforts and the subsequent importance of US political and material support of the UK. It also offers new insights into previously under-examined issues, such as Reagan's alleged last-ditch effort to achieve a negotiated settlement in the war by means of five-point peace plan. In all, this case study provides a useful opportunity to analyse the impact of a Latin American crisis upon a renewal in Anglo-American relations in the early 1980s.

The question of sovereignty

The Falkland Islands were charted by Spanish, British and Dutch explorers in the sixteenth century, but it was not until the late seventeenth century, in 1690, that the British named the islands after Viscount Falkland, the Treasurer of the British Navy. Some fourteen years later, in 1764, the French occupied and claimed sovereignty over the islands.[2] In 1765, the British formally declared possession of the islands and a settlement was established. During this time both British and French settlements remained on the islands. Spain subsequently laid claim to the islands and demanded that France give up its settlement. Between 1765 and 1766 negotiations between France and Spain saw France agree to transfer its colony to Spain in return for a reimbursement of expenses incurred in establishing the French settlement. France also insisted that Spain prevent the British from claiming the islands.[3] Despite Spanish demands for their expulsion, the British settlement remained on the island until 1774 when it became economically unviable for it to continue. In 1790, the British signed the Nootka Sound Convention with Spain, which effectively renounced Spanish colonial claims to South America and its adjacent islands, including the Falklands.[4] Notwithstanding this agreement, Argentina, then known as the United Provinces of El Rio de la Plata (the River Plate), took formal possession of the islands in 1820 as the successor to Spain following the dissolution of the Spanish Empire. The British protested Argentine possession and forced the expulsion of the Argentine settlers from the islands in 1833.[5] The islands were re-occupied by the British to use as a hunting and shipping base in the South Atlantic. Thus, began a long and complicated dispute between the UK and Argentina over the sovereignty of the Falkland Islands that lasted throughout the nineteenth and twentieth centuries.

During the 1960s Argentina repeatedly raised the question of sovereignty with the British and brought the issue before the UN. In December 1965, UN General Assembly (UNGA) Resolution 2065 called for bilateral negotiations under the auspices of a 1960 UN Declaration on the Granting of Independence to Colonial Countries and Peoples. As a result of these declarations, Argentina lobbied for sovereignty over the islands throughout the 1960s and 1970s. In 1974, a British-led geological survey determined that the islands could potentially have vast oil reserves, which again reignited the sovereignty issue. In September 1975, the British government under Harold Wilson commissioned a survey to carry out an economic study of the islands. The team, led by Lord Edward Shackleton, arrived in the Falklands in January 1976 much to the consternation of Argentina.[6] Anglo-Argentine tensions escalated in the aftermath of the Shackleton expedition. Argentina's occupation of Southern Thule (part of the South Sandwich Islands also contested by Argentina and the UK as part of the Falkland Island Dependencies) in December 1976 exacerbated such tensions. Anglo-Argentine talks continued in the aftermath of this incident with ministerial and working group talks in Rome, New York, Lima and Geneva from 1977 to early 1979.[7] However, these talks failed to resolve the issue and the Falkland Islands remained a point of contention for the new Thatcher government in May 1979.

Thatcher comes to power

The UK's new Minister of State at the FCO, Nicholas Ridley, visited the islands in July 1979 in a bid to try to resolve the matter. British Foreign Secretary Lord Peter Carrington simultaneously pressed Parliament for discussions on the issue, but was informed that it would not be discussed until after the question of Rhodesian independence had been resolved. Argentine impatience continued to grow and, on 18 March 1980, Argentina's Ambassador to the UK, Carlos Ortiz de Rozas, gave an address in Canning House (a long-standing forum used to debate matters concerning the Latin American region) during which he declared that the Malvinas issue was Argentina's 'number one foreign policy issue'.[8] Meanwhile, Ridley continued to seek a solution in the form of a long-term lease-back of the Falkland Islands. The plan envisaged Argentine sovereignty over the islands with continued British administration. However, the Cabinet abandoned the idea following strong opposition in the House of Commons on 2

December 1980 from three Tory right-wing backbenchers, Julian Amery, John Farr and Bernard Braine. The Falkland Island Joint Councils similarly rejected the lease-back idea on 7 January 1981 and looked instead for a sovereignty freeze effectively halting Anglo-Argentine discussions.

Britain's subsequent decision to withdraw HMS *Endurance*, a Royal Navy ice patrol vessel in the South Atlantic, due to budgetary constraints and the announcement that the British Antarctic Survey would close its station on South Georgia (a British overseas territory that lies some 800 miles southeast of the Falklands and is governed as part of the Falkland Island Dependencies) the following year had unforeseen consequences for the UK. Argentina interpreted these decisions as a relaxation of Britain's commitment to the entire region.[9] Carrington suggests of the planned withdrawal of HMS *Endurance*: 'I think John [Nott] made a mistake with *Endurance*. I don't think that was critical at all but it was a mistake. It gave the wrong signal. But, whether it would have made any difference, I don't know.' He laughingly suggests: 'The real problem wasn't ours; it was Galtieri's.'[10] Nonetheless, these decisions, coupled with the British decision to grant independence to Belize in September 1981 (see Chapter 4), contributed to an Argentine impression that British power and interests in the region were waning.

Meanwhile, Argentina under President Jorge Rafael Videla enjoyed improved relations with the Reagan administration. The US was determined to secure a strong anti-communist ally in Latin America in order to protect American hemispheric interests, in particular, the battle against Soviet influence in the region. It hoped that if Argentina was allied with the US it could help to ensure the safety of the South Atlantic region against possible Soviet maritime activities.[11] Thus, the Reagan administration lifted the arms embargo placed by President Carter on Argentina and sent many high-ranking officials, such as US Ambassador at Large General Vernon Walters, and US Ambassador to the UN Jeane Kirkpatrick, to Argentina in a bid to improve bilateral relations. According to a report of a White House Interagency Group Meeting on Argentina on 23 February 1981, the US action plan for Argentina included among others: a US Army Chief of Staff visit (5–11 March); high level nuclear consultation; and periodic security consultation focusing on the security of the South Atlantic.[12] Videla was succeeded by General Roberto Eduardo Viola on 29 March 1981. However, this military dictatorship lasted a mere months, as Viola was ousted by a military junta led by General Leopoldo Fortunato Galtieri on 10 December 1981.

Under Galtieri there was a hardening of Argentine attitudes towards the sovereignty issue. The junta inherited a flagging economy, a devaluation in the peso, rising unemployment, inflation, falling wages and a rising trade deficit. Argentina needed a cause that would unite the country and would also distract public attention from the government's many failings. As a result, Argentina's socioeconomic problems along with a rising sense of nationalism were important factors in the Argentine decision to invade the Falkland Islands. Galtieri steadfastly championed the sovereignty issue, and 1982 was declared the year of the Malvinas. He appointed Dr Nicanor Costa Méndez as Argentina's Foreign Minister, who subsequently played a key role in exchanges involving Carrington, the British Ambassador in Buenos Aires, Anthony Williams, the US Ambassador in Buenos Aires, Harry Schlaudeman, and the US Secretary of State, Alexander Haig.

In early 1982 Carrington sought to enlist the help of the US in mediating the dispute, in particular, the good offices of the US Assistant Secretary of State for Inter-American Affairs, Thomas O. Enders. This was simply a precautionary measure as the FCO had determined, in conjunction with intelligence reports, that 'an Argentine attempt to invade the Falklands was unlikely in the near future'.[13] Nevertheless, the UK continued to engage in talks with Argentina, and negotiations in New York from 26 to 27 February resulted in a decision by both countries to reaffirm their resolve to find a negotiated solution to the sovereignty dispute.[14] The delegations led by Richard Luce (who had taken over from Ridley as Minister of State in the FCO after a Cabinet reshuffle in September 1981), Enrique Ros, the Argentine Deputy Foreign Minister, and Ambassador de Rozas succeeded in drafting a communiqué on the establishment of a Negotiating Commission on the Falklands issue.[15] These talks were, unbeknown to the UK, the last bilateral negotiations held before the Argentine invasion.

After New York the Argentine position hardened and Thatcher later admitted: 'With hindsight this was a turning point.'[16]

A few weeks later, on 19 March, a diplomatic crisis was triggered in South Georgia when an Argentine scrap-metal merchant named Constantino Davidoff, along with several Argentine soldiers, landed at Leith Harbour, South Georgia, under the guise of disassembling an abandoned whaling station. Davidoff had been approached by high-ranking Argentine officials in December 1981 with promises of a crew and free passage to South Georgia aboard an Argentine icebreaker to help him fulfil his contract. When the Davidoff party arrived on the island on 19 March on board the *Bahía Buen Suceso*, members of the British Antarctic Survey team working on the island became suspicious of men in army-style fatigues who raised the Argentine flag. The British team immediately contacted the Governor of the Falkland Islands, Rex Hunt, who ordered the Argentines to leave South Georgia and informed the FCO in London of events. The UK's reaction was one of disbelief. Cecil Parkinson recalls that the UK was 'taken by surprise', but suggests that Argentine actions did not worry the UK too much at this point:

> I think that we had been uneasy about this funny group who had landed on South Georgia and were allegedly collecting scrap metal. It didn't ring true, but nobody had any reason to take it too seriously because there were so few of them and the place was so many miles from anywhere.[17]

Carrington confirms the view that the UK was taken by surprise because 'all the intelligence said it wasn't going to happen'. He admits that the mistake he made 'was to rely too much on the intelligence'.[18] Argentina's actions were also unforeseen by John Nott, who later wrote that the Falkland Islands were not at the forefront of his concerns at the time. The Defence Secretary was, at the time, preoccupied with other matters such as the bi-annual meeting of NATO's Planning Group and the problems surrounding Britain's acquisition of the Trident D5 SLBM from the US.[19] The UK reacted with a flurry of diplomatic exchanges, followed by formal protests and the dispatch of HMS *Endurance* stationed at Port Stanley, East Falkland, to monitor the situation. The *Bahía Buen Suceso* left South Georgia on 21 March along with most of the party with the exception of twelve Argentines who remained on the island. A worried Carrington minuted his Cabinet colleagues on 24 March that Britain 'could not exclude the ultimate possibility of military action'.[20] Indeed, on 25 March, another Argentine vessel, the *Bahía Paraíso*, landed at Leith with Argentine marines on board. The British began to fear the growing possibility of an Argentine invasion of the Falkland Islands. Thatcher rang Carrington on 28 March to express her anxiety over the situation. The following day, the Prime Minister agreed to send a nuclear-powered submarine to the South Atlantic to reinforce HMS *Endurance*. Thatcher later wrote: 'My instinct was that the time had come to show the Argentines that we meant business.'[21]

Across the Atlantic, the Reagan administration was keen to diffuse the potential of war between two of its allies. On 28 March, Haig asked Ambassador Schlaudeman to urge Argentina not to take further steps to aggravate the situation. On 29 March, Ambassador Henderson contacted Deputy Secretary of State Walter Stoessel in order to convey British concerns. Stoessel informed Henderson that 'the USA did not wish to take sides between the UK and Argentina. They merely wished to counsel patience on both parties.'[22] In response, Carrington sent a message to the US Deputy Chief of Mission in the American embassy, London, Edward J. Streator, stating that the US appeared to be treating Britain on the same level as Argentina.[23] At this point, the US favoured a dovish approach to the developing crisis. Carrington believes that this was 'exceedingly annoying' and 'disgraceful'.[24] On 30 March, the US sent messages to the Argentine junta and to the Argentine Ambassador to the US, Esteban Takacs, stating that further action could seriously damage US–Argentine relations.[25]

On 31 March, British intelligence reports detailed the dispatch of Argentine frigates, the *Drummond* and *Granville*, and the sailing of the Argentine fleet. Nott immediately contacted Thatcher to arrange a meeting in her rooms in the House of Commons. A hastily arranged group, including Thatcher, Luce, Antony Acland, Permanent Under-Secretary of State at the FCO, and Humphrey Atkins, Lord Privy Seal (standing in for Carrington who was in Israel), were informed of the imminent invasion. Nott was alarmed and informed the group of the Ministry of Defence's (MOD) view that once the Falklands were seized they could not be retaken. This was unacceptable to Thatcher who replied: 'If they are invaded, we have got to get them back.'[26] Discussions regarding the assembling of a British Task Force ensued and an urgent message was drafted to Reagan asking him to intervene with Galtieri in the hope that he might dissuade further Argentine actions. The Thatcher government believed that the US would not hesitate to support its transatlantic ally in a possible war with Argentina. It assumed that the close bonds of friendship, a shared political and military history, and both leaders' commitment to the Special Relationship would predispose the Reagan administration to support British sovereign interests. The UK failed to comprehend the strategic importance of Argentina as a Latin American ally to the US.

Initial US neutrality

The US desire to improve its relations with Argentina was helped by the existence of a distinctly pro-Latin American faction in the State Department, of which Kirkpatrick and Enders were most prominent. Both were keen to ensure traditional US neutrality on the Falklands issue as they feared that US support for the British position would confirm suspicions in Latin America that the US would support European interests over those of its closest neighbours.[27] However, Enders' role and influence in affecting the US response to the Falklands crisis should not be overestimated. Although he shared many of Kirkpatrick's concerns, it was Kirkpatrick who was the principal champion of Latin American concerns in the White House. Kirkpatrick was the one who warned Reagan and US National Security Advisor William P. Clark that to support the UK in the Falklands War 'would engender a hundred years of animosity in Latin America'.[28] The distinction between Kirkpatrick and Enders did not go unnoticed by the British. Nicholas Henderson later wrote that Enders was 'more fascist than fool', whereas Kirkpatrick was 'more fool than fascist'. The Ambassador also lambasted Kirkpatrick as 'one of America's most reliable own goal-scorers: tactless, wrong-headed, ineffective'.[29] This damning accusation highlights the extent of British umbrage with Kirkpatrick at the time. Elsewhere in the Reagan administration, officials such as US Secretary of Defense Caspar W. Weinberger fought tirelessly to promote British interests in the South Atlantic. Under-Secretary of State for Political Affairs Lawrence Eagleburger was also a strong advocate of the British position, as he believed the US should support its NATO ally, the UK.[30]

The obvious disunity among the Reagan administration, coupled with overarching US foreign policy interests in Latin America, made initial US neutrality in the case of the Falklands inevitable. In addition, Argentina was at that time helping the CIA to train anti-Sandinista counter-revolutionaries, or 'contras', in Nicaragua (such activities will be examined in Chapter 5). The US did not want to jeopardise this assistance nor did it want to draw unwelcome attention to its Latin American policies by declaring support for either Argentina or the UK. This is a view shared by Neil Kinnock, who suggests that the US had already:

> got their jersey caught on the barbed wire over the Contras and other CIA operations in Central and Latin America. That was generating antagonism even in fairly right-wing political circles in the continent and they just didn't want the bother of it. That was the reason for being much more sotto voce than they should (in my view) have been with the Argentines.[31]

The reluctance to draw attention to its Latin American policies also fed into the US desire to distance itself from British interests in Latin America, in particular, those in the Falklands, which were seen by many in the hemisphere as outdated, colonial aspirations. As Adrian Beamish suggests:

> The hemisphere was not only the US backyard but also a sort of chasse gardée. And that meant that non-US initiatives, however well-meaning, were not much appreciated. For the British to be starting a

war in the chasse gardée was deeply unwelcome and required a lot of hasty readjustment on the part of the State Department policy wonks. This was a factor in the tensions between the US and the UK that Reagan and Thatcher had to work to overcome. In principle, the US is anti-colonial hence its agnosticism on the question of sovereignty over the Falkland Islands . . . Whatever the political realities might be it was important to the State Department to maintain a posture that did not jar too much with the anti-colonial and Third World posture and rhetoric of the Latin American republics . . . As the Falklands crisis deepened, the UK needed US support but the US did not need to be seen to be in bed with the British.[32]

An important question arises here. Why did Argentina decide to invade the Falkland Islands? Apart from the obvious sovereignty issue, the growing frustration of Argentina in the protracted negotiation process, the approaching 150th anniversary of British occupation of the islands, its own domestic problems and a view that Britain was unlikely to agree to the transfer of sovereignty willingly, there were also misconceptions of Britain's commitment to the islands. Argentina's plan to occupy the Falklands, or Operation 'Rosario' as it is otherwise known, was based upon the assumption that capturing the islands would be quick and bloodless, and that the UK would not use force to retake them.[33] Galtieri and his junta believed that due to the logistical problems that came with orchestrating a war in the South Atlantic and the considerable financial costs of such an operation, the British would not retaliate. This was a fundamental miscalculation by Argentina.[34] Argentina also believed that the US would not side with the British in a war as this would damage US–Argentine relations and would endanger Argentine support of the contras in Nicaragua. Furthermore, there is strong evidence to suggest that Kirkpatrick played a role in Argentine assumptions of American neutrality. It has been suggested that she unofficially provided assurances to the junta that the US supported the Argentine position in the Falklands.[35] Kirkpatrick certainly informed Argentina's Ambassador to the UN Eduardo Roca that she believed it would be impossible for the UK to bring a crisis in the Falklands before the UN. Henderson discussed Kirkpatrick's actions with Haig and claimed that Kirkpatrick informed Ambassador Roca that the US would not criticise Argentine actions in the Falklands in return for continued Argentine support of the US in Nicaragua. Haig assured an irate Henderson that this was not the case.[36]

The imminent invasion and Anglo-American consultation

Reagan responded to Thatcher's request for help on 31 March and assured the Prime Minister that attempts to contact Galtieri were under way. The President also assured her that the US would 'do what we can to assist you'.[37] Thatcher was encouraged as she believed US help was vital in dissuading Argentina from action as the US could, if it chose, put considerable financial and political pressure on the junta. Anglo-American consultation continued on 31 March when Haig met with Henderson in Washington to discuss the developing situation. According to Henderson, it was during this meeting that Haig decided to become more actively involved in the burgeoning crisis. Enders, who was also present at the meeting, reiterated that Argentina had assured him that it was not launching an attack and reminded those present that 'Argentina had been helpful to the USA over El Salvador'.[38] A thinly veiled reminder of the importance the US attached to its relationship with Argentina in the context of wider US–Latin American relations.

Haig met briefly with Ambassador Takacs on 1 April and argued that Argentina's use of force would reverse US–Argentine cooperation in Central America and that the Americans would have to side with the British. Haig informed Takacs that US–Argentine relations would be 'back to the worst days'.[39] Following numerous failed attempts to contact Galtieri by telephone, Reagan finally succeeded in the early hours of 2 April, the day Argentina invaded the Falklands. During their conversation Reagan stated that the US had 'solid information' that Argentina was planning to take military action. He appealed against such actions and offered the good offices of the US, which included the possibility of sending Vice-President George H. W. Bush to Buenos Aires to discuss the matter directly with Galtieri. The Argentine President refused the offer and informed Reagan that after 149 years of the UK refusing to relinquish sovereignty 'time had run out'.[40] Upon hearing of this, Henderson telephoned Thatcher directly and informed her of the conversation's substance. The Prime Minister was already aware of its import as during a late-night meeting with Carrington, who had returned from Israel, Haig had telephoned to convey the news.[41] Nonetheless, Reagan wrote to Thatcher to outline in detail his conversation with Galtieri and informed her that Galtieri had left him with the clear impression that he had 'embarked on a course of armed conflict'. Reagan assured the Prime Minister: 'while we have a policy of neutrality on the sovereignty issue, we will not be neutral on the issue involving Argentine use of military force'.[42]

The UK's delegation in the UN led by Sir Anthony Parsons initiated efforts to garner support for the British position in the Falklands and to seek collective condemnation of Argentine actions. The US joined nine other countries in adopting the British-sponsored UN Security Council Resolution (UNSCR) 502 on 3 April demanding an immediate and unconditional withdrawal by Argentina from the Falklands. UNSCR 502 provided the basis for what Parsons termed the 'three planks' of the UK's policy towards the Falklands: international support; economic and political measures against Argentina; and British military action under Article 51 of the UN Charter, that is, the right of individual or collective self-defence.[43] International support for UNSCR 502 was vital to the British as without it, as Nott later wrote, the UK 'would have been in trouble, as well as making our task in Parliament infinitely more difficult'.[44] However, UNSCR 502 alone was not enough for the UK. Thatcher drafted numerous messages to various world leaders to try to secure additional support for the UK in the form of sanctions against Argentina. As a result, the UK secured support from its European neighbours with the establishment of an embargo on military equipment to Argentina. When Argentine forces invaded and took South Georgia on 4 April, the UK again looked towards the US for support. It requested that the US condemn the attack, withdraw Schlaudeman from Buenos Aires, embargo arms shipments to Argentina and take the issue to the OAS. Much to the UK's dismay, the US cautioned against such action.[45] In light of this reaction, Henderson intensified his efforts in the US to raise awareness for the British position and appeared in a number of radio and television interviews denouncing Argentine aggression.

In the UK, Thatcher wasted little time in establishing a Task Force to set sail for the islands. The Task Force eventually consisted of over 100 ships and 27,000 personnel and set sail amid much ceremony from Portsmouth on 5 April. This was a defiant show of strength to Argentina and the wider international community. With the Task Force on its way, Carrington, who had been openly criticised for his failure to forecast the invasion, resigned along with FCO ministers Richard Luce and Humphrey Atkins. Carrington's resignation was a blow to Thatcher, who had counted on him for his sage analytical and decision-making abilities. The Prime Minister, along with her Deputy Prime Minister William Whitelaw and the government's Chief Whip, Michael Jopling, had tried unsuccessfully to persuade Carrington to remain as Foreign Secretary.[46] Carrington later wrote of his decision:

> It was a difficult as well as a painful decision and it was entirely my own ... As to the responsibility for the invasion itself, in the sense of having left undone something we should have done which would have pre-empted it, I could not with honesty and soul-searching feel much.[47]

Carrington was replaced by a leading Tory 'wet', the Lord President of the Council, Francis Pym; a man Thatcher had little time for. Their dislike was mutual. As David Owen put it, 'To him she was below the salt; to her he was a snob.'[48] Indeed, there was in Nott's words, 'a frequent clash of wills' between Thatcher and her new Foreign Secretary.[49] Pym favoured a diplomatic resolution to the crisis, whereas Thatcher was determined to oust the Argentines from the islands. Carrington contends that Pym was 'much more emollient about the Falklands than she was. He was always trying to get it settled and she wasn't.'[50] Notwithstanding this, Thatcher appointed Pym on the basis of his experience in foreign affairs and defence. Pym was seen as the sort of man who would be 'just right in a crisis'. However, as Thatcher later wrote: 'I was to have reason to question that judgement. Francis's appointment undoubtedly united the Party. But it heralded serious difficulties for the conduct of the campaign itself.'[51] Despite the obvious tension between Thatcher and Pym, the British government as a whole worked at maintaining a united front during the crisis, with the Cabinet meeting an additional two times a week in order to be kept informed of developments.

One of the Prime Minister's first objectives was to establish a War Cabinet to determine Britain's military strategies in a possible war with Argentina. The South Atlantic subcommittee of the Overseas and Defence Policy Committee of the Cabinet, or ODSA as it was otherwise known, included Thatcher, Whitelaw, Nott, Pym, Acland and Parkinson. ODSA also included Chief of Defence Staff Admiral Sir Terence Lewin, Cabinet Secretary Sir Robert Armstrong, Permanent Under-Secretary of State at the MOD Sir Frank Cooper and Special Adviser to the Prime Minister Sir Michael Palliser. Other important figures such as Attorney General Sir Michael Havers also attended the daily, sometimes twice daily, meetings of the War Cabinet. As Chancellor of the Exchequer, Sir Geoffrey Howe was not included in the ODSA. The decision to exclude him was made on the advice of former Prime Minister Harold Macmillan (who counselled Thatcher at the time). Thatcher recalled in her memoirs that Howe was 'upset', but the decision was based upon not wanting to compromise the security of British forces for financial reasons.[52] Parkinson, for his part, suggests that Howe was 'very bruised that he missed out on the War Cabinet'.[53]

Thatcher again contacted Reagan on 6 April with a request for the US to place economic sanctions on Argentina. The US responded by placing an arms embargo, but not a trade embargo as envisaged by the UK. The Prime Minister later concluded that at that stage 'the Americans were anxious to achieve a settlement that would prevent them having to choose between Britain, their natural ally, and their interests in Latin America'.[54] Indeed, Haig wrote to Reagan on 6 April regarding possible US mediation of the dispute and suggested that the US should act before it was placed 'in an untenable position of having to compromise our impartiality if we are to be responsive to escalating British requests for assistance'. Haig acknowledged that this would be a 'high-risk mission', but it was one he believed the US 'must take if we are not to suffer a major setback to our policies in this hemisphere'.[55] Haig's ensuing 'shuttle diplomacy' between Washington, London and Buenos Aires represented a US effort to resolve the situation by diplomatic means whilst securing vital US interests. Haig wanted a solution wherein Argentina could withdraw and Galtieri could save face thereby avoiding a potential power vacuum in Argentina. To that end, before leaving for London, Haig met with Henderson to discuss the possibility of establishing an international commission under the aegis of the OAS to remove the Argentine troops from the Falklands. Henderson was aghast at the suggestion and rejected it immediately.[56] This was an inauspicious start to the negotiating process. In fact, Henderson was doubtful of Haig's abilities as Secretary of State. He had previously described him in unenthusiastic terms: 'Haig is not firmly in the saddle: he does not have the President's trust in the way that Weinberger does, and is actively distrusted by Reagan's closest White House advisers . . . He has also proved a consistent own-goal scorer.'[57]

Haig's desire to keep Galtieri in power cast an unwelcome shadow over his subsequent talks with the British. As David Gompert, a member of Haig's mediation team put it: 'important American interests were on a collision course with one another: on the one hand, the Anglo-American special partnership and the principle of non-aggression, on the other, our Latin American relationships and our ability to maintain peace and tranquility in this hemisphere'.[58] In contrast to Haig, Weinberger made repeated attempts in NSC meetings throughout April 1982 to persuade his colleagues that 'there would be no support by other South American countries for Argentina; that there would be no adverse reactions by any of those countries' if the US decided to help Britain.[59]

Haig's shuttle diplomacy

Haig, accompanied by Streator, met with Thatcher and Pym on 8 April in Downing Street. During the meeting Thatcher informed

Haig that there was 'total determination' in the UK to use 'military strength if needed'. She expressed concern at American neutrality, but was appreciative of US help in intelligence matters.[60] Haig seemed to unofficially align the US with the UK in the crisis as he assured Thatcher that he was certain that she 'knew where the President stood. We are not impartial.'[61] Haig was determined to avoid active engagement between British and Argentine armed forces, and warned the Prime Minister that once engagement began it would become 'an increasingly difficult burden to protect principle'.[62] He proposed the withdrawal of Argentine forces, an interim administration including representatives from the US, Canada and two Latin American countries, and the resumption of negotiations. However, Thatcher refused to relinquish British authority over the islands and Haig informed Reagan that 'the Prime Minister has the bit in her teeth'.[63] Thatcher's doggedness was unnerving to Reagan as he wrote to Haig in response: 'The report of your discussions in London makes clear how difficult it will be to foster a compromise that gives Maggie enough to carry on and at the same time meets the test of "equity" with our Latin neighbors.'[64] This statement reveals the delicate position in which the US found itself. Reagan was obviously keen to support the British, but was fearful of alienating the US from its Latin American neighbours. This predicament was illustrated in Haig's interaction with British and Argentine officials during the mediation process. According to Henderson's memoirs, Haig repeatedly assured him that the US 'would not let its ally down as Washington had done over the Suez crisis'.[65] However, during a meeting with the Argentine President, Haig informed Galtieri of Thatcher's demand that the Argentines should withdraw before she would consider negotiating. Haig informed Galtieri: 'I told her [Thatcher] I was sure you could not accept this – and frankly I don't believe you should. The British position is tantamount to an ultimatum.'[66]

Following a visit with the Argentine government, Haig met with Thatcher again in London on 12 April with a revised proposal based on UNSCR 502 calling for: both sides to withdraw; a clause stating that no future military forces would be introduced on the islands; the establishment of a Special Commission including British, US and Argentine representatives; the lifting of economic sanctions against Argentina; and a call for the continuation of negotiations under the auspices of the UN charter to be completed by 31 December 1982.[67] During the meeting tensions began to surface between Haig and Thatcher with regard to stopping the Task Force prior to any Argentine withdrawal. Thatcher claimed that if she did so she would not survive in the House of Commons.[68] Meanwhile, Pym continued to search for a resolution to the conflict in tandem with Haig. On 12 April, the UK established a Maritime Exclusion Zone around the Falklands as a way to halt the incursion of Argentine vessels into waters surrounding the islands. Pym's suggestion that the exclusion zone should be delayed until after the US mediation efforts, so as not to offend Haig, was met with incredulity by his colleagues. Nott saw this as 'an absurd suggestion' as, according to him, to delay the establishment of the exclusion zone 'would have been disastrous because it was vital that we [the UK] showed determination at the outset to take the islands back'.[69]

As the crisis deepened Haig increasingly misinterpreted the British position. He wrote to Reagan on 14 April stating that he was 'convinced that Mrs. Thatcher wants a peaceful solution and is willing to give Galtieri a fig leaf'.[70] Reagan contacted Galtieri on 15 April and urged both parties to show 'flexibility and restraint' in the days ahead. Reagan reiterated US neutrality, but warned Galtieri that if fighting broke out this would be 'much more difficult'.[71] Following this discussion, Reagan wrote to Thatcher and referred yet again to the difficulties the US faced in its relationship with Argentina. Reagan thanked Thatcher for being receptive to US efforts to try to find common ground between the UK which was one of the US' 'closest allies, and Argentina, with whom we would like to be able to cooperate in advancing specific interests in this hemisphere'.[72] Thatcher responded to Reagan on 16 April to reaffirm that the UK's 'earnest aim' was to avoid conflict (this was written on the same day the ODSA discussed possible rules of engagement for a war with Argentina). The Prime Minister ended her letter with a cautionary message: 'it is essential that America, our closest friend and ally, should share with us a common perception of the fundamental issues of democracy and freedom which are at stake'.[73] Reagan rang Thatcher the following day to inform her that he had contacted Haig in Buenos Aires to tell him to return home if there was no break in the Argentine position.[74] Despite such reassurances, Thatcher was keen to impart to the US the importance she attached to its support. Accordingly, British concerns regarding US neutrality were expressed during a meeting between William P. Clark and Henderson in Washington on 17 April. During the meeting Clark expressed concern at reports that British opinion was critical of American neutrality. Clark could not understand this because 'America was helping in all sorts of ways but had to remain neutral in public while the talks were going on'.[75]

Haig wrote to Pym on 19 April to outline a revised proposal put forward by Argentina during his recent visit to Buenos Aires. The proposal included a link between the interim period of administration and the negotiations process. It also argued that 'the rights of the inhabitants refer only to individual rights and not a "collective" right of self-determination'.[76] Thatcher was singularly unimpressed by the proposal. For her, the right to self-determination of the islanders was paramount. In a diary entry dated the same day Reagan wrote: 'I don't think Margaret Thatcher should be asked to concede anymore.'[77] A US tilt towards the UK was becoming increasingly apparent. A member of Haig's mediation team, NSC official James 'Jim' Rentschler, argued in a message to Clark on 20 April that it was essential for the US to back the UK for reasons that 'transcend the already compelling ties of history, language, and formal alliance. Our strategic imperatives in the East– West context and the stakes we have in asserting the primacy of our Western leadership require it.'[78]

Argentina approached the OAS on 20 April to pass a resolution in favour of invoking the Rio Treaty (Inter-American Treaty of Reciprocal Assistance) against Britain (this was largely in response to the EEC's one-month ban on imports from Argentina). The OAS' subsequent resolution on 21 April urged the US not to aid Britain 'in deference to the principle of hemispheric solidarity'.[79] However, the resolution did not go as far as Argentina hoped, as it failed to impose sanctions against the UK. It was, instead, a rather lacklustre response by the OAS to the Falklands crisis. This worried Argentina greatly as it needed strong OAS support given Thatcher's success in the EEC and the growing support for the British position in US political circles. Indeed, Democrat Senator Daniel Patrick Moynihan had on the same day introduced a draft resolution to the Senate calling for a US trade embargo against Argentina.

Anglo-American tensions resurfaced on 21 April when Henderson informed Haig of the British decision to retake South Georgia. He was told quite firmly that the British were informing, not consulting him. Haig suggested informing Argentina of this news, but was allegedly dissuaded by Henderson from doing so.[80] In fact, the UK's former Head of the Chancery in Washington, Robin Renwick, later wrote that some 'violent remonstrances' were required by the British to prevent Haig from informing Argentina.[81] However, the official British historian of the Falklands War, Lawrence D. Freedman, suggests that Haig did warn the junta about the British decision in order to warn the Argentines about the 'possible consequences of their intransigence'.[82] When questioned about the possibility of such information being leaked to Argentina, Nott suggests:

> I'm afraid I do believe that . . . The State Department saw its policies towards South America going down the tube. I was very much against informing the Americans that we were about to attack South Georgia but we were persuaded by Francis Pym that it was courteous to do so. Haig then said that he felt that he was under an obligation to inform the Argentinians, which was a ridiculous suggestion really.[83]

The suggestion that Haig may have leaked such information to Argentina is strengthened by his conversation with Clark on an open line a few days earlier. After this call Haig wrote to Clark explaining: 'I called you on open line with clear recognition that Argentines would monitor. In order to break impossible impasse this morning on force withdrawal modalities, I created impression [sic] that British military action was about to take place.' Haig suggested that this was 'somewhat over-theatrical', but had the 'virtue of being true in the context of first British units steaming toward South Georgia island'.[84]

Haig invited Pym to Washington on 22–23 April to engage in more bilateral discussions. On 23 April, during a meeting between Clark, Pym and Henderson at the White House, a surprising US offer was made. Clark suggested the idea of a trusteeship for the islands by the US for a period of five years, after which the US would be prepared to guarantee the status the islanders decided upon. This suggestion was championed by Reagan, but an outraged Pym promptly dismissed the idea. The Foreign Secretary was offended by the lack of consultation extended by the US on such an important issue. In its place a new proposal was put forward by Haig to be brought back to London by Pym.[85] On 24 April, in what was later called 'the final drama of the Haig negotiations', Pym presented an amended set of proposals to the War Cabinet.[86] These proposals included the possibility of a negotiated transfer of sovereignty whilst affording the Falkland islanders the right to choose between independence and the right to associate with either Argentina or the UK. This meant that the islanders' situation would never return to normal as the British saw it. The proposals also called for a joint withdrawal of forces, an end to sanctions against Argentina and the establishment of an interim authority on the islands with representatives from the Argentine government. Pym argued strongly for the War Cabinet to accept these proposals. Thatcher was appalled at the suggestion and saw the terms of the proposal as completely unacceptable. A quick-thinking Nott suggested that the proposals should be put forward first to Argentina for acceptance. If Argentina rejected them (as anticipated by the British) the UK could then lean on the US to publicly support its position in the Falklands. This was a calculated move; one that allowed the diplomatic process to continue and also allowed British forces to retake South Georgia on 25 April without fear of diplomatic admonition.

Haig presented his final peace plan to Argentina and sought a response by midnight on 27 April. This deadline was encouraged by the approaching British Task Force to the exclusion zone. As anticipated in London, the junta rejected the proposal by declaring on 28 April that Argentina's objective was 'the recognition of its sovereignty over the Malvinas' and that this was an 'un-renounceable goal'.[87] Following this announcement,

Thatcher wrote to Reagan on 29 April to seek his support: 'I cannot conceal from you how deeply let down I and my colleagues would feel if under these circumstances the US were not now to give us its full support.'[88] Reagan responded to this letter the same day yet again promoting a peaceful solution to the crisis and offering US assistance in achieving the same. More importantly, he stated that the US would give its full 'support for you and the principles of international law and order you are defending. You can count on that support in whatever forum this issue is debated. You can also count on our sympathetic consideration of requests for assistance.'[89] US support was all but assured for the UK.

On 30 April, an NSC meeting was held based upon the State Department paper 'Next Steps on the Falklands'. During the meeting a number of possibilities regarding US support for the British position whilst limiting possible adverse effects on US–Argentine relations were reviewed. Deputy National Security Advisor Robert 'Bud' McFarlane opened the meeting by declaring that the Falklands dispute had reached a watershed. Haig outlined the dilemma that the US felt regarding the 'growing pressures at home and abroad' to support the UK and the need to manage its relations with Argentina. He advised that the US did not want to 'close the door on diplomacy', and warned that the US needed to be careful in how it raised its 'tilt' towards the UK. However, Haig's miscalculation of Thatcher's position on the Falklands issue was again apparent as he suggested that the Prime Minister was 'reasonably satisfied' with the US position up to that point.[90] In reality, nothing was further from the truth. The NSC meeting was followed by a press statement issued by Haig on 30 April announcing formal US support of the British in the Falklands. This was a turning point in Anglo-American relations during the Falklands War.

Thatcher was overjoyed as the UK could proceed with its plans to retake the Falklands militarily safe in the knowledge of assured US diplomatic and material support. Furthermore, Haig's irksome mediation efforts had come to an end. Indeed, Haig's efforts had not been well received by many in the Cabinet, including the Prime Minister. In Charles Powell's words:

They were a huge hindrance. Margaret Thatcher hated them. She thought that they were just trying to get us to accept in some form or another Argentine sovereignty over the Falklands which she was never going to be prepared to concede . . . But did she for one minute welcome them? No she did not! And she made that very clear to Haig. She was not one to mince her words when it came to dealing with that issue.[91]

Bernard Ingham similarly adds:

I consider Al Haig's machinations a blithering nuisance. Instead of acting as an ally he strode the world as a mediator, no doubt wishing to go down in history as the man who avoided hostilities, regardless of the terms of that avoidance. The only realistic terms would have left the Argentines in possession of the Falklands. That would have solved nothing.[92]

Geoffrey Howe suggests of the mediation efforts that: 'They weren't discussed much in Cabinet . . . except for Margaret Thatcher's reaction. She was unenthusiastic about going much along that road. Francis Pym on the other hand was more disposed to do so.'[93] Parkinson for his part contends: 'We all thought that he [Haig] was hopelessly optimistic . . . Haig did his very best but he was flogging a dead horse.' He also suggests that Thatcher gave Haig 'an absolutely impossible negotiating mandate . . . it was ridiculous'.[94]

Why then did Thatcher entertain Haig's mediation efforts? Was it simply in deference to her close relationship with Washington? Put simply, the answer is no. This was not an attempt by the UK to merely appease the US. The Haig mediation efforts allowed the UK to concentrate on the deployment of the Task Force essentially buying them time before British forces could land on the islands. Parkinson suggests: 'The diplomacy was backed up by the force. Because it took them eight weeks to get there, the diplomats had eight weeks.'[95] Nott supports this view: 'As Defence Secretary I was happy with this long protracted business because it diverted the attention of the world from the progress of our Task Force towards the Falklands.'[96]

Another important question arises here. Why did the US choose to support the British at such a late stage in the crisis? The failure of mediation process undoubtedly contributed to the American about-face. However, this alone was not enough to sway the US position. Increasing domestic pressure also contributed to the US tilt in favour of the UK. In fact, support for the British position had grown substantially in American political circles. The House Foreign Affairs Committee had adopted a resolution sponsored by Democrat Congressman Stephen J. Solarz days earlier which called for Argentina to withdraw its troops from the islands. It also proposed full US diplomatic support of the UK in its 'efforts to uphold the rule of law' in the event of the failure of diplomatic talks (the House of Representatives later adopted the resolution on 4 May).[97] This is a view supported by Michael Heseltine, who believes that American public opinion 'became very much supportive of Britain's position and that persuaded President Reagan to move his initial scepticism'.[98] The US also feared that should the Argentines remain in the Falklands, Thatcher would be forced to step down as Prime Minister. This would leave a vacuum in the UK that the anti-nuclear Labour Party would be happy to fill. This possibility did not appeal to the Reagan administration given its existing ideological compatibility with the Conservative Thatcher government. The US needed Thatcher as a strong ally within NATO and as a champion of US interests in Europe.[99] This, combined with growing British frustration with US neutrality, in particular the Prime Minister's, greatly impacted the American position. Thatcher played a pivotal role in persuading the US to support its long-standing ally, the UK. This is a view shared by many of her former colleagues such as Ingham, who argues that the Prime Minister 'put the hard word on Ronald Reagan' over the Falklands. He further contends:

> Mrs Thatcher told Reagan bluntly that if he did not support a democracy against a junta and allowed a junta to march into the Falklands with impunity then he would not be able to stop other dictatorships marching all over small states. She made him stand up for the principle of free determination.[100]

Powell suggests that 'over time she wore President Reagan down'. Moreover, he believes that Thatcher's ability to persuade Reagan, whilst 'obviously very important', 'took longer than you might have thought given their basic ideological similarity and their basic friendship'. Powell also suggests that the US decision to support the UK 'had to be fought out within the American administration and finally Reagan had to come down on one side or the other. He came down on the right one.'[101]

On a personal level, Reagan's support of the British position was unquestionable. He was torn between maintaining the Anglo-American Special Relationship and establishing firm ties with the Argentine junta. Argentina's rejection of Haig's final proposals presented Reagan with the opportunity he needed to come out in public support of the UK. Indeed, as Reagan later wrote: 'the depth of this special relationship made it impossible for us to remain neutral during Britain's war with Argentina over the Falkland Islands in 1982, although it was a conflict in which I had to walk a fine line'.[102] As Beamish suggests:

> For the US a number of possible outcomes would have been acceptable. In Mrs. Thatcher's case there was only one acceptable outcome, Argentine evacuation of the islands. Anything less would have been a failure and a humiliation and could have brought her premiership to an end. So for her the stakes could not have been higher nor the goal clearer. This was an asset in her dealing with Reagan and she exploited it fully. He had the weaker hand . . . Reagan was not troubled to lose points in his dialogue with Mrs. Thatcher because he recognised that she was fighting for principles both held dear and in his case dearer than the short-term objective of the State Department's Latin American policies.[103]

Whatever the motivations behind US formal support of the UK in the Falklands War, the decision was welcomed in London. The first British air operations on the Falkland Islands began on 1 May with operation 'Black Buck 1' in which Port Stanley airfield was bombed by a British Vulcan strategic bomber aircraft. This operation was followed by various Sea Harrier attacks on the Stanley and Goose Green airfields. Given the escalation in the crisis and subsequent international criticisms, American support (both material and otherwise) was vital to the British.

International reactions to the war

International reactions to the crisis were divided. The Soviet Union was open in its condemnation of what it saw as colonialism at work in the Latin American hemisphere, and announced its 'complete support for Argentine action to regain sovereignty' over the Falkland Islands.[104] This was disconcerting to the British and the Americans, who feared the possible involvement of the Soviet Union, or its proxy Cuba, in the war by arming Argentina. Unsurprisingly, Commonwealth members such as Canada, Australia, New Zealand, Belize and Dominica were quick to condemn Argentine actions. Guyana, for its part, pledged 'complete solidarity' with any UK or Commonwealth initiatives to restore the status quo in the Falklands.[105] In Europe, the reaction to events in the South Atlantic was more restrained.[106] Italy expressed its condemnation of the 'act of strength' made by Argentina whilst encouraging the withdrawal of armed forces and a resumption of negotiations. Following weeks of procrastination, Italy finally agreed to place an embargo on arms exports to Argentina but, importantly, it did not publicly support the British position.[107] This was in deference to Italy's historical cultural, economic and political ties with Argentina. West Germany, under Chancellor Helmut Schmidt, made its support of EEC sanctions against Argentina dependent upon Britain's interest in continued diplomatic negotiations. This was inspired by a West German wish to re-establish friendly relations with Argentina in the aftermath of the EEC sanctions.[108] France was the most vocal European advocate of the British position. French President François Mitterrand was the first foreign leader to ring Thatcher directly to offer support. In doing so, France provided the British with important intelligence on French Exocet anti-ship missiles that the Argentine Navy possessed. France also sent French planes to the UK so that British pilots could train against them.[109] However, European support was not unequivocal as seen in the Spanish response to the crisis. While Spain supported the Argentine claim to the Falklands, it was torn between its former claim to the islands, its historical ties with Argentina and the wider Latin American region, and its ongoing desire to become a member of the EEC. Added to this, Spain did not want to alienate itself from the UK, as it was then involved in ongoing negotiations with the UK over the contested territory of Gibraltar on the Iberian Peninsula. As a result, Spain abstained from UNSCR 502 and called for a ceasefire in the crisis.[110]

In Latin America, too, the reaction to the crisis was mixed. Cuba issued a statement on 1 May declaring its 'solidarity' with Argentina.[111] Guatemala supported Argentina inspired by its long-standing feud with the UK over territorial claims to Belize (see Chapter 4). Guatemalan President General Fernando Romeo Lucas García even placed 350 paratroopers and marines on standby to be flown to Port Stanley to engage in combat against the UK should the need arise.[112] Venezuela specified that if armed conflict took place between Argentina and the UK, then the Venezuelan government would provide assistance to Argentina and would break its diplomatic relations with the UK.[113] In another marked show of solidarity with Argentina various Latin American countries, including Nicaragua, Peru, Ecuador, Bolivia and Colombia, increased their trade with Argentina to compensate for European sanctions.[114] While Mexico condemned Argentina's use of force, it supported Argentine efforts in seeking to obtain 'acknowledgement of its sovereignty' over the Malvinas. Brazil also offered to send military equipment, but not troops, to Argentina in the fight against the British.[115] On the other hand, the UK found allies in the region in the guise of Uruguay and Chile. Uruguay helped the UK to evacuate wounded servicemen during the conflict via its capital city and chief port, Montevideo.[116] Uruguay was, in Gloria Hooper's words, 'particularly helpful to the British forces in terms of servicing ships' during the Falklands crisis. Hooper asserts that Chile, under the leadership of Pinochet, was a keen supporter of the UK. She suggests that Pinochet was 'a military strategist and followed with great interest the campaign'.[117] In fact, Pinochet instructed his government, within the context of its neutrality, to provide whatever assistance it could to its 'friend and ally'.[118] This support was influenced by Chile's ongoing border dispute with Argentina over the Beagle Channel. Chilean intelligence proved very useful to the British, but its support was not unlimited. When the UK approached Chile regarding the possibility of stationing Nimrod maritime patrol aircraft in their airfields during the war it was unsuccessful in this request. Nott describes Chile as a 'cautious' ally given the strong opposition of other South American countries.[119] Parkinson argues a more active Chilean involvement in events as he suggests that 'Chile was intercepting Argentinian intelligence and was relaying it to ours [the UK]'.[120]

US material support

US material help was instrumental in helping the British to victory in the war. However, the timing and extent of American material support is a matter of some debate. According to Pym, the US was 'active on our behalf behind the scenes'.[121] Argentina has claimed that the US provided intelligence to the British prior to the beginning of the war in April 1982; a claim fervently denied by the Americans. In Haig's words, 'we provided no intelligence support before the collapse of negotiations'.[122] However, former US Secretary of the Navy John Lehman argues that the US role was never in doubt when Argentina invaded the Falklands. He suggests that the conflict was a 'textbook case of the special relationship in action ... Britain took a stand on principle and the United States provided the help expected of a close ally'. It appears that the Pentagon, unbeknown to many in Washington, provided significant intelligence support to the UK during the early stages of the conflict. Lehman argues that it was 'highly unlikely' that anyone in the White House or State Department understood the extent of communications and intelligence assistance provided by the US to Britain.[123]

The US certainly provided the UK with significant signal and satellite intelligence (SIGINT) during the war. This intelligence was provided under the auspices of the 1947 UK/USA Agreement, which closely linked British and American intelligence capabilities from then onwards. Anglo-American intelligence cooperation included the CIA, the British Defence Staff and the US National Reconnaissance Office, which all shared vital information during the South Atlantic war.[124] It was later claimed that the true extent of US involvement in intelligence gathering during and prior to the collapse of negotiations was deliberately kept quiet. The British were supposedly protecting the US in order not to implicate their allies and also to protect the code-breaking mechanisms the US provided.[125] Nevertheless, the consensus within British circles is that the US provided significant SIGINT during the crisis. Ingham agrees that the US gave 'abundant intelligence support' to the British.[126]

The British had an intelligence group in South America that routinely reported to the Joint Intelligence Committee (JIC) throughout the crisis. Information was also relayed to the CIA from naval and defence attachés and from intelligence 'friends' (spies) in Argentina, which was passed on to the British.[127] The vast majority of intelligence came from the US tracking station in southern Chile, and was relayed to the National Security Agency (NSA) in Washington and then directly to the UK Government's Communications Headquarters (GCHQ) in Cheltenham. This intelligence was enhanced by material received from the Her Majesty's New Zealand Ship (HMNZS) station, the SIGINT base on Ascension Island and the US SIGINT base on Galeta Island off the coast of Panama.[128] Despite all these sophisticated intelligence networks, the US ultimately failed to inform the British of Argentine plans to invade. Nonetheless, US intelligence support proved fruitful when the Reagan administration was persuaded by the UK to change the direction of the orbit of a US SIGINT satellite in order to provide important satellite imagery of the region. The American willingness to change the satellite's orbit reflected the fact that despite the regional importance of Argentina to the US, the UK was globally important in terms of shared bases and intelligence cooperation. Nott argues that the US was not prepared initially 'to shift their satellite', and argues that it 'gave very little intelligence support' to the UK during the war. He recalls: 'I don't remember recovering any special intelligence reports from the United States other than the general relationship which was very close.'[129] This statement appears somewhat at odds with the general perception of the level of American intelligence support during the Falklands

War. Nott is quick to point out, however, that Weinberger was 'extremely helpful in providing facilities'. In Nott's words:

> We had great support from the Pentagon, none really from the State Department or the Security Council. It was not until later when Reagan realised that Congress and the American people were on our side that there was support from the American government generally. In fact, Weinberger and the Defense Department were very much working on their own.[130]

Interestingly, minutes of the NSC meeting held on the Falklands on 30 April record an exchange between Weinberger and Deputy Director of the CIA Admiral Bobby Ray Inman regarding US military aid to the UK. When questioned on this aid by Inman, Weinberger replied that 'nothing was pending but believed that more fuel would be requested for Ascension, plus ground support on Ascension and perhaps more specialized ammunition'.[131] This would suggest that US material support was provided to the British before the end of Haig's mediation efforts. Indeed, the British had been expeditiously granted the use of American military facilities on the British-owned (but US-leased) Ascension Island, which was located roughly half way between Britain and the Falkland Islands. Ascension allowed the Royal Air Force (RAF) to use the island's Wideawake airfield as a staging post to conduct over 600 sorties by both VC10 and Hercules aircraft in its military campaign and supply drops in the Falklands and South Georgia. These sorties allowed the movement of over 5,800 people and over 6,600 tons of supplies.[132]

The US also provided invaluable material provisions to the British, including aviation fuel, spare parts and the provision of 150,000 square yards of matting in order to create a temporary airstrip on Ascension.[133] US covert communications links enabled portable radio transmitters to contact controllers by a direct satellite link and were used by Britain's Special Air Service (SAS) teams during the war.[134] In addition, the Reagan administration supplied anti-aircraft Stingers and radar-seeking Shrikes for use by the Vulcans. It also provided HMS *Illustrious* with the Vulcan Phalanx anti-missile gun system. It was estimated that the US provided at least US$120 million of material in the month of May 1982 alone to the British forces in the South Atlantic.[135]

Weinberger proved himself a worthy ally and a committed Anglophile in enabling the provision of vital US material support to the British. Howe recalls that US material support was 'inspired by Cap Weinberger. Of course he was a willing partner.'[136] Weinberger himself believed that 'if the British were going to mount a counterattack and try to retake the Islands, we should, without any question, help them to the utmost of our ability'.[137] To that end, Weinberger authorised the provision of over 12 million gallons of aviation fuel, 200 Sidewinder air-to-air missiles and copious amounts of ammunition.[138] The Sidewinders were important as they supplemented and improved the capabilities of the Sea Harriers. The US also provided 200 MK-46 torpedoes for use against Argentine submarines.[139] In order to provide such material, Weinberger had to bypass the normal channels of the supply authorisation process by approaching Reagan directly. In doing so, he succeeded in reducing the transfer time needed to authorise and dispatch supplies from a two-week period to a mere twenty-four hours. In all, Weinberger eliminated fifteen stages from the supply authorisation process.[140]

Weinberger even proposed sending the USS *Eisenhower* to support the British in the South Atlantic by acting as a mobile runway for RAF aircraft. According to Parkinson, 'At that point we said, "No" . . . that would be very provocative.' Parkinson further suggests: 'I've always felt that he [Reagan] knew what Weinberger was up to.'[141] Henderson recalls Weinberger's offer as one 'of spontaneous and practical generosity that must be unique in the annals of the Washington–London relationship'.[142] These provisions inspired Thatcher to later gush of Weinberger: 'America never had a wiser patriot, nor Britain a truer friend.'[143] In recognition of his loyalty to the UK during the Falklands War, Weinberger was given an honorary knighthood by the Queen in 1988. Howe recalls that the ceremony was an intimate affair: 'It was a very personal occasion. Everyone knew that quote unquote, that Cap Weinberger had really been on our side, Al Haig not.'[144]

The Peruvian proposals

The US continued to play a role in pursuing a peaceful settlement of the crisis even after the failed Haig mediation efforts. Peruvian President Fernando Belaúnde Terry contacted Haig on 2 May to ask for US assistance in drafting new proposals for the settlement of the Falklands crisis. Haig willingly agreed as he wanted not only to resolve the crisis, but to salvage some domestic and international credibility in the wake of his tender of resignation on 25 June (he agreed to stay on in the position until 5 July).[145] On 2 May, one of Britain's most controversial actions during the Falklands War was undertaken. The Argentine cruiser, the *General Belgrano*, was sunk by the UK nuclear attack submarine, HMS *Conqueror*, some thirty miles outside the exclusion zone. The loss of 321 crew members quickly dispelled any hope of a negotiated settlement. Following the sinking of the *General Belgrano* condemnation was rife amongst the international community. The Irish government called for an end to EEC sanctions against Argentina and called for the UN to request an immediate cease-fire. Italy, Germany and Denmark also voiced concerns regarding the escalation in fighting.[146] Despite Galtieri's rejection of the Peruvian initiative on 3 May, Haig and Belaúnde Terry persisted. However, Galtieri's intransigence, along with the Argentine sinking of HMS *Sheffield* on 4 May with the loss of twenty-one crew members, made the possibility of a successful negotiated outcome to the crisis increasingly unlikely.

Haig was undeterred and met with Henderson in Washington on 5 May to discuss the latest proposals put forward by Pym. The proposals which suggested a ceasefire included a reference to the restoration of the former (British) administration of the islands and the need for the wishes of the islanders to be respected. However, Haig refused to put Pym's proposals forward to Peru and Argentina as he did not consider that there was the 'slightest chance' that Peru would agree to them. Haig insisted that there was 'no conceivable chance' of reaching an agreement if the UK insisted on such language in the proposal.[147] Henderson and Haig had a 'prolonged argument' about respect for the wishes of the islanders, including the issue of the future administration of the islands.[148] Instead, Haig put forward proposals, in conjunction with Peru, that included: the immediate cessation of hostilities; a joint withdrawal and non-reintroduction of forces; a neutral administration of the islands on a temporary basis by a contact group comprising of representatives from the US, Brazil, Peru and West Germany; a joint recognition of each other's differences regarding the status of the Falkland Islands; an acknowledgement of the islanders' aspirations and interests; and a deadline for the contact group to reach a definitive agreement by 30 April 1983.[149]

The initiative to internationalise the islands was espoused by the State Department and Reagan. The President wrote to Thatcher on 5 May to encourage her to accept these proposals as he believed that it was the best way in which to achieve a peaceful settlement and avoid more lives being lost.[150] The Prime Minister was unimpressed with the proposals and outlined her misgivings in her response to Reagan on the same day. Thatcher argued that the proposals did not provide 'unambiguously for a right to self-determination'. In order to temper Haig's proposals, the Prime Minister suggested that the interim administration must consult with the locally elected representatives on the islands. Thatcher would agree to Haig's proposals if such changes were incorporated.[151] Haig agreed to incorporate the changes and the UK tentatively accepted the UNSCR 502-based Peruvian proposals. However, this agreement was short-lived as Argentina ultimately rejected the original Peruvian proposals on 6 May based upon the inclusion of the US in negotiations on the future of the islands and the continued British demands regarding the rights and wishes of the islanders.[152] The UK was unfazed by Galtieri's rejection of the proposals. Parkinson recalls: 'I don't think Belaúnde's proposals really had the slightest chance of running. They just gradually disappeared in the wash.'[153] Nott describes them as 'an understandable distraction from our objective which was to recapture the islands by force'.[154]

Anglo-American consultation and Reagan's five-point peace plan

Anglo-Argentine tensions continued to grow when the UK extended the perimeter of the exclusion zone to twelve miles from Argentina's coast on 7 May. In response, Argentina declared a 'war zone' in the South Atlantic on 11 May. In the US, Reagan re-emphasised his support of the UK when he signed National Security Decision Directive (NSDD) 34, 'US Actions in the South Atlantic Crisis', on 14 May. This suspended all US military exports to Argentina and withheld new Export–Import Bank credits, insurance and guarantees to Argentina.[155] The UK presented a final set of proposals to the UN on 17 May, which called for a complete Argentine withdrawal within fourteen days in return for the lifting of the exclusion zone and the lifting of economic measures against Argentina. Argentina responded on 19 May with a call to extend the withdrawal to thirty days.[156] This was unacceptable to the British.

During this time, UN Secretary General Javier Pérez de Cuéllar also tried to mediate the dispute by seeking to provide an alternative to the failed Peruvian proposals. His subsequent proposals were based upon a cease-fire, a mutual withdrawal of forces from the islands and an end to all sanctions against Argentina. Despite such attempts to broker a settlement, the Secretary General was unable to find a compromise acceptable to both the UK and Argentina.[157] On 19 May, Parkinson recalls that Thatcher telephoned the Secretary General to thank him for his efforts in trying to resolve the dispute and to 'her horror' he responded: 'Mrs Thatcher, thank you for those wonderful words. I really feel I owe it to you to make one further effort.' This, according to Parkinson, was said at the time that the UK had already given the orders to land in the islands in forty-eight hours.[158] Pérez de Cuéllar had misinterpreted Thatcher's words as a signal for another peace proposal initiative. Thatcher was worried as the War Cabinet had planned to deploy British ground forces on the Falklands on 21 May. However, having failed to get an Argentine response to yet another new set of proposals, the UN Secretary General informed the UNSC on 20 May that his peace efforts had come to an end.[159] British forces launched an amphibious assault on 21 May at San Carlos Water, off the coast of East Falkland Island. This assault marked the first landing of British ground forces and the beginning of Anglo-Argentine hand-to-hand combat in the Falklands War.

Anglo-Argentine fighting escalated and on 25 May the British fleet suffered a significant blow when the *Atlantic Conveyor* was hit by Argentine Exocet missiles and HMS *Coventry* was sunk by Argentine Skyhawk attack aircraft.[160] By this stage, the US began to fear that the UK would not agree to any concessions with Argentina. Haig wrote to Reagan on 26 May informing him that the latest US exchanges with the British confirmed that 'they are currently not of a mind to work toward a negotiated settlement which gives anything at all to the Argentines before they retake the Islands'. Haig suggested that the US should 'conserve our leverage with Mrs Thatcher until it can be used to produce results, i.e., when the islands are effectively in British hands'.[161] This message was sent on the same day that Ireland put forward a resolution in the UN calling for a cessation of hostilities and a return to negotiations. The resulting UNSCR 505 was unanimously adopted and reaffirmed UNSCR 502. It called for Pérez de Cuéllar to undertake a renewed mission of good office and to submit an interim report on the crisis to the UNSC by 2 June.

Anglo-American relations were strained during a late-night telephone conversation between Reagan and Thatcher on 31 May when the President asked the Prime Minister to strike a deal with the junta. Reagan hoped that such a deal would help to avoid complete Argentine humiliation. The deal was based upon the suggested establishment of a UN trusteeship on the islands and was originally put forward by Chief of the Argentine Air Force and junta member, Brigadier Basilio Lami Dozo, who feared a possible Argentine move towards the Soviet Union and Cuba. Lami Dozo approached Kirkpatrick with the plan, who in turn presented it to Reagan.[162] (Kirkpatrick wanted to avoid the possibility of a US veto in line with the UK of any future UNSCR demanding a ceasefire in the Falklands which could further endanger wider US–Latin American relations.) During his conversation with Thatcher, Reagan outlined his concern that the junta might fall in Argentina only to be replaced with leftist Peronists.[163] This was unacceptable to the Prime Minister. British troops were at that moment closing in on the last remaining undefeated Argentine garrison in Port Stanley. Thatcher firmly rejected Reagan's suggestion and was left feeling dismayed by her exchange with the President. She rang Henderson to vent her considerable frustrations and denounced Reagan's proposals as 'pure Haigism'.[164]

In the UN, Panama and Spain sponsored a resolution calling for an immediate ceasefire and for Pérez de Cuéllar to implement UNSCRs 502 and 505 in their entirety. The resolution was to be voted on in the UN on 4 June. Argentina tried to influence the Latin American faction in the State Department in a bid to sway the US position away from an anticipated veto in line with the UK. Enrique Ros contacted Enders to try to convince the US to abstain from the vote in order to safeguard US–Argentine relations.[165] Meanwhile, Reagan and Thatcher were due to attend a Western G7 Summit in Versailles on 3–4 June. It was rumoured that the President would present Thatcher with a five-point peace plan as a final attempt to negotiate a settlement in the Falklands before the UN vote. It was anticipated that Reagan would present the plan to Thatcher during private talks planned with her on 4 June. The peace plan was allegedly intended to involve countries such as Jamaica and Brazil in a peace-keeping operation in the Falklands following a proposed Anglo-Argentine withdrawal from the islands.[166] However, there is some confusion as to whether or not Reagan proposed such a plan to Thatcher. The pair certainly discussed the situation in the Falklands during a meeting in Versailles, but as the customary note-takers were not present during this meeting there is, to date, no documentary evidence to prove that Reagan did present a five-point peace plan to Thatcher. If such evidence does exist, it remains classified. Furthermore, Thatcher and Reagan spoke about the Falklands during a private meeting in the US embassy in Paris on 4 June, but again there is no evidence to suggest that a five-point peace plan was presented by the President.[167] Parkinson laughingly suggests of Reagan's possible presentation of such a plan to Thatcher:

I don't think he would have dared. Oh, no. I've always felt he was playing a bit of a game. He was really on our side but he was persuaded by Enders and Co. to try to be even-handed. He wasn't really. His whole instinct was to support us . . . Margaret had certainly never said to me that Reagan had given this five-point peace plan.[168]

Nott provides an alternative viewpoint when questioned about this possibility:

I suspect so, because when we were already on the islands . . . making progress across the Island to Port Stanley, Reagan telephoned Thatcher and other messages were sent, trying to persuade us at that final moment to do a deal. It was, of course, an absurd idea that when we'd already got three-quarters of the way that we should at the last moment come to some compromise agreement. Yes, Reagan was putting pressure on us and on Thatcher to agree to a late deal but Thatcher rejected it out of hand.[169]

The UN vote on 4 June proved to be an irritant in Anglo-American relations. As anticipated, the UK and the US vetoed the resolution. Nevertheless, the resolution was adopted by a vote of nine in favour (Spain, Panama, Ireland, Japan, Poland, China, Zaire, the Soviet Union and Uganda) with four abstentions (France, Togo, Guyana and Jordan). US support of the British was overshadowed by a subsequent declaration made by Kirkpatrick. Minutes after casting the US vote, Kirkpatrick declared that she would like it noted that given the opportunity the US would have abstained. The US was essentially unofficially withdrawing its support of the UK.[170] This was an affront to British interests and a public betrayal by its Special Relationship partner. A few moments prior to the vote Haig had tried to contact Kirkpatrick to tell her to abstain from voting on behalf of the US. The message had not reached the ambassador in time. Haig had succumbed to pressure from the Latin American faction and Argentina. Thatcher later claimed that the announcement actually helped the UK on that day in the UN, as it helped to distract media attention from the British veto. The Prime Minister was magnanimous upon hearing that Reagan did not know of the proposed change in vote and

Figure 3 Meeting at 10 Downing Street during the Falklands War, 9 June 1982

refused to be quoted on the matter when questioned by journalists in Versailles. She later wrote that she 'had no intention of rubbing salt into a friend's wounds'.[171] In the aftermath of this minor irritant in bilateral relations, both Thatcher and Reagan endeavoured to show a united front. During the President's official visit to London on 8 June, Reagan gave a speech to both Houses of Parliament. The President spoke of the efforts of the British troops fighting in the South Atlantic for the 'belief that armed aggression must not be allowed to succeed'.[172] Reagan's words were received with rapturous applause by those present.

In the Falklands, British troops made significant advances, which culminated in Argentina's surrender on 14 June 1982. Thatcher was triumphant and the British public rejoiced in the UK's victory over Argentina. In a letter to Thatcher on 18 June, Reagan offered his congratulations and offered US support in assisting the UK in the aftermath of the war: 'A just war requires a just peace. We look forward to consulting with you and to assisting in building such a peace.'[173] The Reagan administration had two specific objectives at this point: to 'heal the wounds' in US–Latin American relations, whilst continuing to provide support to the British.[174] To that end, Reagan was keen to broach the subject of the future of the Falkland Islands with Thatcher during her official visit to Washington on 23 June. The US wanted to 'lay down a marker' by noting that US support for the British (in terms of the sovereignty issue) could continue only if there was eventual progress towards a negotiated settlement.[175] This was bound to infuriate the Prime Minister. In fact, when Reagan tried to discuss the issue with Thatcher during their meeting, she quickly interrupted him and spoke of the many sacrifices Britain had made during the war. Reagan again reasserted his desire to help the British with the future of the Falklands in a 24 June letter to Thatcher: 'The news of your victory in the South Atlantic is most welcome. I look forward to working with you on a lasting solution to the situation there.'[176] Close relations appear to have been restored as a more genial Thatcher replied to Reagan on 29 June: 'The last three months have been a difficult period and I remain most grateful for all the support and help which we have received from the United States.'[177] However, this Anglo-American accord was short-lived as Argentina's new leader began to call for renewed negotiations.

Following Galtieri's resignation on 18 June, Alfredo Oscar Saint-Jean was elected as interim President of Argentina. He was succeeded on 1 July 1982 by General Reynaldo Benito Bignone. Under his leadership Argentina began to call for a resumption of negotiations on the Falklands under UN auspices. While the UK was determined not to engage in further negotiations, the US supported Argentina's calls. Anglo-American tensions quickly reignited. Argentina's proposals were discussed in a heated meeting between Edward Streator and the Political Director of the FCO, Julian Bullard, in London on 17 August. Bullard informed Streator that the British intended to stonewall such efforts in New York and that Thatcher was 'unalterably opposed' to the idea of further negotiations.[178] In late October, Argentina again called for the resumption of negotiations on the Falklands in the UNGA. It drafted a resolution which reaffirmed the principles of the UN Charter concerning the non-use of force; took into consideration the de facto cessation of hostilities; stated that the interests of the islanders should be taken into account; and eliminated references to colonialism and to statements by the Non-Aligned Movement.

The draft resolution was 'wholly unacceptable' to the British, and Thatcher wrote to Reagan on 25 October requesting US support for the British position.[179] Reagan responded to Thatcher's letter on 1 November in a non-signed message delivered via the American embassy in London. In it Reagan outlined the importance the US attached to negotiations, but tempered his approach by flattering the Prime Minister:

> Margaret, I know how you have anguished over this conflict from the beginning. Your courage and leadership throughout have been a source of deep personal inspiration to me. I count it as a privilege to have been able to support you and Britain at this critical moment. You may be absolutely confident that I would do it all again the same way.[180]

The President wrote again to Thatcher the following day, this time a personally signed letter, in a bid to further explain US support of the Argentine proposals. He tentatively began: 'I fully understand that negotiations are not acceptable to you, having just paid so much in blood and treasure to repulse the Argentine invasion.' Reagan tried to alleviate British concerns by stating that the US representative in the UN would put on record US views that force should not be used again to solve the dispute, that the sovereignty issue should not be prejudiced by the resolution and that the aspirations of the islanders must be taken into account. Reagan ended his letter with an apology, but remained committed to the US stance: 'I am truly sorry that we disagree on this matter and for my part will do everything in my power to make sure this resolution is not abused.'[181] Reagan's attempts to mollify the Prime Minister were met with disdain. Thatcher was rankled and wrote to him that a vote on such a resolution would be received by the British with 'utter incomprehension'.[182] Despite such objections, on 4 November UNGA Resolution 37/9, 'Question of the Falkland Islands (Malvinas)', was adopted by a vote of ninety in favour (including the US), twelve against (including the UK), with fifty-two abstentions. Following the vote, Deputy US Ambassador to the UN Kenneth Adelman delivered a statement in the UNGA in which he referred to the US' 'closest relationship of friendship with Great Britain'.[183] This attempt to appease the British was an exercise in futility.

An incandescent Thatcher wrote to Reagan on 4 November. The President responded swiftly and tried to reassure Thatcher of US intentions: 'I can assure you Margaret that the United States did not make a decision to support Argentina against Britain. Neither did we abandon the principle of self-determination.' He emphasised their 'shared faith in the Anglo-American relationship' and their 'shared commitment to the same fundamental principles and values' in a bid to restore improved bilateral relations.[184] These assurances did not placate the Prime Minister. Thatcher's immense displeasure was again communicated weeks later to the new US Secretary of State, George P. Shultz (who was appointed following Haig's resignation), via Britain's new Ambassador to the US, Sir Oliver Wright. Shultz had been the one to persuade Reagan to vote in favour of a 'balanced resolution' on the Falklands and Wright angrily remonstrated with him. Shultz later recalled in his memoirs that his meeting with Wright was 'stormy'.[185] Shultz met with Thatcher in Downing Street on 16 December, and the Prime Minister took a final opportunity to address the disagreeable support of Argentina in the UN by the US on 4 November. Shultz listened patiently to Thatcher, but stated firmly his view that, while the US was right to support the UK during the Falklands War, the time had come to repair the damage this support had done to US interests in South America. With both sides' grievances aired, normal Anglo-American relations could resume. In fact, Shultz left London with the belief that 'the special relationship between America and Britain was going to be stronger than ever . . . because it was flanked by the Reagan–Thatcher personal relationship'.[186]

Despite British disenchantment with the US over UNGA Resolution 37/9, political diplomacy prevailed and Anglo-American equanimity was restored as both countries made decisive efforts to improve bilateral relations in the immediate aftermath of the Falklands War. Improved relations would arguably have been more difficult to achieve had it not been for the close bonds of personal diplomacy between Reagan and Thatcher and the provision of material and intelligence support to the UK by the US during the Falklands War. After all, American support was seen in the UK as evidence that the US was willing to forego its own strategic interests in Latin America in deference to its Special Relationship partner, the UK. Such was the extent of US material support during the crisis that it compensated, in the eyes of the British, for its initial neutrality, Haig's mediation efforts, its contentious announcement following the UN vote on 4 June and its support of renewed Anglo-Argentine negotiations following Britain's victory. Improved US–UK relations in the aftermath of the Falklands War would prove to be all-important in helping to overcome the effects of subsequent challenges emanating from Latin America upon the Special Relationship's at times tentative equilibrium. This was particularly evident in the case of the US invasion of Grenada the following year.

Notes

1. It has been argued that Thatcher's determined stance during the Falklands War increased her popularity with the British public. The Prime Minister was seen as a strong and capable leader who would defend British interests at all costs. This had a positive impact on Thatcher's ratings in the June 1983 general election and is often referred to as the 'Falklands factor'. However, the extent to which the 'Falklands factor' played a role in Thatcher's auspicious rise in popularity is widely debated. The Conservative Party's landslide victory of 397 seats to Labour's 209 is seen by many as the result of a combination of factors, including gradual

economic improvement in the UK, Thatcher's success against the trade unions, the decline in popularity of the Labour Party (due to its pursuit of unilateral disarmament) and the apparent increase in the Soviet threat during the 1980s. For more information on the 'Falklands factor', see: Timothy Heppell, *The Tories: From Winston Churchill to David Cameron* (London: Bloomsbury, 2014), p. 86; Simon Jenkins, *Thatcher and Sons: A Revolution in Three Acts* (London: Penguin, 2007), pp. 76–7; Norman Tebbit, *Upwardly Mobile* (London: Weidenfeld & Nicolson, 1988), p. 196; Hugh Bicheno, *Razor's Edge: The Unofficial History of the Falklands War* (London: Phoenix House, 2007), pp. 96–7.

2. Christoph Bluth, 'The British resort to force in the Falklands/Malvinas conflict 1982: international law and war theory', *Journal of Peace Research*, 24(1) (March 1987): 5–20, at p. 6.
3. Roberto C. Laver, *The Falklands/Malvinas Case: Breaking the Deadlock in the Anglo-Argentine Sovereignty Dispute* (The Hague: Martinus Nijhoff, 2001), pp. 30–3.
4. Max Hastings and Simon Jenkins, *The Battle for the Falklands*, 2nd edn (London: Pan Books, 1997), p. 17.
5. Lord Edward Shackleton, 'The Falkland Islands and their history', *Geographical Journal*, 249(1) (March 1983): 1–4, at p. 3.
6. The results of the Shackleton expedition were outlined in May 1976 in a two-volume report entitled the 'Falkland Islands Economic Study'. For a concise assessment of the motivations behind the Shackleton expedition along with the report's principal recommendations, see Klaus Dodds, *Pink Ice: Britain and the South Atlantic Empire* (London: I. B. Tauris, 2002), pp. 148–54.
7. TNA, FCO 7/3805, brief on Anglo-Argentine talks in New York, 28–30 April 1980, n.d.
8. TNA, FCO 7/3726, Ortiz de Rozas address, 18 March 1980, p. 1.
9. D. George Boyce, *The Falklands War* (Basingstoke: Palgrave Macmillan, 2005), p. 24. Similar views are outlined in Jimmy Burns, *The Land that Lost its Heroes: How Argentina Lost the Falklands War*, 2nd edn (London: Bloomsbury, 2002), p. 139; Moore, *Not For Turning*, p. 672.
10. Interview with Peter Carrington.
11. Richardson, *When Allies Differ*, p. 114.
12. Haig to Reagan, 13 March 1981, p. 1, file: (03/17/1981) President Viola Argentina (2), box 90125, Roger W. Fontaine Files, Ronald Reagan Library.

13. Lord Carrington, *Reflect on Things Past: The Memoirs of Lord Carrington* (London: William Collins, 1988), p. 362.
14. TNA, FO 973/231, FCO background brief 'Militarism and Repression in Argentina', April 1982, p. 3.
15. Richard Luce, *Ringing the Changes: A Memoir* (Norwich: Michael Russell, 2007), p. 138.
16. Margaret Thatcher, *Thatcher's War: The Iron Lady on the Falklands* (London: HarperCollins, 2012), p. 6.
17. Interview with Cecil Parkinson.
18. Interview with Peter Carrington.
19. John Nott, *Haven't We Been Here Before? Afghanistan to the Falklands: A Personal Connection* (London: Discovered Authors, 2007), p. 25. The Trident D5 deal was intended to replace Britain's aging Polaris nuclear defence system. It was secured in March 1982 through a series of letters between Reagan and Thatcher and their respective secretaries of defence.
20. Carrington, *Reflect on Things Past*, p. 365.
21. Thatcher, *Thatcher's War*, pp. 9–10.
22. Henderson, *Mandarin*, p. 447.
23. Lord Franks, *Falkland Islands Review: Report of a Committee of Privy Councillors*, Cmnd. 8787 (London: HMSO, 1983), p. 63.
24. Interview with Peter Carrington.
25. Alexander M. Haig, Jr, *Caveat: Realism, Reagan, and Foreign Policy* (London: Weidenfeld & Nicolson, 1984), p. 263.
26. Thatcher, *Thatcher's War*, p. 11; Robin Renwick, *A Journey with Margaret Thatcher: Foreign Policy under the Iron Lady* (London: Biteback, 2013), p. 42.
27. Lawrence D. Freedman, 'The special relationship, then and now', *Foreign Affairs*, 85(3) (May/June 2006): 61–73, at p. 65.
28. LeoGrande, *Our Own Backyard*, p. 293.
29. TNA, PREM 19/652, Henderson valedictory despatch, 27 July 1982, p. 12.
30. Lawrence D. Freedman, 'The impact of the Falklands conflict on international affairs', in Stephen Badsey *et al.* (eds), *The Falklands Conflict Twenty Years On: Lessons for the Future* (Abingdon: Frank Cass, 2005), p. 16.
31. Interview with Neil Kinnock.
32. Author's correspondence with Adrian Beamish, 3 August 2011.
33. Patrick Bratton and Wallace Thies, 'When governments collide in

the South Atlantic: Britain coerces Argentina during the Falklands War', *Comparative Strategy*, 30(1) (2011): 1–27, at p. 3.

34. Argentina's miscalculation regarding the British response is referred to in Caspar W. Weinberger, with Gretchen Roberts, *In the Arena: A Memoir of the 20th Century* (Washington, DC: Regnery, 2001), pp. 374–5. The junta believed that there would be minimal, if any, response by the British to Argentine actions. This, along with the belief that Washington would not become militarily involved in a war over the Falkland Islands and that the US would ally itself with Argentina as opposed to the UK, is discussed in Burns, *Land that Lost its Heros*, pp. 143–4.

35. This suggestion is discussed in Michael C. Desch, *Power and Military Effectiveness: The Fallacy of Democratic Triumphalism* (Baltimore, MD: Johns Hopkins University Press, 2008), p. 145.

36. Kirkpatrick's meeting with Ambassador Roca is discussed in Richard C. Thornton, *The Reagan Revolution II: Rebuilding the Western Alliance* (Oxford: Trafford Publishing, 2004), p. 67; Richard C. Thornton, *The Falklands Sting: Reagan, Thatcher, and Argentina's Bomb* (London: Brassey's, 1998), pp. 126–7. Haig's meeting with Henderson is discussed in Haig, *Caveat*, p. 269.

37. Reagan to Thatcher, 1 April 1982, file: United Kingdom PM Thatcher (8202120–8205267), box 35, Executive Secretariat NSC Head of State Files, Ronald Reagan Library.

38. Henderson, *Mandarin*, p. 448.

39. Department of State to US embassy in Buenos Aires, 2 April 1982, available at: www.margaretthatcher.org/document/114267, accessed 27 March 2013.

40. Department of State to US embassy in Buenos Aires, 2 April 1982, available at: www.margaretthatcher.org/document/114266, accessed 27 March 2013.

41. Moore, *Not For Turning*, pp. 668–9.

42. Reagan to Thatcher, 2 April 1982, available at: www.margaret thatcher.org/document/109401, accessed 1 November 2011.

43. Anthony Parsons, 'The Falklands crisis in the United Nations, 31 March–14 June 1982', *International Affairs*, 59(2) (Spring 1983): 169–78, at p. 172.

44. Nott, *Haven't We Been Here Before?*, p. 42.

45. Haig, *Caveat*, p. 266; Richardson, *When Allies Differ*, p. 118.

46. Kenneth Baker, *The Turbulent Years: My Life in Politics* (London: Faber & Faber, 1993), p. 69; William Whitelaw, *The Whitelaw Memoirs* (London: Headline Books, 1990), pp. 266–7.

47. Carrington, *Reflect on Things Past*, p. 368.
48. Owen, *Time to Declare*, p. 574.
49. Nott, *Haven't We Been Here Before?*, p. 68.
50. Interview with Peter Carrington.
51. Thatcher, *Thatcher's War*, p. 22.
52. Thatcher, *Downing Street Years*, p. 188.
53. Interview with Cecil Parkinson.
54. Thatcher, *Downing Street Years*, pp. 187–8.
55. Haig to Reagan, 6 April 1982, file: Falklands Crisis 1982, RAC box 5, Dennis C. Blair Files, Ronald Reagan Library.
56. Moore, *Not For Turning*, p. 686.
57. TNA, PREM 19/1152, Henderson to FCO, 11 July 1981.
58. David C. Gompert, 'American diplomacy and the Haig mission: an insider's perspective', in Alberto R. Coll and Anthony C. Arend (eds), *The Falklands War: Lessons for Strategy, Diplomacy and, International Law* (London: George Allen & Unwin, 1985), p. 110.
59. Caspar Weinberger, *Fighting for Peace: Seven Critical Years in the Pentagon* (New York: Warner Books, 1990), p. 207.
60. US embassy in London to State Department, 8 April 1982, pp. 2–4, available at: www.margaretthatcher.org/document/114333, accessed 5 April 2013.
61. *Ibid.*, p. 4.
62. Freedman, 'Special relationship', p. 66.
63. Haig to Reagan, 9 April 1982, file: Falklands War, Box 91365, Executive Secretariat NSC Country Files, Falklands War, Ronald Reagan Library.
64. *Ibid.*, Reagan to Haig, 9 April 1982.
65. Henderson, *Mandarin*, p. 444.
66. Document titled 'Talking Points: Galtieri', n.d. (the document was located in a file detailing correspondence from 1 March to 30 April 1982), file: United Kingdom 1982 (03/01/1982–04/30/1982), RAC box 6, Dennis C. Blair Files, Ronald Reagan Library.
67. Text of Haig's peace proposals, 12 April 1982, available at: www. margaretthatcher.org/document/123117, accessed 5 April 2013.
68. Thatcher, *Downing Street Years*, p. 197.
69. Interview with John Nott.
70. Haig to Reagan, 14 April 1982, file: United Kingdom (4/1/82– 7/31/82) (3/6), box 20, Executive Secretariat NSC Country Files, Europe and the Soviet Union, Ronald Reagan Library.
71. Memcon. of Reagan–Galtieri discussion, 15 April 1982, file:

Falklands Crisis 1982, RAC box 5, Dennis C. Blair Files, Ronald Reagan Library.

72. *Ibid.*, Reagan to Thatcher, 15 April 1982.

73. Thatcher to Reagan, 16 April 1982, available at: www.margaretthatcher.org/document/122860, accessed 5 April 2013.

74. Ronald Reagan, *The Reagan Diaries*, ed. Douglas Brinkley (New York: HarperCollins, 2007), p. 80.

75. Henderson to FCO, 17 April 1982, available at: www.margaretthatcher.org/document/123057, accessed 3 April 2013.

76. Haig to Pym, 19 April 1982, file: Falklands War, box 91365, Executive Secretariat NSC Country Files, Falklands War, Ronald Reagan Library.

77. Reagan, *The Reagan Diaries*, p. 204.

78. Rentschler to Clark, 20 April 1982, file: United Kingdom 1982 (03/01/1982–04/30/1982), RAC box 6, Dennis C. Blair Files, Ronald Reagan Library.

79. John Norton Moore, 'The Inter-American system snarls in the Falklands War', *American Journal of International Law*, 76(4) (October 1982): 830–1. For more information on OAS considerations on the Falklands, see Gordon Connell-Smith, 'The OAS and the Falklands conflict', *World Today*, 38(9) (September 1982): 340–7.

80. Thatcher, *Downing Street Years*, p. 204.

81. Renwick, *Journey with Margaret Thatcher*, p. 59.

82. Freedman, 'Special relationship', p. 67.

83. Interview with John Nott.

84. Haig to Clark, 18 April 1982, file: (Cables 09013, 09100, 091154, 091640, 181715, 91650, 181715, 191754, 192115), box 30, Executive Secretariat NSC Country Files, Latin America, Falklands War, Grenada, Ronald Reagan Library.

85. Henderson, *Mandarin*, p. 454.

86. John Nott, *Here Today, Gone Tomorrow: Recollections of an Errant Politician* (London: Politico's, 2002), p. 292.

87. Haig, *Caveat*, p. 293.

88. Thatcher to Reagan, 29 April 1982, available at: www.margaretthatcher.org/document/122861, accessed 3 April 2013.

89. Reagan to Thatcher, 29 April 1982, available at: www.margaretthatcher.org/document/122862, accessed 27 March 2013.

90. NSC meeting minutes, 30 April 1982, file: Meeting File, box

91284, Executive Secretariat NSC Meeting Files, Ronald Reagan Library.

91. Interview with Charles Powell.

92. Interview with Bernard Ingham.

93. Interview with Geoffrey Howe.

94. Interview with Cecil Parkinson.

95. *Ibid.*

96. Interview with John Nott.

97. TNA, PREM 19/624, UK embassy in Washington to FCO, 5 May 1982.

98. Interview with Michael Heseltine, 25 May 2011.

99. Similar arguments have been put forward by Kathleen Burk, 'Old world, new world: Great Britain and American from the beginning', in John Dumbrell and Axel R. Schäfer (eds), *America's 'Special Relationships': Foreign and Domestic Aspects of the Politics of Alliance* (Abingdon: Routledge, 2009), pp. 36–7; Boyce, *Falklands War*, p. 57.

100. Interview with Bernard Ingham.

101. Interview with Charles Powell.

102. Reagan, *An American Life*, p. 357.

103. Author's correspondence with Adrian Beamish.

104. American embassy in Buenos Aires to Secretary of State in Washington, 23 April 1982, file: Falkland File (04/02/1982) (1), box 19, Executive Secretariat NSC Cable File Records, Ronald Reagan Library.

105. *Ibid.* American embassy in Georgetown to Secretary of State in Washington, 23 April 1982, file: Falkland File (04/05/1982) (4), box 19. Australia's and New Zealand's reactions and offers of help to the British are detailed in Martin Middlebrook, *The Falklands War: 1982* (London: Penguin, 2001), pp. 182–3. Canada's reaction to the war is examined in Timothy C. Winegard, 'Canadian diplomacy and the 1982 Falklands War', *International History Review*, 35(1) (2013): 162–83.

106. Much is written on the European response to the Falklands crisis. The individual responses of Ireland, Italy, Spain and Denmark are examined in Stelios Stavridis and Christopher Hill, *The Domestic Sources of Foreign Policy: West European Reactions to the Falklands Conflict* (Oxford: Berg, 1996). See also Michael Parsons, *The Falklands War* (Stroud: Sutton Publishing, 2000), p. 98. For information on EEC sanctions against Argentina, see Lisa L. Martin, 'Institutions and cooperation: sanctions during

the Falkland Islands conflict', *International Security*, 16(1) (Spring 1992): 143–78.

107. Prime Minister Giovanni Spadolini to Thatcher, 10 April 1982, available at: www.margaretthatcher.org/document/123265, accessed 27 March 2013.

108. Lawrence D. Freedman, *The Official History of the Falklands Campaign, vol. II: War and Diplomacy*, revised edn (London: Routledge, 2007), p. 445.

109. Interview with John Nott; Aldrich, *GCHQ*, p. 415.

110. Lawrence D. Freedman, 'The Falklands/Malvinas conflict', in Andrew Dorman and Greg Kennedy (eds), *War and Diplomacy: From World War I to the War on Terrorism* (Dulles, VA: Potomac Books, 2008), p. 137; Lawrence D. Freedman, *Britain and the Falklands War* (Oxford: Blackwell, 1988), pp. 40–1.

111. TNA, FO 973/262, FCO background brief 'The Falklands Crisis: Soviet, Cuban and East European Reactions', August 1982.

112. George Black *et al.*, *Garrison Guatemala* (London: Zed Books, 1984), p. 164.

113. TNA, PREM 19/959, UK embassy in Caracas to FCO, 14 April 1982.

114. FCO Situation report (Sitrep.), 18 April 1982, available at: www.margaretthatcher.org/document/123058, accessed 27 March 2013.

115. José López Portillo to Thatcher, 20 April 1982, available at: www.margaretthatcher.org/document/123280, accessed 27 March 2013. FCO Sitrep, 24 April 1982, available at: www.margaretthatcher.org/document/123083, accessed 27 March 2013.

116. Thatcher to President Gregorio Álvarez of Uruguay, 15 July 1982, available at: www.margaretthatcher.org/document/123416, accessed 28 March 2013.

117. Interview with Gloria Hooper, 3 February 2011.

118. Freedman, *Official History of the Falklands Campaign, vol. II*, p. 394.

119. Interview with John Nott.

120. Interview with Cecil Parkinson.

121. Francis Pym, *The Politics of Consent* (London: Hamish Hamilton, 1984), p. 25.

122. Haig, *Caveat*, p. 296.

123. John F. Lehman, Jr, 'The Falklands War: reflections on the "Special Relationship"', *RUSI Journal*, 157(6) (December 2012): 80–5, at p. 83; John F. Lehman, Jr, *Command of the Seas* (Annapolis, MD: Naval Institute Press, 1988), p. 269.

124. Dumbrell, *A Special Relationship*, pp. 168–9.
125. Derrik Mercer *et al.*, *The Fog of War: The Media on the Battlefield* (London: Heinemann, 1987), p. 163.
126. Interview with Bernard Ingham.
127. Hastings and Jenkins, *Battle for the Falklands*, p. 75. The JIC directed the UK's national intelligence organisations on behalf of the UK's Cabinet.
128. Lawrence D. Freedman and Virginia Gamba-Stonehouse, *Signals of War: The Falklands Conflict of 1982* (Princeton, NJ: Princeton University Press, 1991), p. 86.
129. Interview with John Nott.
130. *Ibid.*
131. NSC meeting minutes, 30 April 1982, file: Meeting File, box 91284, Executive Secretariat NSC Meeting Files, Ronald Reagan Library.
132. HMSO, MOD, *The Falklands Campaign: The Lessons*, Defence White Paper, Cmnd. 8758, p. 6.
133. Thatcher, *Downing Street Years*, p. 227.
134. Duncan Campbell, *The Unsinkable Aircraft Carrier: American Military Power in Britain*, 2nd edn (London: Paladin Grafton Books, 1986), p. 146.
135. TNA, PREM 19/633, UK embassy in Washington to FCO, 1 June 1982.
136. Interview with Geoffrey Howe.
137. Weinberger, *Fighting for Peace*, p. 205.
138. Dimbleby and Reynolds, *An Ocean Apart*, p. 335.
139. Lehman, 'Falklands War', p. 82; Richardson, *When Allies Differ*, p. 126.
140. Dimbleby and Reynolds, *An Ocean Apart*, p. 335.
141. Interview with Cecil Parkinson.
142. Henderson, *Mandarin*, p. 443.
143. Thatcher, *Downing Street Years*, p. 188.
144. Interview with Geoffrey Howe.
145. Haig stayed on as Secretary of State in order to deal with the crisis surrounding Israel's invasion of Lebanon. Haig later wrote that his efforts in the Falklands dispute ultimately cost him his job as Secretary of State. For more information, see Haig, *Caveat*, pp. 298–9.
146. Freedman, *Britain and the Falklands War*, p. 55; Boyce, *Falklands War*, p. 106.
147. Henderson to FCO, 5 May 1982, p. 2, available at:

www.margaretthatcher.org/document/123062, accessed 28 March 2013.

148. *Ibid.*, p. 4.
149. Henderson to FCO, 5 May 1982, available at: www.margaretthatcher.org/document/123063, accessed 28 March 2013.
150. Reagan to Thatcher, 5 May 1982, file: United Kingdom 1982 (03/01/1982–04/30/1982), RAC box 6, Dennis C. Blair Files, Ronald Reagan Library.
151. Thatcher to Reagan, 5 May 1982, available at: www.margaretthatcher.org/document/122864, accessed 28 March 2013.
152. Douglas Kinney, 'Anglo-Argentine diplomacy and the Falklands crisis', in Alberto R. Coll and Anthony C. Arend (eds), *The Falklands War: Lessons for Strategy, Diplomacy, and International Law* (London: George Allen & Unwin, 1985), p. 101.
153. Interview with Cecil Parkinson.
154. Interview with John Nott.
155. NSDD 34, 'US Actions in South Atlantic Crisis', 14 May 1982, file: NSDD 34, box 91311, Executive Secretariat NSC NSDD Files, Ronald Reagan Library.
156. HMSO, *Britain and the Falkland Islands* (London, 1983), pp. 40–2.
157. For more on these proposals see Moore, *Not For Turning*, pp. 722–9.
158. Interview with Cecil Parkinson.
159. Moore, *Not For Turning*, p. 732.
160. Boyce, *Falklands War*, p. 123.
161. Haig to Reagan, 26 May 1982, file: Falklands Crisis 1982, RAC box 5, Dennis C. Blair Files, Ronald Reagan Library.
162. Thornton, *Falklands Sting*, p. 235; Boyce, *Falklands War*, p. 135.
163. Telcon. of Reagan and Thatcher discussion, 31 May 1982, file: United Kingdom (4/1/82–7/31/82), box 20, Executive Secretariat NSC Country Files, Ronald Reagan Library.
164. Henderson, *Mandarin*, p. 466.
165. Freedman and Gamba-Stonehouse, *Signals of War*, p. 350.
166. The peace plan is briefly referred to in Hastings and Jenkins, *Battle for the Falklands*, p. 296; Parkinson, *Right at the Centre*, p. 210; Duncan Anderson, *The Falklands War 1982* (Oxford: Osprey, 2002), p. 2; Nicholas Wapshott and George Brock, *Thatcher* (London: Futura, 1983), p. 249.
167. Renwick, *Journey with Margaret Thatcher*, p. 75.

168. Interview with Cecil Parkinson.

169. Interview with John Nott.

170. David Lewis Feldman, 'The United States role in the Malvinas crisis, 1982: misguidance and misperception in Argentina's decision to go to war', *Journal of Interamerican Studies and World Affairs*, 27(2) (Summer 1985): 1–22, at p. 12.

171. Thatcher, *Downing Street Years*, p. 232.

172. Address to British Members of the British Parliament (MPs), 8 June 1982, the Public Papers of President Ronald W. Reagan, Ronald Reagan Library, available at: www.reagan.utexas.edu/archives/speeches/1982/60882, accessed 4 June 2010.

173. Reagan to Thatcher, 18 June 1982, file: United Kingdom PM Thatcher Cables (1/4), box 34, Executive Secretariat NSC Head of State Files, Ronald Reagan Library.

174. Haig to Reagan, 19 June 1982, file: United Kingdom (4/1/82–7/31/82) (5/6), box 20, Executive Secretariat NSC Country Files, United Kingdom, Ronald Reagan Library.

175. Clark to Reagan, 22 June 1982, file: 84, Meeting with Prime Minister Thatcher (6/23/1982), box 12, Charles P. Tyson Files, Ronald Reagan Library.

176. Reagan to Thatcher, 24 June 1982, file: United Kingdom PM Thatcher Cables (1/4), box 34, Executive Secretariat NSC Head of State Files, Ronald Reagan Library.

177. Thatcher to Reagan, 29 June 1982, file: United Kingdom PM Thatcher, box 35, Executive Secretariat NSC Head of State Files, Ronald Reagan Library.

178. Streator to Shultz, 17 August 1982, file: United Kingdom 1982 (08/01/1982–10/03/1982), RAC box 6, Dennis C. Blair Files, Ronald Reagan Library.

179. L. Paul Bremer (Executive Assistant to Haig) to Clark, 30 October 1982, file: United Kingdom PM Thatcher (8207592–8300964), box 35, Executive Secretariat NSC Head of State Files, Ronald Reagan Library.

180. Reagan to Thatcher, 1 November 1982, file: United Kingdom 1982 (08/01/1982–10/03/1982), RAC box 6, Dennis C. Blair Files, Ronald Reagan Library.

181. Reagan to Thatcher, 2 November 1982, file: United Kingdom PM Thatcher Cables (1/4), box 34, Executive Secretariat NSC Head of State Files, Ronald Reagan Library.

182. Freedman, 'Special relationship', p. 69.

183. US Mission in New York to Secretary of State in Washington,

5 November 1982, file: United Kingdom 1982 (11/03/1982–12/16/1982), RAC box 6, Dennis C. Blair Files, Ronald Reagan Library.

184. Reagan to Thatcher, 4 November 1982, file: Falklands War (UN/Kirkpatrick/Haig 06/06/1982–11/04/1982), box 3, William P. Clark Files, Ronald Reagan Library.

185. George P. Shultz, *Turmoil and Triumph: My Years as Secretary of State* (New York: Charles Scribner's, 1988), pp. 152–3.

186. *Ibid.*, pp. 153–4.

3 Friend or Foe? The US Invades Grenada

The US-led invasion of the Caribbean island of Grenada at the alleged behest of the Organisation of Eastern Caribbean States (OECS) on 25 October 1983 had a profound negative impact upon the development of the Special Relationship under Reagan and Thatcher. The dubious legality of the intervention was widely criticised by the international community, most notably the UK. And yet, it was the Thatcher government that bore the scars of considerable domestic criticism regarding the unlawful US involvement in the internal affairs of a member of the British Commonwealth. The US invasion of Grenada, or operation 'Urgent Fury' as it is otherwise known, raised important questions regarding the limits of British credibility and importance within the Anglo-American alliance.

Britain was outraged at such a blatant American disregard for its legal authority and history in Grenada, and the relationship suffered a serious crisis of confidence. The lack of US consultation with the UK, and America's obvious intention to mislead Thatcher and her Cabinet of its true intentions towards Grenada resulted in a mistrust of American policies and scorn towards the ensuing platitudes. Thatcher was placed in the unenviable position of having to save face in the light of both party and public criticism of the US while simultaneously striving to maintain close transatlantic ties. Despite her marked displeasure over Reagan's deception, the Prime Minister wanted to continue to pursue close Anglo-American relations. This was difficult as the US appeared to have favoured unilateralism over transatlantic cooperation and consultation. Britain's credibility as a close ally of the Reagan administration and as an important actor in the Caribbean was questionable to say the least. Anti-Americanism flared throughout the UK as American strategic interests were criticised by many, including the general public. Questions were raised regarding the ability to trust the Reagan administration, in particular, with regard to the forthcoming placement of US Cruise missiles in British bases. Thus, the US invasion of Grenada possessed potentially far-reaching negative consequences for the Special Relationship and its future development.

This chapter will analyse the implications of US actions in Grenada upon the development of the Special Relationship, with a particular emphasis on the level of bilateral consultation (or lack thereof) that occurred prior to the brief three-day invasion. It will also examine US and UK relations with Grenada prior to the invasion, the reasons behind the US decision to intervene, and will assess the legality of the invasion itself. Through the extensive analysis of newly released primary documents in the US and the UK (including documents released by the TNA in August 2013, such as the PREM 19/979, PREM 19/1048, PREM 19/1049, PREM 19/1151, CAB 128/76/30 and CAB 128/76/31 file series), the chapter will reveal new information relating to the role of the US in orchestrating both the OECS and the Governor General's requests to intervene in Grenada. In addition, it will elucidate previously guarded British views on US actions, and will assess efforts made by both countries to try to resume close bilateral relations in the aftermath of this potentially divisive Latin American crisis.

British and American relations with Grenada

Grenada's turbulent political history played a key role in the US decision to intervene militarily on the island. Grenada lies some 1,500 miles southeast of the US coastline, and in 1983 it had a population of around 110,000 people. The island came under British rule in 1763, but acquired the right to self-government from the UK in 1967 under the leadership of Sir Eric Gairy. Full independence was later granted to Grenada by the UK on 7 February 1974.[1] During the mid-1970s an internal political struggle developed on the island, leading to the creation of a new opposition party, the New Joint Effort for Welfare, Education and Liberation, or 'New Jewel Movement' (NJM), under the leadership of Maurice Bishop. The NJM launched a successful coup d'état against the Gairy government on 13 March 1979, and Bishop assumed the role of Prime Minister. A People's Revolutionary Government (PRG) was subsequently established followed shortly by a 'Declaration of Revolution', which suspended the constitution and promised an early return to constitutional rule following a referendum in the near future. However, this promise did not materialise and the PRG committed itself to a 'socialist-orientated path of development'.[2] The US monitored events in Grenada carefully, and Cyrus Vance contacted the UK on 17 March to outline the US desire to coordinate its approach to the PRG with other concerned governments, especially Caribbean Community (CARICOM) countries, the UK and Canada.[3] The US modified its position in late March when it stated in a telegram to the FCO that its main purpose was to 'keep Grenada from drifting into the Cuban orbit'.[4] Cuba announced that it had established diplomatic relations with the PRG on 16 April. On 2 May, tripartite US/UK/Canadian talks in the State Department examined events in Grenada and the Caribbean in close detail.[5] The PRG saw these talks as an effort to undermine the legitimacy of its new regime.

The Carter administration formed a subcommittee of the Special Coordination Committee of the NSC to monitor developments in Grenada. It offered US Peace Corps volunteers along with a Special Development Activity Fund to the new Bishop government. In theory, this would have allowed the US to monitor events from within Grenada. Bishop refused the offer and began to speak of US attempts to undermine his regime. Britain, meanwhile, did not enjoy particularly close relations with the PRG as it felt that it had adopted 'a foreign policy hostile to the UK and its allies'.[6] However, the UK was measured in its position towards the PRG as British relations with Grenada afforded the UK some, albeit limited, influence in the region. Such influence was important given Britain's ongoing negotiations with Argentina over the Falkland Islands and with Guatemala over Belize. As a result, the UK, under the direction of the newly elected Thatcher government, continued to provide a limited amount of aid to Grenada in 1979.

With Thatcher in power the PRG attempted to improve its relations with the UK. To that end, the High Commissioner for Grenada, Fennis Augustine, met with the head of the Mexico and Caribbean Department in the FCO, A. J. Payne, on 5 August 1980. Augustine informed Payne that the PRG believed that the US and UK had jointly set out to attempt a 'new experiment in isolation' with Grenada.[7] Augustine continued to approach British officials on the matter and met with Nicholas Ridley in London on 24 September. During this meeting Augustine hastened to assure Ridley that Grenada did not regard Britain with the same suspicion as it did the US.[8]

In January 1981, US policy intensified towards Grenada as the Reagan administration was convinced that Grenada was in the process of becoming a Soviet beachhead in the region. This fear was fed as Grenada began to develop close relations with Cuba, the Soviet Union, North Korea and other communist countries. Thus, the new regime in Grenada was placed within the wider context of the East–West conflict by the Reagan administration.[9] The US lobbied to exclude Grenada from loans available from the Caribbean Development Bank and the World Bank in order to place economic pressure on the Bishop government. In Grenada, anti-US rhetoric continued to grow and the US/NATO amphibious operation 'Ocean Venture 81' from 1 August to 15 October 1981 did not improve matters. The Caribbean phase of the operation simulated the invasion of an island group known as 'Amber and the Amberines' in order to overthrow a Marxist regime to rescue US hostages, a thinly veiled reference to Grenada and the Grenadines.[10] To Bishop this constituted a US threat of invasion. Infuriated, he wrote to Reagan in late August 1981 to express his 'deep concern' over recent hostile US actions towards Grenada. Bishop looked for high-level talks between the governments of both countries to explore a normalisation of relations. Despite this, the US continued to monitor events closely as it was concerned about the 'solidifying' Cuban presence and influence in Grenada.[11] Cuba's perceived involvement in Grenada became the linchpin of US policy towards Grenada during the Reagan administration. In fact, in a speech to the OAS on 24 February 1982 Reagan unveiled his Caribbean Basin Initiative (CBI) and expressed his concern over 'the tightening grip of the totalitarian left in Grenada'.[12] Reagan excluded Grenada from the CBI; an indication of his anxiety over the situation there.

US–Grenadian relations continued to deteriorate throughout 1982 and into 1983. Reagan administration officials believed that the situation in Grenada was detrimental to US national security interests. William P. Clark wrote to Reagan in early 1983 that Bishop had 'Marxist/opportunistic revolutionary tendencies' and suggested a 'more active program' to reduce Bishop's influence in Grenada.[13] In contrast, the UK sought to improve its relations with the PRG. A Foreign Affairs Select Committee report on the Caribbean and Central America recommended that the UK should improve its representation in Grenada and that the security requirements of the area 'should be judged in terms of indigenous problems rather than as part of global East/West conflict'.[14] There was a clear asymmetry in Anglo-American views towards Grenada during this time.

Reagan's address before a Joint Session of Congress on 27 April 1983 again highlighted US concerns over its national security interests. Reagan argued that if the US did not respond to threats near its own borders, US credibility in the wider international community would be damaged. He stated:

The national security of all the Americas is at stake in Central America. If we cannot defend ourselves there, we cannot expect to prevail elsewhere. Our credibility would collapse, our alliance would crumble, and the safety of our homeland would be put in jeopardy.[15]

This was seen as a justification to use force in Latin America, in this case Grenada, by the Reagan administration. This type of justification was consistent with the 'credibility gap' theory associated with US foreign policy.[16]

In a bid to try to improve US–Grenadian relations, Grenada's Ambassador to the OAS, Dessima Williams, suggested the idea to the PRG of a visit by Bishop to Washington. Williams met with strong opposition from PRG party hardliners, who believed that Grenada should not bow to US pressure. Nevertheless, it was arranged that the Congressional Black Caucus would invite Bishop to speak at the sixth Annual TransAfrica forum in Washington, DC, in June. Bishop would also give a speech to the OAS Permanent Council.[17] Bishop arrived in Washington on 30 May and immediately requested an audience with Reagan. This request was refused and he was instead granted a meeting with Clark and US Deputy Secretary of State Kenneth W. Dam at the State Department on 7 June. During the meeting Dam reiterated to Bishop that a normalisation of US–Grenadian relations would depend upon Grenada's actions 'in the key areas of improving individual liberties, cutting Cuba/Soviet presence and toning down anti-US rhetoric'. Bishop replied that the US must reciprocate as he saw 'Grenada as David being attacked by Goliath, the US'.[18]

Bishop's promise to tone down anti-US rhetoric was quickly broken as he was quoted in a *New York Times* article on 10 June as saying that 'the timing of the [US] threat has been pushed back', but that 'we don't think the threat has been entirely removed'.[19] Bishop returned to a tumultuous political environment in Grenada. The PRG became embroiled in an internal struggle for power with Bishop and his supporters, on one side, and the more Marxist Deputy Prime Minister Bernard Coard, on the other. Bishop's trip to Washington had antagonised party hardliners. On 26 August, during an emergency meeting of the Central Committee (CC), it was alleged that sections of the party had begun to rebel against 'the higher organs of the party'.[20] Bishop's role as Prime Minister was under threat. On 14 September, a vote was held in the CC in favour of the creation of a joint leadership in Grenada. Bishop would retain the chairmanship of the CC and his position as Prime Minister, whereas Coard would gain control of the functions and direction of the party, the Politburo and the party's Organising Committee.[21] Bishop tried to rally support against such a move, and the Army Chief of Staff, Einstein Louison, organised strikes and demonstrations against the joint leadership deal.[22] However, the idea was approved by a majority vote in the CC on 25 September.

In the US, Reagan signed NSDD 105, 'Eastern Caribbean

Regional Security Policy', on 4 October, which effectively authorised the destabilisation of Bishop's government. The NSDD
referred to the possible use of the island as a 'base for subversion'
in the eastern Caribbean. It also stated: 'The United States should
maintain sufficient military presence in the Eastern Caribbean to
deter aggression . . . and to respond to any such aggression, as
necessary.'[23] On 8 October, Bishop returned to Grenada from
an overseas trip to Czechoslovakia, Hungary, East Germany, the
Soviet Union and Cuba, during which he had decided to renege
upon the joint leadership deal. Bishop announced his decision
and claimed that Coard and some of his followers were planning
to assassinate him. During a CC meeting on 12 October, it was
decided to place Bishop under house arrest and to detain those
spreading 'rumours'.[24] Coard subsequently resigned as Deputy
Prime Minister. Bishop's arrest resulted in civil unrest and demonstrations broke out across the island. On 19 October, followers loyal to Bishop decided to free him from house arrest and
proceeded to the garrison at Fort Rupert in order to free other
detained party members. At Fort Rupert the followers encoun-
tered armed troops loyal to Coard. Fighting erupted and many
were killed, including Bishop and three of his former ministers. Shortly afterwards, Radio Free Grenada announced that a
Revolutionary Military Council (RMC) had been established by
Coard with one of his closest supporters, General Hudson Austin,
as its nominal head. A twenty-four-hour shoot-on-sight curfew
was implemented and journalists who had arrived on the island
were deported.[25] Panic quickly enveloped the island.

The US became increasingly concerned for the safety of both
American and foreign citizens on the island. There were an estimated 600 US medical students studying at St. George's Medical
School on the island. The UK was also concerned about the
developing situation and determined during a Cabinet meeting on
20 October that the RMC was likely to be 'even more Marxist/
Leninist than its predecessor'.[26] The island's airport was closed
and flights were turned away, heightening concerns for those on
the island. Reaction in the wider Caribbean and Latin American
community was immediate. Jamaica broke its diplomatic relations with Grenada, while Barbadian Prime Minister Tom Adams

issued a statement condemning the murders of Bishop and his ministers.[27]

As Coard's grip tightened over Grenada, events unfolded in the Middle East that would further inspire the US to invade Grenada. On 23 October, a suicide truck bomber drove into the US marine headquarters in Beirut killing 241 American servicemen. Two miles away, the French military headquarters was also attacked with the loss of fifty-eight French paratroopers. The loss of so many American servicemen in Beirut made the US even more determined to prevent any possible danger to US citizens in Grenada.[28] The Reagan administration had faced considerable condemnation regarding its foreign policy objectives in the Middle East. Political pressure to justify the presence and sacrifice of so many American lives in Lebanon was inevitable after the Beirut bombing. By intervening in Grenada, the US could be seen as the guardian and saviour of American lives. As such, Grenada provided an opportunity to draw the public's focus away from the catastrophe in the Middle East. This was obvious to many in the international community, but none more so than Thatcher who later wrote: 'The humiliation inflicted on the United States by the Beirut bombing undoubtedly influenced its reaction to the events which were taking place on the island of Grenada in the eastern Caribbean.'[29]

Legitimacy of the intervention and the OECS request

The OECS's official request was the legal basis for the Reagan administration's invasion of Grenada. The request, along with a desire to restore peace and democracy and a wish to protect American citizens on the island, allowed the US to justify its involvement in an island it deemed as Marxist. The OECS request gave validity to US involvement as the intervention was characterised as a regional collective security measure. The OECS argued that in taking lawful collective action it was free to call upon other concerned states, including the US, to maintain peace and security in the region. Assistance given in response to such a request was therefore deemed lawful by the OECS. Furthermore, as US involvement permitted the safe evacuation of American citizens the intervention was 'justified by well-established principles of international law'.[30] However, there are a number of flaws in this legal justification. The primary one being that the US, Jamaica and Barbados were not members of the OECS. Thus, the OECS treaty did not apply to the US in this instance (the OECS comprised Antigua-Barbuda, Dominica, Grenada, the Grenadines, St. Kitts-Nevis, St. Lucia, St. Vincent and Montserrat).[31] In addition, Article 6 of the OECS treaty stipulates that actions of the organisation are not binding on member states unless all member states have either approved or abstained the proposed action. This provision was clearly ignored as Grenada did not agree to the intervention and St. Kitts-Nevis chose not to participate in the vote that decided upon intervention as the best course of action. The US justified OECS actions on the basis that when governmental authority ceases to exist in a member state it is considered impossible to obtain its approval or abstention on a decision made by the organisation, in this case the OECS. In such a case, the organisation is not precluded from acting.

Another flaw is evident here, in that Article 8 of the OECS treaty specifies that collective defence is justified when there is a need to preserve peace and security against 'external aggression'.[32] As Grenada was a member of the OECS, there was no external threat and therefore the argument of collective defence did not apply. Moreover, the international norm of non-intervention, which prevents states from intervening in the internal or external affairs of other states unless there is a legitimate argument for self-defence, there are violations of human rights, there is a definite request for intervention by that state and on condition that all other peaceful forms of action have been examined, was not applied in this decision.[33] A case could be argued for the human rights violations aspect here as a curfew had been imposed and some citizens were harmed on 19 October, but this argument is outweighed by the combined failure of the OECS and the US to address the situation on the island by peaceful and diplomatic means.

Furthermore, members of the OECS are party to the provisions of the OAS, which specifies in Article 8 of its charter that 'no state or group of states has the right to intervene, directly or indirectly, for any reason whatever, in the internal or external affairs of any other state'. The OAS charter also specifies in Article 20 that the 'territory of a member state is inviolable and therefore may not be the object, even temporarily, of military occupation or of other measures of force taken by another state, directly or indirectly, on any grounds whatever'.[34] In addition, the UN forbids intervention in the internal affairs of a state. Despite the apparent concern of the OECS and the US regarding the situation in Grenada, there was no attempt made by either party to bring the matter before the OAS or the UNSC for consideration.[35] These facts, coupled with the UN Charter which permits self-defence measures only when an attack occurs (which was not the case in Grenada), refute the legal basis of the intervention.[36] Both the UN and the OAS later condemned the actions by the joint forces. The OAS denounced it as a 'violation of both international law and of the principle of non-intervention in the domestic affairs of member states'.[37] Notwithstanding this, the US justified collective action based upon the 'unique and unprecedented nature of the situation in Grenada as a collapse of governmental authority'.[38] Such was the illegality of the intervention, the Secretary General of the OAS, Alejandro Orfila, resigned during the November 1983 session of the General Assembly as he believed that the organisation had lost its effectiveness in the region.[39]

There is also an undesirable unilateral element to US actions in Grenada. US unilateralism was referenced by US Assistant Secretary of State for Western Hemisphere Affairs Langhorne 'Tony' Motley in a statement before the House Armed Services Committee on 28 January 1984. Motley outlined US plans prior to its final decision to intervene. He pointed to the unilateral plan of the US to invade the island, which was only multilateral at the last minute on receipt of the OECS request:

> We had been planning unilaterally, focusing on the safety of our own citizens. But when we were approached by the member nations of the OECS to assist them to restore peace and security to the Eastern Caribbean, we shifted into a multilateral mode.[40]

This statement would strongly suggest that the OECS request was the legal pretext under which the US decided to intervene, but had it not been issued the US would have intervened on a unilateral basis.

In the days preceding the invasion requests for US intervention in the crisis came from many sources. It is here that the legitimacy of the origins of the OECS request can be called into question. On 19 October, the White House Situation Room received a cable from the American embassy in Bridgetown, Barbados, which acted as American representation in the region (the US did not have an embassy in Grenada). The cable detailed Prime Minister Adams' request for US military intervention in Grenada in order to rescue Maurice Bishop and other political detainees.[41] This cable was closely followed by a recommendation by US Ambassador in Barbados Milan Bish for the possible emergency evacuation of American citizens from the island.[42] Following a meeting with Adams in Bridgetown on 20 October, Bish forwarded a situation report to the White House in which he stated:

> I believe that sentiment in [the] Eastern Caribbean for action is now so strong that it might be possible to elicit a public invitation from the region's collective leadership to the US to act for the sake of human decency and human rights (assume department is consulting Allies and others, as appropriate). I did not discuss the prospect with the heads of Government, but I believe that the Organization of Eastern Caribbean States might well agree to be the multi-national umbrella under whose aegis a peacekeeping intervention might be mounted. Friendly non-members, such as Barbados and Jamaica, would almost certainly join in.[43]

It appears from this cable that Bish recognised the advantage of a possible OECS request and the formation of a multinational intervention force. Consequently, it might be argued that the US played a role in soliciting the 'invitation' by the OECS and that its justification of US involvement in the invasion as a measured response to a genuine OECS request is questionable.

Meanwhile, the White House continued to receive calls for US intervention in the crisis. The Deputy Prime Minister of St. Kitts-Nevis called for direct US intervention on 20 October, indicating a direct opposition to the violence in Grenada.[44] On the same day, the Reagan administration's Crisis Pre-Planning Group (CPPG) met in response to the increasing calls for action and perceived escalation of the crisis on the island. The CPPG meeting was chaired by Robert McFarlane and discussed the possibility of using force in Grenada.[45] The CPPG's recommendations were then passed on to the administration's Special Situation Group (SSG), which was chaired by Vice-President Bush. The SSG endorsed the recommendations of the CPPG and the US prepared to invade Grenada. In preparation for such action, Bush sent an NSDD to Reagan for his signature.[46] Reagan signed NSDD 110, 'Grenada: Contingency Planning', on 21 October, which outlined the US position on 'a situation which could lead to the further radicalization of Grenadian society and increased Cuban/Soviet presence and activities on the island'. The NSDD detailed a US naval, air and marine amphibious forces plan to conduct a non-combatant evacuation operation (NEO) on Grenada. NSDD 110 stated:

> The Secretary of State, in concert with the Secretary of Defense and the Director of Central Intelligence, will initiate contact with the Allies and other regional governments, as appropriate, to determine their assessment of the situation on the island and their willingness to participate in a multi-lateral force to restore order on Grenada. The Department of State will also prepare associated diplomatic, legislative and public affairs plans regarding this contingency.[47]

It appears from this document that the Reagan administration initiated the idea of a multilateral force to justify conveniently and retrospectively their intervention in Grenada. Indeed, the timing of Reagan's signature of NSDD 110 was fortuitous. On 21 October, in Barbados, government heads of the OECS, along with representatives from Jamaica and Barbados, met to discuss the situation in Grenada at the behest of the OECS chairman, the Prime Minister of Dominica, Eugenia Charles.[48]

On 22 October, Major Christopher Stroude of the RMC made a statement on Radio Free Grenada calling for national unity. Stroude stated that Grenada would continue its independent non-aligned foreign policy and wished to continue efforts to improve relations with the US. He reiterated that peace and order had been restored on the island and that no person or group in Grenada would be victimised.[49] This was a clear attempt by the RMC to prevent any possible external intervention in Grenada. Bish met with Prime Minister Adams on 22 October to discuss again the possibility of intervening in Grenada. During this meeting Bish informed Adams that the US was prepared to be 'fully cooperative and supportive' of any action that the region might call for. Bish emphasised to Adams that the countries of the Caribbean would 'have to take the lead'.[50] That same day, the OECS formally resolved to form a 'multinational Caribbean force to undertake to depose the outlaw regime on Grenada by any means, including intervention by force of arms; and, secondly, to ask the United States and other friendly countries for the necessary assistance and means to do this'.[51] This was to happen under the auspices of Article 8 of its treaty. In the US, on 22 October, troops were assembled in preparation for an operation in Grenada. The 1st Ranger Battalion and the 75th Infantry at Hunter Army Airfield, Georgia, were assembled in response to a warning order for the operation. These groups were later joined by infantry units from the 2nd Ranger Battalion and the 75th Infantry from Fort Lewis, Washington.[52]

The OECS announced sanctions against Grenada on 23 October, which effectively ended all OECS cooperation with Grenada's military rulers until the island was ruled by a 'democratically elected Government'.[53] The US was aware of the potential lack of support for a multinational intervention in Grenada, and Shultz sent a cable to the American embassy in Bridgetown on 23 October requesting an emergency meeting of the Permanent Council of the OAS in order to pre-empt a 'possible hostile invocation of OAS machinery'. The cable also stated: 'we are dubious that an OAS Permanent Council meeting would produce a very strong endorsement of OECS sanctions'. The cable included a draft text of an invitation for US government assistance to which the Secretary of State added: 'We would not contemplate a US note of support, since it is unnecessary and potentially counterproductive.'[54] The cable suggested that a possible visit by an OECS representative to Washington would be advisable under the circumstances:

to provide emphasis that US is responding to OECS plus other request to join together to restore constitutional democracy in Grenada, visit of PM Charles or other designated representative on Tuesday would be highly desirable. Prime Minister would meet with President to convey request in person and then appear before press along with President after meeting; Prime Minister could also be in position to bring case personally before OAS. We would like to have their views on this.[55]

It is clear from this cable that the US played a key role in not only orchestrating an OECS request, but also in organising Eugenia Charles' visit to Washington. This was a calculated decision made by the US to help to justify its intervention in Grenada. Shultz' cable could be viewed as invalidating the US assertion that it was the OECS that approached the Reagan administration for assistance. This is a claim refuted by both parties including Prime Minister Charles who later stated emphatically: 'the OECS asked the US to intervene and not the other way around'.[56]

In order to determine the need for US involvement in a multinational force, the administration sent its special emissary, Ambassador Frank McNeil, to Barbados on 23 October to consult with Prime Minister Adams and Prime Minister Edward Seaga of Jamaica and other officials. Bish was also present at the meeting. During this meeting McNeil found these leaders to be 'unanimous in their conviction that the deteriorating conditions on Grenada constituted a threat to the entire region'.[57] Seaga outlined his concern that a US military intervention would 'raise the hackles' of the world leftist movement. Therefore, the strongest possible justification for intervention should be put forward. According to informal minutes of that meeting, in Seaga's view such a justification would be 'foreign interference'. The suggestion was that the overthrow of Bishop was accomplished by forces hostile to the values of the Caribbean. 'Russians and Cubans' were mentioned in the minutes. However, for Adams the question was 'not quite so blunt', as he argued that the OECS charter provided adequate legal basis for an intervention.[58] The participants also discussed the future administration of the island and the deportation of foreign nationals such as Cubans. Barbadian Foreign Minister

Louis Tull, with the help of a drafting committee, produced a new document for consideration as the OECS letter of request to the US. After several minor adjustments were made, it was agreed that McNeil would carry this letter back to Washington.[59] Reagan's Press Secretary Larry Speakes later wrote in his memoirs that McNeil was on hand to make sure that when the request was issued 'it was sent to the right address. You might also say that we RSVP'd in advance.'[60]

The official OECS request for US help was issued on 23 October. The Reagan administration's response was unsurprisingly swift. On the same day, Reagan signed NSDD 110A, 'Response to Caribbean Governments' Request to Restore Democracy on Grenada', which authorised a US landing with allied Caribbean military forces on Grenada no later than dawn on 25 October.[61] Across the Atlantic in the UK, the British government was seemingly unaware of US intentions. However, it was sceptical of the origins and timing of the OECS request. A Foreign Affairs Select Committee report later claimed: 'We have reason to believe that discussions about possible collaboration were held between United States officials and the Barbadian Government and OECS leaders not later than the evening of Thursday 20 October.'[62] Clearly, there was a distinct lack of US consultation with the British regarding its intentions towards Grenada during this time. The lack of consultation contravened the very nature of the Special Relationship between both countries, which relied upon continuous and frank discussions and cooperation on matters of joint concern.

The US was aware that their involvement in Grenada was tenuous at best and lacked any meaningful legality. A memo sent by US Assistant Attorney General Theodore B. Olson to his superior, US Attorney General William French Smith, titled 'International Law Ramifications of US actions in Grenada', detailed the legal ambiguity of US actions in Grenada. This particular memo referred to an assessment of US actions as outlined by a legal adviser at the State Department on 26 October. This assessment cited the Doctrine of Humanitarian Intervention and provisions in multilateral treaties regarding collective action as reasons to justify US actions in Grenada.[63] The subsequent memo concluded:

the arguments made in the legal advisor's October 26, 1983 memorandum would benefit from substantial additional factual and possibly legal support. The 'humanitarian intervention' argument, properly elaborated, provides support for the United States actions, but that principle is limited to the duration of its factual predicate. The argument based upon the provisions of the collective security treaties could be made much stronger if presented more rigorously, if supported by subsequent events and if placed in the context of the actions of Cuba which may have partially occasioned the responsive intervention.[64]

This document alludes to the lack of legal justification for US actions. More importantly, it alludes to what is perhaps the real reason behind US actions, that is, Cuba's perceived influence in Grenada.

Cuba's involvement in the construction of an extended runway at Port Salines airport in the southwest of the island certainly played a key role in US actions. The runway was being constructed with the help of Cuban funding and up to 300 Cuban labourers, and was purportedly designed to promote tourism on the island.[65] However, the Reagan administration believed the runway to have more ominous objectives, such as facilitating the movement of Cuban troops to Africa and allowing the shipping of materials to revolutionaries throughout Latin America. The construction of a road between the airport and the nearby military base at Calivigny contributed to such fears.[66] These fears alone were not enough to justify US involvement in Grenada. One of the principal reasons used to justify the intervention (along with the OECS request) was the decision to protect US medical students and approximately 400 other US citizens who were on the island at the time of the unrest. The US termed the intervention a 'rescue mission' to protect the lives of innocent US citizens. The terminology used to describe US actions is important here. A 'rescue mission' vindicated US involvement in Grenada, at least in the eyes of the Reagan administration. The President himself hated the term 'invasion'. He later stated: 'To call what we did in Grenada an invasion, as many have, is a slur and a misstatement of fact. It was a rescue mission, plain and simple.'[67] In fact, Reagan referred to an 'invasion' in his diary entry of 22–23 October: 'I've spent the day in meetings on this [Beirut] and Grenada. We're going to go on with the invasion.'[68]

The US decision to intervene

Records show that the US decision to intervene began as early as 10 October when Motley and his colleagues at the Latin America Bureau convened an interagency group meeting in order to evaluate the situation in Grenada. This meeting was followed on 13 October by an NSC meeting during which Special Assistant to the President on Latin America Constantine C. Menges summarised the situation in Grenada and proposed a plan to restore democracy to the island and rescue American citizens.[69] Following this meeting, a Restricted Interagency Group (RIG) of the State Department began to review a standard evacuation plan for Grenada on 14 October. Motley wrote to McFarlane on 17 October suggesting possible US action in Grenada:

> The confused situation of divided loyalties poses an opportunity for a third force representing democracy and freedom. If we ever entertained the option of supporting, covertly or otherwise, such a force, now would seem to be the time to act . . . The next ten days provide a window of opportunity.[70]

The Joint Chiefs of Staff (JCS), led by General John 'Jack' Vessey, began reviewing contingency plans for an evacuation operation. The Commander in Chief Atlantic (CINCLANT), Admiral Wesley McDonald, was contacted in order to 'investigate the possibility of conducting US Naval presence and possible non-combatant evacuation operation if the need arose to evacuate American citizens from the island'.[71] On 18 October, Menges presented a plan to McFarlane regarding a possible US military operation in Grenada. Menges then met with US Ambassador to the OAS William Middendorf, to determine the possible reaction by the OAS to such an operation, a reaction which was not expected to be favourable.[72] On 19 October, the RIG began to plan in more detail for a non-permissive evacuation, which would require 'the use of military assets and the securing of military targets on Grenada'.[73]

The White House Situation Room continued to receive updates on the situation on the island. On 21 October, a cable was received from US intelligence in Havana which detailed Cuba's response to the events in Grenada. Castro denied any Cuban involvement in the recent events on the island and declared 'our political relations with those now responsible for ruling Grenada must undergo a serious and profound analysis'.[74] The Soviet Union also denied any involvement in the crisis, and more reports on 22 October cited no danger to foreigners on the island. In a Grenada situation report sent by Shultz to American embassies in the region, the Secretary of State stated that: 'We have received no reports of additional violence in Grenada', and 'We continue to receive assurances from various sources that US citizens at the medical school in St. George's are safe.'[75] It appeared at this point that there was no immediate danger to American citizens in Grenada. An offer to privately evacuate the US medical students from the island was put forward on 22 October by President and Chairman of the board of Nation-Wide World-Wide Emergency Return, Joseph Travis.[76] This offer was declined by the US. Geoffrey Howe comments on alleged US fears regarding the safety of the medical students that: 'We couldn't really quite understand why the Americans were being so whooped up about it. The student presence was a convenient addition to their reasons for being concerned. But actually, the real anxiety was the potential of a Communist airbase.'[77]

Anglo-American consultation and the Governor General's 'request'

As conditions deteriorated on the island, the UK assumed that the Reagan administration would keep Britain informed of US intentions. Richard Luce (in place for Howe who was in Athens on other ministerial business at the time) oversaw Anglo-American consultations in the days preceding the invasion. It was Luce's job to relay British concerns regarding possible US intervention in Grenada to the Reagan administration. In a bid to keep all parties fully informed of events, telegrams received by the British during this time were repeated to Bridgetown, Washington and to Howe in Athens. In Washington, British embassy officials also remained in contact with their American counterparts in order to keep abreast of the developing situation. And yet there was some confusion in British circles regarding developments in Grenada. Howe was seemingly unaware of OECS and US intentions and even sent a cable to the British High Commissioner to Barbados, Giles Bullard, on 22 October tentatively floating the idea of engaging in negotiations with either Coard or Austin in the hope of restoring a constitutional government in Grenada.[78] However, records released by the TNA in August 2013 suggest that the FCO received information on 22 October that 'indicates that OECS Heads of Government have agreed to send a united military force to Grenada'. This information was relayed to Thatcher on the same day by a No. 10 duty clerk.[79] The wording of this note is important as it does not specify a direct intervention in Grenada, nor does it specify direct US involvement. Oliver Wright did, however, inform the FCO on 22 October that a US carrier group led by USS *Independence* with 1,900 marines on board en route to Lebanon from Norfolk, Virginia, had been diverted to the eastern Caribbean. But Wright was assured by the US that the deployment was made on a 'contingency basis'.[80] Again, there was no direct confirmation of a US-led invasion of Grenada. This deployment was announced publicly by the US as a purported signal to local authorities on Grenada 'of US concern for their nationals on the island'.[81] Later that day Wright was informed by American officials that the US had made 'no decisions going beyond these contingency plans', and that 'there would be consultation if the Americans decided to take any further steps'.[82] Wright was again informed by US officials on 23 October that no decision had been taken on further action. The Ambassador relayed this information directly to the FCO in London.[83] Furthermore, when Robin Renwick called on the Director of the State Department's Bureau of Political-Military Affairs, Admiral Jonathan T. Howe, on 22 October he was informed that no decision to intervene had been taken and that the US was 'proceeding cautiously'.[84] While the

FCO might have had an idea that an intervention was planned at this stage, it believed US manoeuvres to be precautionary.

The UK, meanwhile dispatched HMS *Antrim* to waters off the coast of Grenada from its Colombian base of Cartagena on 23 October in order to facilitate the possible evacuation of British and other foreign nationals from the island should the need arise.[85] The FCO also maintained close contact with Grenadian officials on the island and was satisfied that the situation was under control. On 23 October, the British Deputy High Commissioner in Barbados, David Montgomery, met with the British Governor General of Grenada, Sir Paul Scoon. During this meeting Scoon did not request any help from the British or any other party, and the UK believed that there was no threat to the Governor General's safety or to the safety of any foreigners in Grenada.[86] The Reagan administration later cited a request by Scoon for US intervention on the island to restore peace as one of the main reasons they decided to intervene militarily on the island. In a statement before the Senate Committee on Foreign Relations on 28 October, Kenneth Dam stated: 'The Governor General made a confidential direct appeal to the OECS to take action to restore order on the island.'[87] The timing of Scoon's alleged request is somewhat difficult to determine as the Governor General himself was initially unsure of when he requested the help of the US/OECS. In a BBC *Panorama* interview on 31 October, Scoon stated: 'I think I decided on Sunday the 23rd, late Sunday evening' when questioned about the timing of his request for help.[88] It is here that a discrepancy emerges regarding Scoon's request for help. The US claimed that the request was made through private channels to Prime Minister Adams who, in turn, informed the US. The US did not publicly release the information due to fears for the Governor General's safety.[89]

The suggestion that it was Scoon who approached Adams is discredited by a cable sent from McNeil to Shultz detailing his meeting in Barbados on 23 October with Prime Ministers Adams and Seaga. McNeil informed Shultz that during this meeting Adams reconfirmed that the Governor General 'was willing to cooperate in every way as soon as he was secured, including formal request for OECS assistance to establish secure peace'.[90]

In addition, Shultz sent a cable to the American embassy in Bridgetown on 24 October in which he provided a draft letter suggesting points that might be made by the OECS in an approach to Scoon requesting a call for assistance in Grenada.[91] The authenticity of Scoon's request is further discredited by another cable sent from the American embassy in Bridgetown to the Secretary of State in Washington on 25 October, which included the 'text of a letter the countries participating in the Caribbean security force propose that the Governor General of Grenada sign and deliver to the OECS, Jamaica, Barbados and the United States'.[92] The proposed letter included the following statement: 'I am requesting your help to assist me in stabilising this grave and dangerous situation. It is my desire that a peacekeeping force should be established in Grenada to facilitate a rapid return to peace and tranquility and also a return to democratic rule.'[93]

Documents released by the TNA in August 2013 shed more light on the dubious authenticity of Scoon's request for help. Scoon's letter to Adams formally requesting help dated 24 October (but made public on 27 October) uses identical wording included in the previously mentioned proposed text letter that was attached to the American embassy cable sent to Shultz on 25 October. Scoon wrote in his letter to Adams: 'I am requesting your help to assist me in stabilising this grave and dangerous situation. It is my desire that a peacekeeping force should be established in Grenada to facilitate a rapid return to peace and tranquility and also a return to democratic rule.'[94] The date of Scoon's official request was questioned by High Commissioner Bullard during a visit with Prime Minister Adams in Bridgetown on 27 October. Bullard commented that although the signature looked genuine, in his opinion, the date was 'almost certainly not that on which the Governor General signed'. He further questioned, if the letter was signed on 24 October by Scoon, why had its appearance been delayed until 27 October? Adams did not have an answer to this question.[95]

In fact, Thatcher herself, believed that the US had persuaded Scoon to issue a 'retrospective invitation to invade' after the Governor General was rescued and taken on board an American aircraft carrier (the USS *Guam*).[96] The suggestion that Scoon's request was retrospective is supported by the Governor General's memoirs. Scoon wrote that draft letters of the request for intervention were handed to him to sign on 27 October at the Port Salines Great House (following his rescue by a team of US Navy Seals and following his brief stay on USS *Guam*) by the Chief of Staff of the Barbados Defence Force and head of the Regional Security System (RSS), Brigadier Rudyard Lewis.[97] Scoon recalled that the letters were meant to have been given to him to sign two days earlier, but the risk was considered too great in view of the 'delicate nature of the preparedness for the military exercise'. Scoon also wrote: 'I perused the letters carefully and made one alteration before signing them. These letters were addressed to Tom Adams, Edward Seaga, Eugenia Charles and Ronald Reagan.'[98] Based on this cumulative evidence, the authenticity of Scoon's request is not only highly questionable; it also appears to have been orchestrated by those countries wishing to invade Grenada, most notably the US under the guidance of Shultz.

As events continued to unfold in Grenada, the White House received an offer from the Cunard cruise line on 24 October to help evacuate American citizens from the island. Yet again, the US declined any such help as they had already decided to intervene militarily in Grenada.[99] In the UK, British officials continued to correspond with the Reagan administration. On 24 October, the British embassy in Washington conveyed its reservations regarding any US action in Grenada to the White House and spoke quite clearly of factors 'which would have to be weighed carefully before any decisions were taken on military intervention'.[100] Thatcher, for her part, was convinced that the US would consult with Britain regarding its plans for Grenada. This conviction was unceremoniously quashed on the evening of 24 October when the Prime Minister received a message from Reagan at 19.15 (local time) stating that he was giving serious consideration to the OECS request and would like the Prime Minister's thoughts on such a move. Reagan finished his message to Thatcher with the statement:

I know that you would want to be kept informed of any role the United States may decide to play in support of the island nations of the Caribbean. I will, therefore, undertake to inform you in advance should our forces take part in the proposed collective security force, or of whatever political or diplomatic efforts we plan to pursue. It is of some assurance to know that I can count on your advice and support on this important issue.[101]

Reagan had, in fact, already dispatched US troops to Grenada. Thatcher immediately instructed officials at No. 10 to draft a reply conveying her strong opposition to an invasion. The Prime Minister intended to review and send this reply to Reagan following her return from a dinner engagement with the US Ambassador to the UK, John J. Louis. During dinner Louis assured Thatcher that he did not have any knowledge of a possible US invasion of Grenada.[102] However, Thatcher did not have an opportunity to send a reply to Reagan's first message. While the Prime Minister was at dinner, Downing Street received yet another message from Reagan stating that he had decided to respond positively to the OECS request. Thatcher received this message shortly after her return to Downing Street around 23.00 (local time). Reagan's second message was much shorter and stated: 'You will appreciate the sensitivity of this information to the security of these operations and the safety of military personnel. We will inform you of further developments as they occur.' Reagan finished his message with the statement: 'The United Kingdom can play an important role in strengthening the new government's position by offering political support and by providing a program of economic assistance.' The second message is notable for its formal tone as Reagan simply signed it 'Ron', that is, without the usual 'with warm regards'.[103]

Thatcher quickly summoned Howe and Heseltine to Downing Street to help draft a reply to this disturbing message. Thatcher's reply was dispatched at around 00.30 (local time), 25 October. The Prime Minister's reply was formal and considered in its tone: 'I must tell you at once that the decision which you describe causes us the gravest concern.' Thatcher asked Reagan to take a number of points into consideration, including reports that suggested that the lives of British and American citizens were not at risk; the UK had not received a formal request from the OECS;

Jamaica and Barbados were not members of the OECS; and the UK had not been able to identify any credible alternative leadership which could be established in the aftermath of a military operation. Thatcher admonished:

> This action will be seen as intervention by a western democratic country in the internal affairs of a small independent nation, however unattractive its regime. I ask you to consider this in the context of our wider East/West relations . . . I cannot conceal that I am deeply disturbed by your latest communication. You asked for my advice. I have set it out and hope that even at this late stage you will take it into account before events are irrevocable.[104]

The Prime Minister signed the message 'Yours Ever, Margaret Thatcher.' She had not used the more informal 'Margaret', which was a feature in her previous correspondence with Reagan.[105]

An impatient Thatcher then decided to telephone the President (who was in a meeting with NSC officials and congressional leaders) at 00.48 in order to express her concerns to him personally. Reagan later wrote that Thatcher asked him 'in the strongest language to call off the operation. Grenada, she reminded me, was part of the British Commonwealth, and the United States had no business interfering in its affairs.' During their brief conversation Reagan did not tell Thatcher that the operation had already begun. Reagan admitted in his memoirs: 'This troubled me because of our close relationship.'[106] During this heated conversation, Thatcher urged Reagan to consider her written reply carefully, but was left despondent when the President replied, 'We are already at zero.'[107] A furious Thatcher launched a verbal attack on the President, leaving him in little doubt of her immense displeasure. A chastised, but impressed, Reagan allegedly held up the telephone for all those present in the meeting to hear and said 'Isn't she wonderful.'[108] The conviction with which Thatcher spoke to Reagan during this conversation is a source of pride and amusement for some former Cabinet officials and close advisers. Carrington recalls that Thatcher was 'bellowing down the telephone' at Reagan.[109] Powell is more descriptive in his account of the conversation. He recalls: 'She came rushing back to No. 10 and telephoned him and gave him one hell of a bollocking.'[110] Ingham suggests: 'Mrs Thatcher was beside herself at Ronald Reagan for acting without telling the Queen as she put it. She hammered away at him over the telephone. However, she was saved in her embarrassment as she felt that she too would have done the same thing in Grenada.'[111] Ingham elaborates upon this view in his memoirs: 'She would probably have given similarly brief notice of the invasion to an ally lest she place her servicemen's lives at risk.' But Ingham admits that Grenada was a 'bruising affair'.[112]

Thatcher received another message from Reagan at 07.45 (local time). The letter was decidedly more conciliatory in its approach as the President began: 'I appreciate your thoughtful message on Grenada.' He then outlined various reasons for US actions, including, among others, the formal OECS request, the weight of national security interests and US concerns regarding Grenada's 'recent drift into the Soviet bloc'. Reagan ended his letter by stating that he shared many of Thatcher's concerns and outlining his hope that the US would have the 'active cooperation' of the UK. The President ended the letter with the more informal 'Warm regards, Ron.'[113] Thatcher later wrote of US actions: 'I felt dismayed and let down by what had happened. At best, the British Government had been made to look impotent; at worst we looked deceitful.'[114] The Prime Minister was bewildered at the lack of consultation by the US with her government and confided in her close friend, Timothy 'Tim' Bell: 'I can't believe he [Reagan] did it without telling me.'[115] It was a betrayal on both a personal and political level. The Reagan administration's deceit of the UK was later examined by the UK's Foreign Affairs Select Committee which investigated events leading up to the invasion. Their report concluded:

> a number of circumstances conspired, during the critical days of 19 to 25 October 1983, to deprive the United Kingdom Government of full information about the intentions of the United States Government and her Caribbean partners and to encourage British Ministers to misinterpret such information as was available to them.[116]

Figure 4 The President meets with Prime Minister Eugenia Charles of Dominica in the White House (George Shultz and Robert McFarlane also visible), 25 October 1983

On 25 October, the Reagan administration deployed 1,900 US marines and soldiers (the number increased to 6,000 by 28 October) in Grenada. The American troops were supported by a token number of 300 Caribbean forces in what was the first major US military operation since the end of the Vietnam War. Prime Minister Charles appeared with Reagan in Washington to make a joint statement on the collective action that afternoon. In the statement Reagan justified the intervention: 'Let there be no misunderstanding, this collective action has been forced on us by events that have no precedent in the Eastern Caribbean and no place in civilized society.'[117] Yet again, the terminology used to describe the actions of the multinational force was defended, this time by Eugenia Charles who stated: 'This is not an invasion.'[118] The joint statement resulted in a barrage of 'hostile questions' (handled by Motley and Speakes) from angry media representatives who, just a day before, had been told by National Security Advisor Admiral John Poindexter that the possibility of an intervention was 'preposterous'.[119] Shultz held a press conference later that evening and when questioned about why the US had disregarded British advice, Shultz was firm in his response: 'The US was always impressed with the views of HMG [Her Majesty's Government] and Mrs Thatcher, but did not always have to agree with them.'[120] Shultz' response again highlighted the unilateral predisposition of the Reagan administration in the Latin American region. US foreign policy, in particular, its application of the Reagan Doctrine, came under intense domestic and international scrutiny in Grenada's aftermath.

US, international and British reactions

The initial reaction of the US media was, for the most part, negative. The *Washington Post*, for example, was vocal in its opposition to the invasion as it termed it 'outrageous' and 'antithetical to open society'. The *New York Times* was similarly critical and called the excuse given for US actions 'flimsy'.[121] This initial reaction changed following the safe return of the American medical students to the US on 27 October. Scenes showing students kneeling and kissing the ground as they disembarked US transport planes resonated loudly with the fiercely patriotic US general public. The emotional return of the students greatly impacted the American public's overall perception of the invasion. Reagan's popularity increased significantly in the backwash of such scenes. Of course, Reagan's renown was greatly helped by his patriotic address to the nation on events in Grenada and Lebanon on the same day.[122] Reagan enjoyed an auspicious spike in Gallup approval ratings from 48 to 53 per cent in a three-week period (26 October–mid-November).[123] The President was effectively lauded by the American public as a guarantor of the safety of American citizens abroad, notwithstanding those killed in Beirut on 23 October.

The reaction within US political circles was mixed. Former Democrat Vice-President Walter Mondale warned that US actions undermined the US ability to criticise what the Soviets had done elsewhere in the world, in particular, in Afghanistan and Poland.[124]

In Congress, many dismissed the idea that Grenada was under Soviet or Cuban influence and therefore denounced the invasion. Congressional opposition focused primarily on the procedural question of the War Powers Act. Both the Democrat Speaker of the House of Representatives, Thomas 'Tip' O'Neill and the Democrat Chairman of the House Foreign Affairs Committee, Clement Zablocki, claimed the War Powers Act was not properly applied in the case of Grenada. Although written notification regarding US intentions was given to both the Senate and the House of Representatives, the notification failed to invoke the consultative provisions as required under Article 4(A)(1) of the act. Thus, an automatic time-limit of sixty days on the deployment of US troops was not applied.[125] O'Neill was particularly vocal in his condemnation of US actions and described US policy in Grenada as 'gunboat diplomacy'.[126] He was joined in his opposition by other influential groups and individuals in Congress, such as Senator Moynihan and the Congressional Black Caucus. Moynihan even asked if the US had the right 'to bring in democracy at the point of a bayonet'.[127] Steadfast opponents to the invasion, including various senators led by Democrat Senator Ted Weiss, went as far as to submit a resolution calling for Reagan's impeachment for violating international law by invading Grenada. These attempts were unsuccessful as O'Neill refused to pursue the matter; the Senate's Republican majority was likely to reject calls for an impeachment. O'Neill later recanted his initial opposition due largely to the report of a congressional study group, which concluded that the invasion was justified based upon the possibility of American citizens being taken hostage in Grenada. On the other hand, Reagan found strong support in Congress from leading Democrat Senators Sam Nunn and Lloyd Bentsen.[128]

The prevailing reaction to the invasion in the international community was negative. Commonwealth countries, such as Australia, India and Canada, openly condemned the invasion. Belize and Guyana were also highly critical of the invasion and looked for support from Trinidad and Tobago and the Bahamas for a UNSC resolution condemning US actions.[129] The Soviet Union was quick to condemn US actions, with its official news agency *Tass* branding the invasion 'an act of open international banditry'.[130] The prevailing reactions in Europe were also widely dismissive of US actions. France forcefully condemned the invasion with acerbic headlines in *Le Monde* such as 'The Malvinas of Reagan' and 'After Grenada, Nicaragua?' Italy's Prime Minister Bettino Craxi also condemned US actions and called for an immediate withdrawal of US troops from Grenada.[131] West Germany was more cautious in its reaction, and issued a statement detailing its regret over the intervention in Grenada and stating that it would have advised against the intervention had it been consulted.[132] There were more robust reactions elsewhere in Europe as Belgium, the Netherlands, Sweden and Greece all condemned the invasion of Grenada. Spain was also critical of US actions as it did not condone military intervention outside the framework of the UN Charter.[133]

On a more regional Latin American level, opinion was divided. Cuba's President Fidel Castro, who had consistently denied any Cuban subversion in Grenada, termed US actions 'an absurd expression of a philosophy of force'.[134] Ecuador, Brazil, Argentina and Bolivia also condemned the invasion. Mexico argued that US actions created 'new dangers for peace in the region'.[135] Costa Rica termed the invasion 'lamentable'; Guatemala expressed 'regret' over US actions, but said it understood the US position; Chile regretted that international organisations were not utilised to prevent such conflicts.[136] Nicaragua was the most vocal opponent of the invasion and asked for an emergency session of the UNSC on 25 October to discuss the matter and call for the withdrawal of foreign troops from Grenada. However, some Latin American countries, such as Uruguay, El Salvador, Paraguay, Honduras and Panama, supported the US.[137]

US actions in Grenada unleashed an outpouring of criticism in the UK. The British press was censorious. Headlines told of a rift in Anglo-American relations and news stories reported of the shock in the House of Commons at the British failure to restrain Washington.[138] The public, too, were outraged at US actions and demonstrations erupted around the UK. In Edinburgh, demonstrators representing the Edinburgh–Latin America Solidarity Campaign gathered outside the consulate general on 26 October, with similar demonstrations taking place outside the US embassy in London.[139] Reagan's failure to consult Thatcher was deeply humiliating and worrisome for the Prime Minister and her Cabinet. Britain's influence in Washington, as seen from British circles, was increasingly marginalised. US actions had indicated an unwelcome proclivity for unilateralism, for power politics. Fears over the direction of Thatcher's pro-American policies arose in the invasion's aftermath, and it was argued that the UK should try to develop closer ties with Europe rather than continuing to align itself with a unilaterally minded Reagan administration.[140]

In Washington, Wright was aware that British condemnation of US actions during the scheduled House of Commons debate on Grenada on 26 October would exacerbate already strained bilateral relations. The US would not appreciate British reproof when American troops were actively fighting to secure democracy in Grenada. Therefore, Wright wrote to the FCO (Howe) before the debate:

> I hope that you will judge that a swift American success, since that is what will most likely achieve our common objectives – the safeguarding of British lives and the return of the island to constitutional rule is also a major British interest at this time and that you will be prepared to say so in the debate.[141]

Following receipt of this cable, Luce wrote to Howe that he agreed, broadly speaking, with Wright's message. Luce suggested:

> The fact is that feelings are very sore on both sides . . . It must now be in our overall interests to make the best of a bad job. This means getting our relations back on a sounder footing and working constructively, politically and diplomatically . . . I hope that this can be borne in mind for the debate.[142]

The US was also keen to resolve any bilateral differences as a result of perceived US bellicosity in Grenada. In order to achieve this, overtures would have to be made to the British, in particular, to an enraged Thatcher. McFarlane suggested a presidential telephone call to the Prime Minister in order to 'help smooth over differences and pay longer term dividends'. McFarlane also recommended that a topic of discussion during the conversation should be the Anglo-American relationship as 'we cannot let a fissure develop between us. If transatlantic differences emerge our enemies could exploit them.'[143] Reagan dutifully rang Thatcher on 26 October to apologise for any embarrassment caused. The telephone call was received by the Prime Minister during the middle of the House of Commons debate. The conversation was notable for its initial awkwardness. It lacked the friendly ease with which both leaders usually conversed, and was made all the more difficult as Thatcher was not in the 'sunniest of moods' when Reagan rang her. The Prime Minister was uncharacteristically uncommunicative and gave 'monosyllabic' replies.[144] The President began quite sheepishly by saying: 'If I were there Margaret, I'd throw my hat in the door before I came in . . . We regret very much the embarrassment caused you.' Reagan tried to reassure Thatcher by explaining: 'When word came of your concerns – by the time I got it – the zero hour had passed, and our forces were on their way.'[145] The conversation ended on a polite, but restrained note with yet another apology from Reagan: 'I'm sorry for any embarrassment that we caused you, but please understand that it was just our fear of our own weakness over here with regard to secrecy.' Thatcher seemed to warm to such sentiments as she told Reagan that it was 'very kind' of him to have rung. She then asked after his wife Nancy and told Reagan that she would have to go to tend to the tricky debate in the House of Commons, to which the President encouragingly joked: 'Go get 'em. Eat 'em alive.'[146]

Thatcher returned to the debate where Labour's spokesman for Foreign Affairs, Denis Healey, launched a scathing attack on her: 'The Prime Minister has made something of a cult of her special relationship with the American President at the expense of British interests, of her relations with our European partners and of our relations with the Commonwealth.' Healey went on to accuse her of 'servility' to Reagan and denigrated her as the President's 'obedient poodle'.[147] This epithet would follow Thatcher in the wake of Grenada. Thatcher was not the only one to face criticism during the debate. Howe, too, faced an angry barrage of accusations as he had denied any knowledge of a planned US invasion in the House of Commons on the very eve of the invasion itself. Howe defended his earlier comments and reiterated that 'we were assured by the US that we should be consulted immediately if the United States decided to take any action'.[148] He then had to give an in-depth account of Anglo-American consultation on Grenada and stated: 'The United Kingdom and a number of Commonwealth Caribbean countries took the view that no action of this kind was required.' Despite his obvious embarrassment, Howe took the same position as the Prime Minister in refusing to openly condemn the invasion. When asked by Labour MP Jack Straw if he condemned what the Americans had done, Howe replied: 'It is no more for me to condemn the United States than it is for them to condemn us.'[149] Howe is surprisingly magnanimous in his recollection of how US actions in Grenada impacted Anglo-American relations. He recalls his 'surprise and dismay' at the US invasion, but contends:

> It remained a kind of permanent thing that both Margaret Thatcher and I remembered, as something that had gone off the rails. It wasn't in itself of huge importance . . . It just ran into the sand . . . It was a revelation to the extent to which one couldn't rely automatically on a kind of close-knit, precisely timed agreement on everything.[150]

Howe also contends: 'The whole thing was relatively insignificant. It was the kind of thing that promoted the questioning, the wider questioning. Hence, the Foreign Affairs Committee investigated it here and so on. It was a pretty rum thing.'[151] These comments are in stark contrast to Howe's memoirs in which he wrote:

> Margaret and I were both confronted with an insoluble dilemma. The United States had followed a course of action which we had both advised against . . . The truth is that the government had been humili-ated by having its views so plainly disregarded in Washington.[152]

Anglo-American relations in the wake of Grenada

On 26 October, Antony Acland in the FCO contacted Ambassador Louis to discuss the importance of the US honouring the constitutional role of the Governor General and to discuss possible future steps for Grenada.[153] Acland informed Louis that HMG was worried about the lack of consultations and wished to coordinate a statement with explanations being offered by the US.[154] Clearly, the lack of US consultation was a sore point for the FCO. Nevertheless, the UK needed US help to contact Scoon. Therefore, Wright met with Lawrence Eagleburger in the State Department on 27 October and asked Eagleburger to provide assistance in establishing contact between British authorities and Scoon in Grenada.[155]

Thatcher faced more criticism in the House of Commons on 27 October. The Prime Minister was again placed in the unenviable position of having to defend Britain's hemispheric interests while also safeguarding the future of the Special Relationship. Determined to weather the storm and maintain close Anglo-American relations, Thatcher firmly stated: 'We stand by the United States and will continue to do so in the larger alliances.'[156] While this was Thatcher's public stance on the matter, privately she was unnerved by Reagan's deception in Grenada: 'After all I've done for him, he didn't even consult me,' she ranted to one of her unofficial advisers, Brian Crozier.[157] However, the Prime Minister was pragmatic in her approach to the crisis as she believed 'whatever our private feelings, we would also have to defend the United States' reputation in the face of widespread condemnation'.[158] This was a calculated decision by Thatcher, who wanted to minimise the negative impact on the future of Anglo-American relations and, to a lesser extent, the impact on her own public image. The Prime Minister needed, and indeed wanted, to reinstate herself as a close confidant to Reagan, regardless of the ignominy she had suffered at the hands of his administration. Of course, there were other important foreign policy objectives to consider. Thatcher wanted to maintain a strong alliance with the US in NATO and was not prepared to allow US actions in Grenada affect such plans. In fact, Thatcher stated in a Cabinet meeting earlier that morning that 'Britain's friendship with the United States must on no account be jeopardised'.[159] The Prime Minister was also keen to abstain from the following day's vote in the UNSC condemning US actions in Grenada. Thatcher believed that a British abstention from the vote would express to the US the British hope that the US might likewise see fit to abstain from the forthcoming 16 November 1983 Argentine-sponsored resolution in the UNGA on the Falkland Islands.[160] To that end, and to the dismay of many backbenchers, opposition and Cabinet members alike, the UK abstained from the UNSC vote condemning US actions on 28 October. This abstention was surprising given the 'chorus of criticism' from other countries, such as Mexico, Guyana, Libya, Nicaragua and Yemen.[161] In the face of such opposition, Jeane Kirkpatrick tried to argue the US case:

> The prohibitions against the use of force in the UN Charter are contextual, not absolute. They provide ample justification for the use of force against force in the pursuit of other values also inscribed in the Charter, freedom, democracy, peace. The Charter does not require that peoples submit supinely to terror, nor that their neighbors be indifferent to their terrorization.[162]

The UK's abstention, along with Togo and Zaire, and a veto by the US effectively quashed the proposed resolution. Britain's abstention was a reflection of the Prime Minister's desire to resume the path of improved Anglo-American relations and to secure vital British interests in both NATO and the UN. As luck would have it, Britain's abstention was tempered by an end to combat in Grenada on the same day. Despite the failure of UN Doc. S/PV 2491 (the draft resolution), the UNGA subsequently declared (2 November) the armed intervention in Grenada as 'a flagrant violation of international law' (UNGA 38/7).[163]

Notwithstanding this abstention, US actions in Grenada were a point of contention on a bilateral ministerial level. During a NATO Nuclear Planning Group meeting in Montebello, Canada, from 27 to 28 October, an indignant Heseltine raised the issue with Weinberger. In Heseltine's words:

> I had one of my most controversial discussions with Cap Weinberger … I took with me the British newspapers so that he could see what had happened as a result of the position in which my colleague Geoffrey Howe had been put, by the impressions at least, that the

President had given to the Prime Minister that there was no such invasion going to happen.[164]

Heseltine dismisses the suggestion that the US invasion of Grenada had any lasting impact on Anglo-American relations. He suggests: 'The event of significance was that Geoffrey was misled into making that statement in the House. That was the big issue.'[165]

Indeed, both Thatcher and Howe were still smarting over the obvious betrayal by the US. During a *Weekend World* television interview on 30 October with former Labour MP Brian Walden, Howe took the opportunity to voice his objections on the Reagan administration's justifications for the invasion. When questioned by Walden whether or not he shared Reagan's view of the necessity of the invasion based upon the need to save American lives and the belief that Grenada was a Cuban/Soviet base, Howe responded: 'We did not share his view for either reason.'[166] Thatcher, too, was not prepared to simply forget about such a public betrayal by the US. During a BBC World Service radio phone-in programme on 30 October, she stated that the British government would be 'sympathetic' to calls for assistance in returning Grenada to democratic rule, but reasserted her belief that US actions were 'ill-advised'. In an uncharacteristically public condemnation of the US, the Prime Minister stated: 'if you are going to pronounce a new law that wherever Communism reigns against the will of the people, even though it has happened internally there, the United States shall enter, then we are going to have really terrible wars in the world'.[167] Members of the Reagan administration were aghast at such comments. NSC member and Deputy Assistant to the President for National Security Affairs Donald R. Fortier termed Thatcher's public recrimination 'politically quite unhelpful' and 'unusually severe and even insulting'.[168] In his memoirs Shultz wrote that Reagan was 'deeply disappointed' by Thatcher's failure to share his judgement on Grenada.[169] However, given the strength of Thatcher's opposition and the overriding value Reagan attached to their relationship, the President was not prepared to voice these concerns directly with the Prime Minister. McFarlane had no such reservations and asked Reagan if he could send a note to Robert Armstrong in London. Reagan agreed and

McFarlane dispatched a 'starchy cable' contrasting US behaviour during the Falklands crisis with the British lack of support for the US in Grenada.[170] Anglo-American relations were not improved by an embarrassing gaffe made by the Director of the US Information Agency, Charles Z. Wick, during a White House press conference when he complained that Thatcher had opposed US actions and refused to lend support because she was a woman. Despite asking the journalists present not to report what he had said, his remarks created quite a stir in the domestic press and were not well received in London.[171]

The invasion also amplified British concerns regarding the scheduled NATO deployment in November 1983 of American Cruise missiles in RAF Molesworth, Cambridgeshire, and Greenham Common, Berkshire.[172] US actions in Grenada resulted in a rising sentiment of anti-Americanism in the UK. British fears of US unilateralism were heightened in the lead-up to the deployment of the missiles. Many feared US involvement in authorising the use of the missiles. These fears were fuelled by the possibility of a Soviet retaliatory attack against the UK should the US decide to launch the missiles against the Soviet Union without consulting Britain. The debate over an Anglo-American dual-key system to operate the missiles reignited in the UK in the aftermath of Grenada. Thatcher, for her part, strongly disagreed with the 'anti-American overtones' surrounding the dual-key debate.[173] An emergency debate on the NATO deployment was held in the House of Commons on 31 October where a vote of 362 in favour and 218 against decided to proceed with the scheduled deployment (which went ahead on 14 November). Despite this vote, US actions in Grenada contributed to an unwelcome rejuvenation in Britain's Campaign for Nuclear Disarmament (CND).[174]

The US realised that overtures would have to be made in the UK. Thatcher's comments during the BBC radio interview had shown that the Prime Minister's loyalty was not absolute. This worried the Reagan administration as Thatcher's support was increasingly important to the US, which was then somewhat isolated abroad as a result of Grenada. In Europe, there was a growing scepticism regarding the OECS and Scoon's requests for help. European concerns needed to be addressed by the US. To that end, the US supplied a one-page factsheet to all of its diplomatic posts to try to address European concerns. Leading members of the NSC's European and Soviet Affairs Directorate, including Jack F. Matlock, Peter R. Sommer and Tyrus W. Cobb, suggested in a memo to McFarlane on 2 November that the 'vague reply' by the US, coupled with its 'less than precise and uniform public statements' on the origins of the OECS and Scoon's request, had hurt the US.[175] More would have to be done by the US to allay European concerns.

The US hoped that its announcement on 2 November that US forces were to begin their withdrawal from Grenada would help to improve its position in Europe. This announcement was followed by a statement revealing that Deputy Secretary Dam was to travel to Europe the following week to visit various European leaders, including Thatcher. It was hoped that this visit would help to repair ties and reinstate European confidence in the forthcoming Cruise missile deployment. A memo sent to McFarlane on 2 November highlighted the importance of Dam's trip:

> As you know, the most serious repercussions have affected our relationship with the British. Mrs Thatcher and Geoffrey Howe have been hurt domestically by what appears to many in the UK to have been our failure to consult adequately with Her Majesty's Government . . . they remain publicly critical of our decision . . . The Deputy Secretary's trip will, we hope, patch up some of the misunderstandings.[176]

The British, too, were keen to improve Anglo-American relations in Grenada's immediate aftermath. Wright noted the impact of the crisis on bilateral relations in a cable to the FCO on 4 November:

> The subsequent fracas has left bruises on both sides. Given the parliamentary reactions in Britain . . . we have been depicted over the last week as the President's leading critic . . . This has produced quite a strong reaction, both on the Republican side and from the American public . . . We have taken steps to put the record straight.[177]

Dam, accompanied by Edward Streator and Assistant Secretary of State for European and Canadian Affairs Richard R. Burt, met with Thatcher, Howe and the FCO's Julian Bullard at the Prime Minister's country retreat, Chequers, on 7 November (Thatcher's Private Secretary Arthur John 'A. J.' Coles was also in attendance). It was a difficult meeting as Thatcher voiced her many concerns over Grenada. The Prime Minister questioned Dam on the timing of Scoon's request and outlined the factors which had led the UK to believe that the US 'was not likely to intervene . . . To say that all this had put us [the UK] in difficulty was to put it very mildly'.[178] Howe, for his part, commented that 'the worrying feature was that, despite our close relationship and good secure communications', the UK had received no indication on 24 October of a 'shift in American thinking'.[179] Thatcher also discussed the impact of US actions in Grenada upon the forthcoming Cruise missile deployment in the UK. In her words: 'in the view of some, if the US does not consult when it goes into the Queen's realm, it might not consult on the use of nuclear weapons'.[180] Thatcher's rebukes did not go unnoticed by Streator, who noted in a message to Shultz on 10 November:

> I am concerned about mounting problems with Thatcher and prospects for US–UK relations in the period immediately ahead . . . I would like authorization soonest to make an informal approach to Howe and Carrington to try to begin to steer Thatcher back toward us . . . Thatcher has been too shrill in reacting on Grenada.[181]

This candid message reveals the extent of American frustration in dealing with a defiant Thatcher post-Grenada.

US concerns over Thatcher's reaction to Grenada were partially assuaged when the UK's Cabinet Office Foreign Affairs adviser, David Goodall, informed officials at the US embassy in London on 15 November that there was a greater 'nervousness' among Thatcher and her advisers about US intentions in general. However, Goodall confirmed that this nervousness 'did not affect Thatcher's belief in the primacy of the Atlantic relationship' as she and her ministers would say publicly in the coming weeks.[182] Thatcher chose to dispel any rumours of a cleavage in Anglo-American relations during a speech she gave when opening the new headquarters of the United Press International Television

News (UPITN) on 9 December. The Prime Minister emphatically stated that as far as she was concerned Anglo-American relations were in 'good heart'. Thatcher further stated: 'It is with friends you can talk frankly; never with rancour; always with friendship; always with understanding. That's the way it is with Britain and the US, and that's the way it always will be.'[183] It is clear that the Prime Minister was determined to consolidate improved Anglo-American relations post-Grenada. This determination, along with that of Reagan, effectively minimised the impact of US actions in Grenada upon the wider Anglo-American relationship. As Powell suggests of the lasting impact of the US invasion:

> It was very brief, the storm. In her [Thatcher's] case of course, it was rather more of the political humiliation which enabled her opponents in Parliament to jeer at her . . . here's the vaunted Special Relationship and this guy doesn't even tell her when he invades the Queen's dominions . . . it made life difficult for her for a time but it was not lasting.[184]

By 15 December 1983, all US combat troops had withdrawn from Grenada, with the exception of a limited number of US military personnel who remained to provide technical and logistical support to the interim administration. The withdrawal of US forces helped to facilitate a speedy return to normalised Anglo-American relations. With Grenada shelved, both leaders could continue to pursue ever-closer diplomatic relations between their respective governments. This joint pursuit of improved relations was a testament to both leaders' commitment to the Special Relationship. After all, the US invasion of Grenada had greatly impacted the relationship by highlighting US unilateralism in a country wherein the UK had vested interests. Moreover, US actions had resulted in considerable embarrassment for the Thatcher government including the Prime Minister, a fiercely proud woman who was not known for her mollifying nature. And yet Thatcher was magnanimous in her approach to the crisis. She chose to pursue improved bilateral relations with the US in deference to her unfailing belief in the importance of the Anglo-American alliance and to her close personal and professional relationship with Reagan; both of which served her interests well as Prime Minister. For Reagan, the crisis had shown that Thatcher was not to be trifled with and the President's admiration for her grew as a result. Reagan could ill-afford to lose such a powerful ally given the widespread international condemnation of US actions. Therefore, while the US invasion of Grenada was temporarily detrimental to the Special Relationship, it also served as a reminder of the growing importance of close transatlantic ties between the US and the UK. Thatcher's and Reagan's recognition of this fact played a key role in both leaders' subsequent foreign policy objectives, particularly in Latin America.

Notes

1. Department of State outline history of Grenada, October 1983, file: Warpowers, Grenada/Lebanon Political Rationale (1/3) (CFOA 1175), Office of the Counsel to the President Records, Ronald Reagan Library.
2. Claremont D. Kirton, 'Grenada and the IMF: the PRG's Extended Fund Facility program, 1983', *Latin American Perspectives*, 16(3) (Summer 1989): 121–44, at p. 121.
3. TNA, FCO 99/356, Cable No. 0753311, proposed statement on Grenada, 17 March 1979, p. 2.
4. TNA, FCO 99/358, American embassy telegram, 31 March 1979, p. 2.
5. TNA, FCO 99/318, cable regarding Cuba–Grenada, 17 April 1979; TNA, FCO 99/361, FCO briefing paper on tripartite talks on Grenada and the Caribbean, 14 May 1979.
6. HCPP, 1983/1984, HC 226, Foreign Affairs Select Committee: Grenada, second report with proceedings, evidence and appendices (received 05/04/1984), p. 45.
7. TNA, FCO 99/568, record of call by Augustine to A. J. Payne, 6 August 1980, p. 1.
8. *Ibid.*, record of call by Augustine to Ridley, 24 September 1980, p. 1.
9. This idea has also been put forward by Joseph Smith, *The United States and Latin America: A History of American Diplomacy, 1776–2000* (Abingdon: Routledge, 2005), p. 157; James Ferguson, *Grenada: Revolution in Reverse* (London: Latin America Bureau, 1990), p. 5.

10. Tony Martin, with Dessima Williams (eds), *In Nobody's Backyard: The Grenada Revolution in its Own Words, vol. II: Facing the World* (Dover, MA: Majority Press, 1983), p. 182; Gregory Sandford and Richard Vigilante, *Grenada: The Untold Story* (Lanham, MD: Madison Books, 1984), p. 101.

11. Bremer to Allen, 18 September 1981, file: Grenada September 1981–December 1981, box 8; Department of State Bureau of Intelligence report, 'Inter-American Highlights: Grenada Storm Signals', 12 August 1981, p. 1, file: Grenada August 1981, box 8, Roger W. Fontaine Files, Ronald Reagan Library.

12. William C. Gilmore, *The Grenada Intervention: Analysis and Documentation* (London: Mansell Publishing, 1984), p. 28. The CBI was first proposed by Reagan in 1982, and was an initiative designed to promote economic development and stability in Latin America through the provision of trade and tariff benefits to various Latin American and Caribbean countries. It was launched in 1983 through the Caribbean Basin Economic Recovery Act (CBERA). For more information on the CBI, see Abigail B. Bakan *et al.* (eds), *Imperial Power and Regional Trade: The Caribbean Basin Initiative* (Waterloo, Ontario: Wilfrid Laurier University Press, 1993).

13. Clark to Reagan, p. 1, n.d., file: Grenada February–April 1983, box 5, Alfonso Sapia-Bosch Files, Ronald Reagan Library.

14. HCPP, 1982/1983, Cmnd. 8819, FCO, Caribbean & Central America, Ministerial Observations on the fifth report of the Foreign Affairs Select Committee 1981/2, p. 14.

15. Address before a Joint Session of Congress on Central America, 27 April 1983, the Public Papers of President Ronald W. Reagan, Ronald Reagan Library, available at: www.reagan.utexas.edu/archives/speeches/1983/42783, accessed 12 February 2014.

16. The term 'credibility gap' emerged in the 1960s as a result of a disinclination by the American public to believe official US statements regarding the Vietnam War. For more information on the credibility gap in relation to the Reagan administration and Grenada, see Cole Blasier, 'Security: the extracontinental dimension', in Kevin J. Middlebrook and Carlos Rico (eds), *The United States and Latin America in the 1980s* (Pittsburgh, PA: University of Pittsburgh Press, 1988), p. 553; Russell Crandall, *Gunboat Diplomacy: US Interventions in the Dominican Republic, Grenada, and Panama* (Lanham, MD: Rowman & Littlefield, 2006), p. 159.

17. Gary Williams, 'Brief encounter: Grenadian Prime Minister

Maurice Bishop's visit to Washington', *Journal of Latin American Studies*, 34(3) (August 2002): 659–85, at p. 663.

18. Dam to Reagan, 7 June 1983, file: Grenada (1/20/81–10/31/83) (5), box 30, Executive Secretariat NSC Country Files, Latin America, Falklands War, Grenada, Ronald Reagan Library.

19. *New York Times*, 10 June 1983, file: Grenada, box 3, William P. Clark Files, Ronald Reagan Library.

20. HCPP, 1983/1984, HC 226, p. 8.

21. *Ibid.*, pp. 8–9.

22. Department of State and Department of Defense preliminary report, 16 December 1983, p. 34, file: Central America, Grenada Preliminary Report, OA 12274, J. Douglas Holladay Files, Ronald Reagan Library.

23. NSDD 105, 'Eastern Caribbean Regional Security Policy', 4 October 1983, file: NSDD 105, box 91291, Executive Secretariat NSC NSDD Files, Ronald Reagan Library.

24. HCPP, 1983/1984, HC 226, p. 9.

25. Shultz, *Turmoil and Triumph*, p. 325.

26. Grenada background fact sheet, 26 October 1983, p. 1, file: Grenada, Background Supplement, 26 October, box 90687, Constantine C. Menges Files, Ronald Reagan Library; TNA, CAB 128/76/30, Conclusions of a meeting of the Cabinet, 20 October 1983, p. 2.

27. Chronology of Grenada events leading to collective action of the Caribbean Peace Force, pp. 2–3, n.d., file: Grenada, Information Packet, box 90687, Constantine C. Menges Files, Ronald Reagan Library.

28. Reagan sent US marines to Lebanon in August 1982 as part of a multinational force (MNF) along with French, Italian and British troops. The MNF was established to supervise the withdrawal of the Palestine Liberation Organisation (PLO) army from Beirut and to prevent wider regional conflict following Israel's invasion of Lebanon.

29. Thatcher, *Downing Street Years*, p. 328.

30. Document titled, 'Legal authority for US action in Grenada', p. 2, n.d., file: Grenada Briefing (10/31/1983) (1), OA 16007, Linas J. Kojelis Files, Ronald Reagan Library.

31. Christopher C. Joyner, 'Reflections on the lawfulness of invasion', *American Journal of International Law*, 78(1) (January 1984): 131–44, at p. 136.

32. Briefing notes on background to legal/political rationale for US

action, p. 3, n.d., file: Grenada (2), box 90517, Christopher M. Lehman Files, Ronald Reagan Library.
33. Joyner, 'Reflections on the lawfulness of invasion', p. 133.
34. Francis A. Boyle *et al.*, 'International lawlessness in Grenada', *American Journal of International Law*, 78(1) (January 1984): 172–5, at p. 173.
35. Joyner, 'Reflections on the lawfulness of invasion', p. 143.
36. Maurice Waters, 'The invasion of Grenada, 1983 and the collapse of legal norms', *Journal of Peace Research*, 23(3) (September 1986): 229–46, at pp. 232–4.
37. W. Raymond Duncan, 'Soviet interests in Latin America: new opportunities and old constraints', *Journal of Interamerican Studies and World Affairs*, 26(2) (May 1984): 163–98, at p. 173.
38. Briefing notes, p. 4, file: Grenada (2), box 90517, Christopher M. Lehman Files, Ronald Reagan Library.
39. Gordon Connell-Smith, 'The Grenada invasion in historical perspective: from Monroe to Reagan', *Third World Quarterly*, 6(2) (April 1984): 432–45, at p. 443.
40. HCPP, 1983/1984, HC 226, p. 68.
41. Cable No. 2922046, PM Adams request, 19 October 1983, file: Grenada Cables (19 October 1983), box 42, Executive Secretariat NSC Cable File Records, Ronald Reagan Library.
42. *Ibid.*, Cable No. 2920001, possible evacuation of American citizens, 20 October 1983.
43. *Ibid.*, Cable No. 2930750, Ambassador's assessment of situation on Grenada, 20 October 1983, file: Grenada Cables (20 October 1983), box 42.
44. *Ibid.*, Cable No. 2930020, Deputy Prime Minister of St. Kitts-Nevis calls for direct United States government (USG) intervention in Grenada, 20 October 1983.
45. *Ibid.*, Cable No. 2940618, Grenada Working Group, 21 October 1983, file: Grenada Cables (21 October 1983) (1), box 42. Shultz, *Turmoil and Triumph*, p. 326.
46. Stephen Kinzer, *Overthrow: America's Century of Regime Change from Hawaii to Iraq* (New York: Times Books, 2007), p. 231; Ronald H. Cole, *Operation Urgent Fury: Grenada* (CreateSpace Independent Publishing Platform, 2013), p. 2.
47. NSDD 110, 'Grenada: Contingency Planning', 21 October 1983, p. 1, file: NSDD 110, box 91291, Executive Secretariat NSC NSDD Files, Ronald Reagan Library.

48. A more detailed account of this meeting is provided in Gary Williams, 'The tail that wagged the dog: the Organisation of Eastern Caribbean States' role in the 1983 intervention in Grenada', *European Review of Latin American and Caribbean Studies (Revista Europea de Estudios Latinoamericanos y del Caribe)*, No. 16 (December 1996): 95–115, at pp. 100–1.

49. Cable No. 063630, Grenada Revolutionary Military Council makes policy statement, 22 October 1983, p. 1, file: Grenada October 1983, classified after review (3), box 90692, Constantine C. Menges Files, Ronald Reagan Library.

50. Cable No. 2950059, approach to Adams regarding Grenada: approach to others tomorrow, 22 October 1983, p. 1, file: Grenada Cables (22 October 1983), box 42, Executive Secretariat NSC Cable File Records, Ronald Reagan Library.

51. *Ibid.*, Cable No. 2950737, OECS formally resolves unanimously to intervene by force if necessary, 22 October 1983.

52. Edgar F. Raines and Richard Winship Stewart, *Operation Urgent Fury: The Invasion of Grenada, October 1983* (Washington, DC: US Government Printing Office, 2008), p. 12.

53. Cable No. 2950126, OECS announces sanctions against Grenada, 23 October 1983, p. 2, file: Grenada Cables (23 October 1983), box 42, Executive Secretariat NSC Cable File Records, Ronald Reagan Library.

54. *Ibid.*, Cable No. 2961841, instructions for dealing with Caribbean friends, 23 October 1983, pp. 4–5.

55. *Ibid.*, p. 9.

56. National Security Records report, 'The Lessons of Grenada', September 1984, p. 2, file: Grenada (1), box 90521, Christopher M. Lehman Files, Ronald Reagan Library.

57. Fact sheet, p. 3, file: Grenada, Background Supplement 26 October, box 90687, Constantine C. Menges Files, Ronald Reagan Library.

58. Cable No. 2982214, informal minutes of meeting between Ambassadors Bish and McNeil with West Indian Heads of Government to discuss Grenada situation, 25 October 1983, pp. 2–4, file: Grenada Cables (25 October 1983) (6), box 42, Executive Secretariat NSC Cable File Records, Ronald Reagan Library.

59. *Ibid.*, p. 14.

60. Larry Speakes and Robert Pack, *Speaking Out: Inside the Reagan White House* (New York: Charles Scribner's, 1988), p. 161.

61. NSDD 110A, 'Response to Caribbean Governments' Request to Restore Democracy on Grenada', 23 October 1983, p. 1, file:

NSDD 110A, box 91291, Executive Secretariat NSC NSDD Files, Ronald Reagan Library.

62. HCPP, 1983/1984, HC 226, p. 13.

63. Attorney General memo regarding Grenada, 2 November 1983, pp. 2–6, file: CO 058 Grenada (609979), WHORM Subject Files, Ronald Reagan Library.

64. *Ibid.*, p. 16.

65. Department of State Bureau of Intelligence and Research report, 'Grenada: Soviet Front Organizations', Appendix A, Chronology, 21 March 1981, p. 1, file: Grenada February–April 1983, box 5, Alfonso Sapia-Bosch Files, Ronald Reagan Library.

66. Jonathan T. Howe to Eagleburger, n.d., file: Grenada Urgent Fury (03/03/1983–10/21/1983), box 90500, Jacqueline Tillman Files, Ronald Reagan Library.

67. Remarks to American troops at Camp Liberty Bell, Republic of Korea, 13 November 1983, the Public Papers of President Ronald W. Reagan, Ronald Reagan Library, available at: www.reagan.utexas.edu/archives/speeches/1983/111383, accessed 11 February 2014.

68. Reagan, *The Reagan Diaries*, pp. 189–90.

69. Shultz, *Turmoil and Triumph*, p. 326; Gary Williams, 'Prelude to an intervention: Grenada 1983', *Journal of Latin American Studies*, 29(1) (February 1997): 131–69, at p. 145.

70. Motley to McFarlane, 17 October 1983, file: Grenada (6/17/1983–10/25/1983) (Too Late to File), box 30, Executive Secretariat NSC Country Files, Latin America, Grenada, Ronald Reagan Library.

71. Williams, 'Prelude to an intervention', p. 147.

72. *Ibid.*, p. 153.

73. National Security Records report, p. 2, n.d., file: Grenada (1), box 90521, Christopher M. Lehman Files, Ronald Reagan Library.

74. Cable regarding Cuba breaks silence on Grenada, 21 October 1983, p. 4, file: Grenada Cables (21 October 1983) (3), box 42, Executive Secretariat NSC Cable File Records, Ronald Reagan Library.

75. *Ibid.* Grenada Sitrep. No. 5, 22 October 1983, pp. 1–2, file: Grenada Cables (22 October 1983), box 42.

76. *Ibid.*, cable regarding offer to evacuate US citizens, 23 October 1983, file: Grenada Cables (23 October 1983), box 42.

77. Interview with Geoffrey Howe.

78. TNA, PREM 19/1048, Howe to Bullard, 22 October 1983.

79. *Ibid.*, duty clerk to Thatcher, 22 October 1983.
80. *Ibid.*, Cable No. 3078, Wright to FCO, 22 October 1983.
81. *Ibid.*, FCO Sitrep., 24 October 1983, p. 2.
82. *Ibid.*, Cable No. 3084, Wright to FCO, 22 October 1983.
83. *Ibid.*, Cable No. 3087, Wright to FCO, 23 October 1983.
84. Renwick, *Journey with Margaret Thatcher*, p. 144.
85. HCPP, 1983/1984, HC 226, Cmnd. 9267, FCO: Grenada ministerial observations on the Foreign Affairs Select Committee, second report 1983/84 (HC 226), p. 3.
86. HCPP, 1983/1984, HC 226, p. 14.
87. TNA, PREM 19/1049, Wright to FCO, 28 October 1983.
88. John Norton Moore, 'Grenada and the international double standard', *American Journal of International Law*, 78(1) (January 1984): 145–68, at p. 148.
89. HCPP 1983/1984, HC 226, p. 68.
90. McNeil to Secretary of State in Washington, 24 October 1983, file: Grenada Invasion October 1983 (1), box 30, Executive Secretariat NSC Country Files, Latin America, Falklands War, Grenada, Ronald Reagan Library.
91. Shultz to American embassy in Bridgetown, 24 October 1983, file: Grenada Cables (24 October) (2), box 42, Executive Secretariat NSC Cable File Records, Ronald Reagan Library.
92. American embassy in Bridgetown to Secretary of State in Washington, 25 October 1983, file: Grenada Cables (25 October) (1), box 42, Executive Secretariat NSC Cable File Records, Ronald Reagan Library.
93. *Ibid.*
94. TNA, PREM 19/1048, Scoon to Adams, 24 October 1983.
95. *Ibid.*, Bullard to MOD, 27 October 1983.
96. Campbell, *Margaret Thatcher, vol. 2*, p. 278.
97. The RSS was created following the signing of a MOU between Barbados, St. Lucia, Antigua and Barbuda, Dominica and St. Vincent and the Grenadines on 29 October 1982. It was created as a collective response to defend the security and defence interests of the signatories.
98. Paul Scoon, *Survival for Service: My Experiences as Governor General of Grenada* (Oxford: Macmillan-Caribbean, 2003), p. 145.
99. Cable regarding Cunard offer of help, 24 October 1983, file: Grenada Cables (24 October 1983) (1), box 42, Executive Secretariat NSC Cable File Records, Ronald Reagan Library.

100. HCPP, 1983/1984, HC 226, Cmnd. 9267, FCO: Grenada ministerial observations on the Foreign Affairs Select Committee, second report 1983/84 (HC 226), p. 4.
101. Reagan to Thatcher (first message), 24 October 1983, file: United Kingdom 1983 (10/24/1983–10/27/1983), box 90424, Peter R. Sommer Files, Ronald Reagan Library.
102. Thatcher, *Downing Street Years*, pp. 330–1.
103. Reagan to Thatcher (second message), 24 October 1983, file: United Kingdom 1983 (10/24/1983–10/27/1983), box 90424, Peter R. Sommer Files, Ronald Reagan Library.
104. *Ibid.*, Thatcher to Reagan, 24 October 1983.
105. *Ibid.*
106. Reagan, *An American Life*, pp. 454–5.
107. TNA, PREM 19/1048, record of Reagan–Thatcher telephone conversation, 25 October 1983.
108. Interview with Cecil Parkinson.
109. Interview with Peter Carrington.
110. Interview with Charles Powell.
111. Interview with Bernard Ingham.
112. Bernard Ingham, *Kill the Messenger* (London: HarperCollins, 1991), pp. 259–60.
113. Reagan to Thatcher, 25 October 1983, file: United Kingdom 1983 (10/24/1983–10/27/1983), box 90424, Peter R. Sommer Files, Ronald Reagan Library.
114. Thatcher, *Downing Street Years*, p. 331.
115. Interview with Timothy Bell, 19 April 2013.
116. HCPP, 1983/1984, HC 226, p. 18.
117. Reagan and Charles joint statement on Grenada, 25 October 1983, file: Grenada Cables (25 October 1983) (5), box 42, Executive Secretariat NSC Cable File Records, Ronald Reagan Library.
118. TNA, PREM 19/1048, Wright to FCO, 25 October 1983.
119. Constantine C. Menges, *Inside the National Security Council: The True Story of the Making and Unmaking of Reagan's Foreign Policy* (New York: Simon & Schuster, 1988), p. 87.
120. TNA, PREM 19/1048, UK embassy in Washington to FCO, 25 October 1983.
121. Crandall, *Gunboat Democracy*, p. 159; Hugh O'Shaughnessy, *Grenada: Revolution, Invasion and Aftermath* (London: Sphere Books, 1984), p. 174.
122. The statement was a masterpiece in political spin cleverly linking a strong anti-communist message with events in Grenada, Lebanon

and the 31 September Soviet downing of the Korean airliner KAL 007 over the Soviet-owned Sakhalin Island in the North Pacific which killed 269 people, sixty of whom were Americans. See 'Address to the Nation on Events in Lebanon and Grenada', 27 October 1983, the Public Papers of President Ronald W. Reagan, Ronald Reagan Library, available at: www.reagan.utexas.edu/archives/speeches/1983/102783, accessed 12 February 2014.

123. Richard A. Brody, *Assessing the President: The Media, Elite Opinion, and Public Support* (Stanford, CA: Stanford University Press, 1991), p. 74.

124. Dinesh D'Souza, *Ronald Reagan: How an Ordinary Man became an Extraordinary Leader* (New York: Touchstone, 1999), p. 157.

125. TNA, PREM 19/1048, Wright to FCO, 27 October 1983. For more information on the War Powers Act in relation to the US invasion of Grenada, see Michael Rubner, 'The Reagan administration, the 1973 War Powers Resolution, and the invasion of Grenada', *Political Science Quarterly*, 100(4) (Winter 1985/6): 627–47.

126. *New York Times*, 28 October 1983.

127. Anthony Payne *et al.*, *Grenada: Revolution and Invasion* (London: Croom Helm, 1984), p. 164.

128. Jonathan Mermin, *Debating War and Peace: Media Coverage of US Intervention in the Post-Vietnam Era* (Princeton, NJ: Princeton University Press, 1999), p. 41.

129. TNA, PREM 19/1048, FCO Sitrep. No. 1, 25 October 1983.

130. *The Guardian*, 26 October 1983.

131. Marlene Cuthbert, 'Ideological differences in press coverage of the Grenada crisis', in Stuart H. Surlin and Walter C. Soderlund (eds), *Mass Media and the Caribbean* (New York: Gordon & Breach, 1990), p. 343; Payne *et al.*, *Grenada*, p. 169.

132. TNA, PREM 19/1048, cable regarding FRG reaction, 26 October 1983.

133. TNA, PREM 19/1049, UK NATO delegation to FCO, 9 November 1983.

134. TNA, PREM 19/1048, Derek Thomas to FCO, 26 October 1983.

135. White House News Summary bulletin, 26 October 1983, file: Grenada (1/3) OA 9450, Edwin Meese Files, Ronald Reagan Library.

136. Briefing notes on worldwide reaction, pp. 1–2, n.d., file: Grenada (8), box 8, Crisis Management Centre NSC Records, Ronald Reagan Library.

137. Mark Adkin, *Urgent Fury: The Battle for Grenada* (Lanham, MD: Lexington Books, 1989), p. 318. Report on summary of diplomatic reactions, 27 October 1983, file: Grenada, Summary of Diplomatic Reactions from 27 October, box 90687, Constantine C. Menges Files, Ronald Reagan Library.

138. Memo on foreign media reaction, 26 October 1983, p. 2, file: Grenada, Foreign Media Reaction 26 October, box 90687, Constantine C. Menges Files, Ronald Reagan Library.

139. Cable No. 2991812, demonstrations against US action in Grenada, 26 October 1983, file: Grenada (10/26/1983) (7/11), box 42, Executive Secretariat NSC Cable File Records, Ronald Reagan Library.

140. John F. Lyons, *America in the British Imagination, 1945 to the Present* (New York: Palgrave Macmillan, 2013), p. 111.

141. TNA, PREM 19/1048, telegram number. (Telno.) 3134, Wright to FCO, 26 October 1983.

142. *Ibid.*, Telno. 3135, UK embassy in Washington to FCO, 26 October 1983.

143. McFarlane memo regarding proposed telephone call to Thatcher, 26 October 1983, file: United Kingdom (11/1/83–6/30/84) (3/3), box 20, Executive Secretariat NSC Country Files, Europe and the Soviet Union, United Kingdom, Ronald Reagan Library.

144. Thatcher, *Downing Street Years*, p. 332; Renwick, *Journey with Margaret Thatcher*, p. 146.

145. Memcon. of Reagan–Thatcher discussion, 26 October 1983, file: United Kingdom (8/1/82–10/31/83) (4/5), box 20, Executive Secretariat NSC Country Files, Europe and the Soviet Union, United Kingdom, Ronald Reagan Library.

146. *Ibid.*

147. House of Commons debate, Grenada invasion, 26 October 1983, available at: www.hansard.millbanksystems.com/commons/1983/oct/26/grenada-invasion, accessed 15 February 2013.

148. Geoffrey Howe opening speech, 26 October 1983, p. 3, file: United Kingdom (11/1/83–6/30/84) (2/3), box 20, Grenada Emergency Debate, Executive Secretariat NSC Country Files, Europe and the Soviet Union, United Kingdom, Ronald Reagan Library.

149. *Ibid.*, pp. 3–4.

150. Interview with Geoffrey Howe.

151. *Ibid.*

152. Geoffrey Howe, *Conflict of Loyalty* (London: Macmillan, 1994), p. 331.

153. Cable No. 070569, Grenada: British thoughts on role of governor general and next steps, 26 October 1983, file: United Kingdom 1983 (10/24/1983–10/27/1983), box 90424, Peter R. Sommer Files, Ronald Reagan Library.

154. Cable No. 2981337, Grenada: UK alarmed at lack of consultations, seeks information urgently, 25 October 1983, file: Grenada Cables (25 October 1983) (3), box 42, Executive Secretariat NSC Cable File Records, Ronald Reagan Library.

155. Cable No. 071995, UK on position of governor general of Grenada, 27 October 1983, file: United Kingdom 1983 (10/24/1983–10/27/1983), box 90424, Peter R. Sommer Files, Ronald Reagan Library.

156. Thatcher statement in the House of Commons, 27 October 1983.

157. Brian Crozier, *Free Agent: The Unseen War, 1941–1991* (Toronto: HarperCollins, 1993), p. 264; Campbell, *Margaret Thatcher, vol. 2*, p. 278.

158. Thatcher, *Downing Street Years*, p. 332.

159. TNA, CAB 128/76/31, conclusions of a meeting of the Cabinet, 27 October 1983, p. 2.

160. *Ibid.*, p. 2.

161. TNA, PREM 19/1048, UK Mission in New York to FCO, 26 October 1983.

162. Kirkpatrick statement in the UNSC, 27 October 1983, p. 1, file: Grenada articles and press releases (1), box 90687, Constantine C. Menges Files, Ronald Reagan Library.

163. Robert J. Beck, *The Grenada Invasion: Politics, Law, and Foreign Policy Decisionmaking* (Boulder, CO: Westview Press, 1993), p. 78.

164. Interview with Michael Heseltine. For more on Heseltine's meeting with Weinberger in Montebello, see Michael Heseltine, *Life in the Jungle: My Autobiography* (London: Hodder & Stoughton, 2000), p. 259.

165. Interview with Michael Heseltine.

166. TNA, PREM 19/1049, Extracts from Howe–Walden *Weekend World* interview, 30 October 1983.

167. Thatcher BBC World Service comments, 30 October 1983, file: Grenada articles and press releases (2), box 90687, Constantine C. Menges Files, Ronald Reagan Library. Hugo Young referred to Thatcher's comments in the phone-in programme as a 'more measured way out of her humiliation'. See Hugo Young, *One of Us* (London: Macmillan, 1989), p. 347.

168. Fortier to McFarlane, 3 November 1983, file: United Kingdom 1983 (11/03/1983–11/06/1983), box 90424, Peter R. Sommer Files, Ronald Reagan Library.

169. Shultz, *Turmoil and Triumph*, p. 340.

170. Robert C. McFarlane and Zofia Smardz, *Special Trust* (New York: Cadell & Davies, 1994), p. 267.

171. Speakes and Pack, *Speaking Out*, p. 159.

172. NATO decided in 1979 to deploy 108 Pershing II and 464 ground-launched Cruise missiles in Europe in response to the Soviet build-up of SS-20 missiles. Deployment of the missiles was due to take place throughout Europe, including the UK, in late 1983. See Aldous, *Reagan and Thatcher*, p. 133.

173. TNA, PREM 19/979, record of Thatcher–Bush discussion, 24 June 1983, p. 1. The dual-key system enabled both British and American operators to insert keys in order to launch Cruise missiles stationed in the UK.

174. The CND campaign emerged in the UK in the early to mid-1980s. Protests against the siting of NATO Cruise missiles in the UK by the Greenham Common Women's Peace Camp, in particular, was a source of ongoing irritation for the Thatcher government.

175. Sommer, Matlock and Cobb to McFarlane, 2 November 1983, file: United Kingdom 1983 (10/28/1983–11/02/1983), box 90424, Peter R. Sommer Files, Ronald Reagan Library.

176. Executive Secretary for Charles Hill (State Department official and adviser to Shultz) to McFarlane, 2 November 1983, file: United Kingdom (11/1/83–6/30/84) (2/3), box 20, Executive Secretariat NSC Country Files, Europe and the Soviet Union, United Kingdom, Ronald Reagan Library.

177. TNA, PREM 19/1151, Wright to FCO, 4 November 1983.

178. *Ibid.*, Memcon. of Dam–Thatcher meeting, 7 November 1983, pp. 2–3.

179. *Ibid.*, p. 4.

180. Situation Room checklist on Dam–Thatcher meeting, 9 November 1983, file: United Kingdom 1983 (11/07/1983–11/19/1983), box 90424, Peter R. Sommer Files, Ronald Reagan Library.

181. Cable No. 023092, Thatcher and the US: where we are, what to do, 10 November 1983, file: United Kingdom 1983 (11/07/1983–11/19/1983), box 90424, Peter R. Sommer Files, Ronald Reagan Library.

182. Cable No. 3201954, US embassy in London to Secretary of State in Washington, 16 November 1983, file: Grenada (11/15/1983–

11/16/1983), box 44, Executive Secretariat NSC Cable File Records, Ronald Reagan Library.

183. Thatcher remarks at the opening of UPITN, 9 December 1983.

184. Interview with Charles Powell.

4 Vested Interests: US Involvement in the Anglo-Guatemalan Dispute

The question of Belizean independence was an important issue for both the Reagan and Thatcher governments in the early 1980s. For the UK, Belizean independence represented an opportunity to reduce its financial obligations in maintaining a former British colony. It also afforded the UK an opportunity to secure a Belizean commitment to the British Commonwealth. The US saw Belizean independence as a means to counter Soviet expansion in the region and as a bulwark against the possible expansion of leftist guerrilla activity from neighbouring Honduras. This was particularly important to the Reagan administration given the perceived communist threat in the region from Cuba, Nicaragua and El Salvador.[1] A democratic Belize would provide the US with a valuable political and ideological ally given its strategic location bordered on two sides by both Honduras and Guatemala. The US also hoped that involvement in the Belizean issue would help it to establish closer ties with Guatemala. Improved US–Guatemalan relations would allow the US to explore the possibilities of renewed US–Guatemalan military trade and, to a lesser extent, the construction of a US naval base in Guatemala.

This chapter will examine the Anglo-Guatemalan dispute over the territorial integrity of Belize. US participation in negotiating a settlement of the Belizean question at the encouragement of the UK will be closely examined, as will the simultaneous developments in US–Guatemalan relations. It will critically assess the impact of US strategic interests in mediating the dispute upon the development of Anglo-American relations during this time. As such, the chapter offers a unique opportunity to assess a previously neglected aspect of Anglo-American relations. To date, there has been little written on the Anglo-Guatemalan territorial dispute with a few notable exceptions detailing the historiography of the dispute prior to 1981.[2] However, the dispute in terms of its importance to the development of Anglo-American relations under Reagan and Thatcher has, until now (to the best of my knowledge), remained unpublished. Accordingly, much of this chapter is based upon the analysis of primary documents accessed in the US and the UK (including documents released by the TNA in August 2013, such as PREM 19/959, PREM 19/1048, PREM 19/1153 file series and in August 2012 from the FCO 46/2848, FCO 46/2850 and FCO 46/2879 file series). The chapter will focus primarily upon the period 1981–3 with regard to the Belizean question as these years marked intensive Anglo-American negotiations with both Belize and Guatemala. It will begin, however, by providing a brief synopsis of the background to the territorial dispute prior to the Thatcher government coming to power in order to provide some historical context.

A question of territory

The dispute between the UK and Guatemala can be dated back to the seventeenth century. From then onwards the UK, Spain and, eventually, Guatemala, all laid claim to the area later known as British Honduras and subsequently Belize. The area served as a base for British buccaneers in the early seventeenth century to carry out acts of piracy against Spanish vessels destined for the European mainland. Following years of use by British buccaneers to harvest logwood in the area, a British settlement was established in the territory. In 1670, the Godolphin Treaty was signed and became the foundation on which the British claim to the territory was laid. Article 7 of the treaty stated that Britain was entitled to the possession of lands, regions, islands and colonies situated in the West Indies and in any places of America. In 1713, Spain issued a royal edict declaring the British logwood trade illegal.[3] However, the Treaty of Paris in 1763 validated the British claim when Spain allowed the British log-wooding to continue. Spain reversed its position yet again in 1779 when, as an ally of

France, Spain declared war on the British and drove the British settlers from the territory. The British settlers returned to the territory following the Treaty of Versailles in 1783 which specified certain areas as open to log-wooding.[4]

Spain saw many of its Latin American possessions gain independence in the early nineteenth century and the Central American Federation was established in 1823.[5] Guatemala claimed possession of the territory under the provision of its independence from Spain and its right to Spanish territories in the region. However, Guatemala failed to mention any claim to the territory when it signed the UK–Guatemala Treaty of 1859 in which both countries agreed to recognise the existing boundaries between the territory and Guatemala.[6] A convention to the treaty in 1863 saw Guatemala agree to cede its territorial rights to Britain on condition that the UK would grant Guatemala access through the territory to the Caribbean Sea.[7] The British failed to construct the road and Guatemala repudiated the treaty. Nevertheless, the territory was declared the colony of British Honduras in 1862 and was declared a Crown Colony in 1871.

Guatemala's claim to British Honduras re-emerged in 1939 under the government of General Jorge Ubico y Castañeda when Guatemala again denounced the 1859 treaty. From 1945 onwards Guatemala made repeated territorial claims to British Honduras. These claims were generally perceived in the UK as a means for Guatemala to engage national pride in the face of domestic unrest and economic difficulties. In 1958, under the leadership of President Miguel Ydígoras Fuentes, Guatemala reinvigorated its territorial claim. This claim coincided with the beginning of a period of intense civil war in Guatemala. In British Honduras, the question of independence became a priority for the general populace and the ruling People's United Party (PUP) under the leadership of George Cadle Price. In 1960, following a meeting between British Honduran and Colonial Office officials in London, an agreement was made to strengthen moves towards the country's self-government. It was decided that British Honduras would remain loyal to the Crown and would become an independent member of the British Commonwealth.[8] Tensions resurfaced and protracted Anglo-Guatemalan negotiations resulted in Guatemala severing diplomatic relations with the UK in 1963.[9] British Honduras achieved full internal self-government a few months later on 1 January 1964.

Guatemala's territorial claim resurfaced in 1965, and the US decided to become actively involved in the negotiating process. President Lyndon B. Johnson appointed former Assistant US Attorney for the Southern District of New York, Bethuel Webster, as a mediator in the dispute. Webster put forward several proposals between 1965 and 1968, all of which were rejected by British Honduras.[10] Guatemala continued to make sporadic threats to invade British Honduras during this time. These threats were offset by a limited British military presence in the country, which formally changed its name to Belize on 1 June 1973. The British military presence in Belize began to increase by the mid-1970s in direct response to perceived Guatemalan aggression. In September 1975, the UK received reports that there was a substantial build-up in Guatemalan activity along part of its shared border with Belize. The UK again approached the US for help. US Secretary of State Henry Kissinger intervened and persuaded the Guatemalans against military action.[11]

Belize began to look towards the international community as a means to weaken Guatemala's territorial claim. On 8 December 1975, the UNGA passed Resolution 3432 regarding the territorial integrity of Belize. It declared that the inviolability and territorial integrity of Belize should be preserved. Notwithstanding this, Guatemala continued to assert its territorial claim. The British garrison in Belize was reinforced in July 1976 to include three Tigercat launchers and six anti-aircraft guns in response to an increasing deterioration in Anglo-Guatemalan relations.[12] Anglo-American discussions on the issue in November 1977 resulted in a proposal to grant Guatemala some territory, including the long-disputed Ranguana and Sapodilla cays (off Belize's south-east coast). Belize refused to cede any territory and rejected the proposal in January 1978.[13] The US State Department put forward additional unsuccessful proposals in February 1978, but the British had concerns that the US was more concerned with meeting the requirements of Guatemala than with those of Belize.[14] Guatemalan frustration continued to grow and was compounded when the UK deployed SAS personnel to Belize in July 1978, thereby augmenting Belizean defence capabilities.[15] A Belize Defence Force (BDF) was created in 1978 to monitor the borders between Belize and Guatemala.

A period of prolonged political violence emerged in Guatemala following the coming to power of General Fernando Romeo Lucas García on 1 July 1978. Under his leadership three leftist guerrilla groups emerged: Organización Revolucionaria del Pueblo en Armas (ORPA, Revolutionary Organisation of the People in Arms), the Fuerzas Armadas Rebeldes (FAR, Rebel Armed Forces) and the Ejército Guerrillero de los Pobres (EGP, Guerrilla Army of the Poor). These groups later combined to create the Unidad Revolucionaria Nacional Guatemalteca (URNG, Guatemalan National Revolutionary Unit), which was responsible for numerous deaths, kidnappings and torture in Guatemala. Violence began to spread throughout the country and extreme right-wing groups, such as the Mano Blanco (the White Hand) and the Ejército Secreto Anti-Comunista (ESAC, or Secret Anti-Communist Army), began to emerge contributing to the increasing numbers of human rights violations in Guatemala. These groups targeted those suspected of being influenced by or involved in leftist guerrilla activities.[16] In the light of its deteriorating domestic situation, the Guatemalan government looked towards resolving the issue of Belize. This would help distract public attention and unite the population in a common cause, much as had happened in Argentina under Galtieri.

US–UK–Belizean–Guatemalan consultation

Upon the Thatcher government coming to power, the UK began to renew its efforts to encourage US support of its territorial claim. It was hoped that US support would help to curtail any possible Guatemalan aggression against Belize. To that end, Nicholas Ridley met with Phil Habib, then a Special Advisor to the Reagan administration, on 5 July 1979 to discuss the Latin American region, including Belize. During this meeting Ridley suggested that the UK should possibly end the deadlock on the Belizean problem. Habib advised against this and suggested that the UK should resume discussions with both Belize and Guatemala. Ridley objected to this as the UK wanted to 'get out of the territory, not just have discussions'.[17] The UK wanted to grant full independence to Belize, which would enable them to withdraw British forces from the country; a considerable drain on British finances at the time. The US, however, was concerned that a British withdrawal from Belize would contribute to further instability in Latin America. The British position was augmented on 21 November 1979 when the UNGA passed Resolution 3438, calling for Belizean independence and a negotiated settlement to the dispute with Guatemala.[18]

Ridley met with a number of US officials, including Cyrus Vance and the new US Assistant Secretary of State for Inter-American Affairs, William G. Bowdler, in Washington on 18 January 1980 to discuss the Central/Latin American region.[19] These exchanges were outlined in a briefing for the then British Secretary of State for Defence, Francis Pym, prior to his forthcoming meeting with Vance on 21 February. According to Pym's briefing notes for this meeting:

These exchanges have allayed American fears of a British intention to bring Belize to early independence without a further attempt to negotiate a settlement with Guatemala. We have been promised US support for further negotiations; they have offered to try to persuade the Guatemalans of the need for early settlement. This helpful attitude denotes a welcome change in US policy which has hitherto been non-committal to Belize.[20]

Despite these notes, Ridley was not entirely convinced of US support at the time. A draft paper on the future of Belize was drawn up for the Cabinet Defence and Overseas Policy Committee (OD) in late February 1980. Ridley reviewed this paper and made a number of handwritten amendments to include in the final draft for the OD. One of Ridley's more striking notes stated:

the US is not going to lean on the Guats [sic] to abandon land cession
– only to encourage it to 'search' for a settlement and the US concern

within the Central Am [sic] applecart will not allow it to kick G [sic] into line. All we have this time from Vance and Co. is neutrality and benevolence.[21]

Nevertheless, Robert Armstrong briefed Thatcher on 1 April that 'the Americans, who have hitherto been carefully neutral in the dispute, now seem ready to back us in looking for a settlement'.[22] This was good news for the Thatcher government, which increasingly focused its attention on the Belizean issue. The UK's position towards Belize was a complex one. While keen to ensure Belizean independence, the UK was reluctant to cede territory to Guatemala. At the same time, it wanted to withdraw British forces from Belize. As Foreign Secretary Peter Carrington explained during a BBC interview on 31 July:

> [There is] no question of Guatemala claiming the whole of Belize. This is not a matter of negotiation. Belize is a British colony and Guatemala says they have some claim over some of the territory of Belize. We are having some conversations with the Belizeans and with the Guatemalans, and I hope very much it will be possible to give independence to Belize in the not too distant future.[23]

Carrington met with George Price in Mexico City on 8 August to discuss Belize's future independence. During this meeting Price was steadfast in his rejection of a possible land cession to Guatemala.[24] Price maintained this position during a similar meeting with Ridley in Miami on 10 August. Ridley subsequently travelled to Guatemala where he met with Guatemalan Foreign Minister Rafael Castillo Valdez on 14 August. During this meeting the territorial issue was discussed without resolution. Despite Britain's diplomatic efforts, the territorial issue continued to gather pace. In a speech before the UNGA on 6 October, Castillo Valdez reaffirmed that Belize was 'an integral part' of Guatemala's national territory.[25] In the face of such Guatemalan intractability, the UK again looked towards the US for help. The UK perceived a positive change in US attitudes towards Belize during a meeting between Ridley and US Deputy Assistant Secretary of State for Inter-American Affairs John A. Bushnell in Washington on 15

October. During this meeting Bushnell acknowledged that the US position on Belize in past years had been 'somewhat indefensible'.[26] A renewed US involvement in the territorial dispute was further evident when Bushnell, along with US Deputy Secretary of State Warren Christopher, met with Castillo Valdez in the State Department on 17 October. Belize was again discussed during this meeting in a bid to open channels of communications between the US and Guatemala on the territorial issue.[27] This meeting provided Guatemala with the perfect opportunity to establish friendlier relations with the US before the Reagan administration came to power in January 1981. Indeed, Guatemala hoped that with Reagan in power improved US–Guatemalan relations would help to underscore Guatemalan territorial claims to Belize.[28]

The Thatcher government watched the developing relations between Guatemala and the US with great interest. Carrington, in particular, realised that Reagan's inauguration could potentially alter the US approach to the territorial dispute. In a cable to the UK embassy in Washington on 23 December, Carrington stated that there were:

> indications that the new [Reagan] administration may be more disposed to lean on Belize rather than Guatemala. It is clearly most important that we should take the earliest opportunity to brief Haig and his advisers on Central America (when these are appointed).[29]

In fact, the UK hoped to make general US support of Guatemala 'conditional upon Guatemalan forbearance over Belize'.[30] Within days of Reagan's inauguration Henderson called on the new Secretary of State to discuss Central America. During this 26 January 1981 meeting with Haig, Henderson discussed British hopes for American support on the Belizean issue. Haig expressed his hope that the US and UK could proceed on this 'in tandem and in step', and welcomed Henderson's suggestion of continued Anglo-American talks on the Caribbean.[31] This was a promising beginning to Anglo-American consultation over Belize under the Reagan administration. In the meantime, the UK continued to try to appease Belizean concerns regarding its future security. To that end, the British Deputy Under-Secretary of State, Derek Malcolm

'D. M.' Day, travelled to Belize in late January 1981 in order to assess the situation with Guatemala and to determine Belizean defence requirements post-independence. Day concluded that Belize would not be able to resist an invasion from Guatemala alone and would need British military support in the aftermath of independence.[32] These security guarantees were to become an integral component of British and American attitudes towards the negotiating process, in particular, the British contribution to the BDF.

Trilateral talks resumed on 5 February when British, Belizean and Guatemalan officials met in New York to discuss the territorial issue. The Guatemalan delegation, led by Ambassador Jorge Skinner-Klee, informed the delegations present that Guatemala would settle for cession of the Sapodilla and Ranguana cays along with a lease of the some land.[33] Guatemala became increasingly frustrated with the lack of progress, and Castillo Valdez was less than hopeful of a successful outcome to the dispute during a Radio-Televisión Guatemala interview on 10 February 1981 when he stated: 'These negotiations have been held for more than ten years and I could not now foresee when they will end.'[34] The New York talks resumed on 12 February, but Belize's proposal to lease Lime Cay (part of the Sapodilla Cay) to the UK, who could then sublet it to Guatemala, coupled with its refusal to cede any of the Ranguana cays, was met with disdain. Guatemala rejected what it saw as a 'derisory offer'.[35] Talks were suspended and the territorial issue remained unresolved. Following these talks, the Guatemalan delegation announced its wish to meet with key members of the Reagan administration, such as Vice-President Bush, Secretary Haig and Richard V. Allen, in order to explain their new negotiating position before the next round of talks.[36]

The Governor of Belize, James Hennessy, wrote to the FCO to outline his concerns on the failure of the talks. According to Hennessy, the Belizean delegation saw Guatemala's move to suspend talks as 'deliberate and calculated', and as a way of diverting domestic attention from Guatemala's civil war. In Belizean eyes, the Guatemalan government was 'aiming to win support at home for a tough anti-Belize policy while looking to the USA for support in the fight against what they call Communist subversion'. As a result, the Belizean delegation had little faith in Guatemalan protestations of good faith.[37] Guatemala's desire to gain US support was worrying to Belize. Thus, Hennessy wrote again to the FCO following a visit on 23 February by the US Ambassador to Belize, Malcolm R. Barnebey. During this visit Barnebey informed Hennessy that the US had formulated its policy towards Belize based upon reports received from the UK and Guatemala following the unsuccessful New York talks. He informed Hennessy that the US had 'tilted towards Guatemala'. The Reagan administration felt that Guatemalan demands were reasonable and Haig had informed Castillo Valdez of this fact during a recent meeting with him (22 February).[38] This apparent US tilt towards Guatemala worried the UK.

The Reagan administration had already begun to seek closer relations with Guatemala. On 23 February, it decided to send its Ambassador to Guatemala, Frederic L. Chapin, to Guatemala sometime in the near future to outline US intentions to approve pending foreign military sales (FMS) licensing requests for cash sales of all helicopter spare parts, routine maintenance, essential equipment modification and to 'entertain favourably fresh requests for FMS cash commercial sales'. It also intended to approve the lease of a small number of helicopters to Guatemala and hoped to exchange intelligence on subversive activities, such as arms shipments and Cuban involvement in the region.[39] Such US objectives would be best served through improved US–Guatemalan relations. The dispute over Belize thereafter provided an excellent forum to achieve closer bilateral relations. Moreover, the US was assured of continued involvement in the dispute given Guatemala's unremitting claims to Belize.

US strategic interests and UK views on Latin America

In fact, the Reagan administration had a number of strategic interests in the Belize dispute. The US was convinced of the need for a British personnel security presence in Belize after it gained independence as it feared Guatemalan–Belizean tension and the possibility of Cuban intervention, which could lead to further regional destabilisation.[40] Cuba's decision to back Belizean independence was a key concern for the Reagan administration. The US could not allow Cuba to gain influence in Belize as they feared this would represent an expansion of Soviet interests in the region. This fed into US views of Guatemala as a country facing the dual problem of a Soviet bloc/Cuban-supported guerrilla movement and the internal violent right.[41] Thus, the US sought to improve its ties with Guatemala so as to monitor the possible spread of communism and insurgency throughout the region. Such fears, according to Gloria Hooper, were 'justifiable', but, she contends: 'With hindsight they may have not been so. But at the time I think it was difficult to know how things would develop.'[42] The Reagan administration thereby sought to convince London of the need to retain the British garrison in post-independent Belize. In accordance with this, US officials spoke with Thatcher in order to help accomplish US objectives in the dispute, which included a settlement by 'diplomatic not military means of a troublesome, potentially dangerous conflict in Central America ... to undercut Cuba's campaign to appear as a major spokesman for Belize's independence, to free us further to act immediately on Guatemala's legitimate internal security problems'.[43] Regardless of the motivations behind US involvement, the UK welcomed US support whilst simultaneously believing that the 'Americans should concentrate on urging continued flexibility on the Guatemalan government'.[44] The Reagan administration also had a vested economic interest in Guatemala in the form of the proposed 'Intermares Trans-Guatemala Pipeline' project. This project (proposed in 1976) was a private-sector initiative that greatly interested the US in terms of its crude oil distribution requirements. The proposed pipeline would provide the US with more oil supply security than it was previously afforded by the transit of oil through the Panama Canal, and represented a possible saving of up to US$766 million per annum (versus shipping oil through the Panama Canal).[45] This was a significant possible saving for the US and it influenced the administration's policy towards Guatemala.

Reagan's preoccupation with the communist threat in Latin

America was not shared by many in the UK at the time, with the notable exception of Thatcher. The British Parliament's Foreign Affairs Committee stated in a 1981 report that: 'the present [US] administration has a paranoid antagonism towards any government in the area which may be remotely described as left wing let alone Marxist'.[46] The Committee believed that the Reagan administration's view of the Central American region in terms of the East–West conflict provided an 'unsatisfactory and insufficient policy framework'. It further argued that such a policy placed too much emphasis on containing communism 'either by destabilising or isolating regimes' and too little emphasis on 'assisting countries in the region to solve their own problems in their own way'.[47] The US, however, was influenced by hardliners such as Jeane Kirkpatrick who saw US objectives in Latin America as:

> the interests of the US require that the influence of the Soviet-bloc powers in the region should be actively resisted. Since the aim of such powers is ultimately the installation of totalitarian regimes hostile to the US, the US should be prepared to back authoritarian regimes friendly to the US – where no clearly stable and democratic alternative exists – rather than weak democratic governments unable to contain subversion.[48]

US policy in Latin America was somewhat contentious from the UK's perspective as it saw its ally become increasingly and unwisely involved in the internal conflicts of many Central American countries in the fight against Soviet expansionism. The Foreign Affairs Select Committee's views on British policy in the region in comparison to those of the US at the time could not have been more different. As the Committee opined:

> We feel that at the present time British policy towards Central America should be particularly concerned that, while our allies, partners may share the broad policy aim of adopting a sympathetic identification with development aspirations of Central American nations and seeking to prevent those from moving into the Soviet orbit, there do exist serious differences of emphasis about the most appropriate ways of achieving these objectives.[49]

The FCO defined British policy in Central America as designed to assist friendly governments in the region, and to help develop their countries 'in a just and equitable fashion'. It was also designed to promote the 'unimpeded operation' of the Panama Canal, to help Belize achieve a stable future and to draw attention to the 'dangers of Communist subversion'. In addition to these objectives, the UK was committed to its condemnation of human rights violations and its desire to alleviate conditions of injustice and poverty in Central America.[50]

In line with its objective to help Belize achieve a stable future, the UK continued to maintain a garrison in Belize to bolster the BDF. In 1981, the UK had an infantry unit, an RAF Rapier Regiment, and Harrier, Puma and Gazelle aircraft in Belize to defend against possible Guatemalan aggression. British defence capabilities in the small country also included armoured reconnaissance, air defence, an engineer and communications unit, and a Royal Navy warship supported by a Royal Fleet auxiliary.[51] This was a considerable British presence given that the population of Belize at the time was in the region of 150,000 people. The British presence was a symbol of its commitment to a former colony. It was also a way in which to promote democracy in line with the US in Latin America. In Thatcher's words: 'In Central America, we keep troops stationed in Belize at that government's request. That is our contribution to sustain democracy in a part of the world so vital to the United States.'[52] The UK's financial commitment to Belize for the fiscal year (FY) 1981 represented £437,000 towards the cost of the garrison and repayment of the MOD for training service personnel.[53] This cost was in addition to a grant of £6 million towards Belizean independence in the same year.[54] This financial commitment was one of the primary reasons the UK wished to grant Belize full independence. In effect, the Thatcher government wanted to relieve itself of a former colonial burden.

Much as with the Haig mediation efforts during the Falklands War, little is known about British views on the subject of Belize. According to John Nott:

We had our liabilities in Belize and we had to carry them out; but we were very stretched in dealing with the Cold War. The most important thing that I want to say about the Falklands and, if you like about Belize, is that people tend to look at these things in isolation, as separate and important issues. But, of course, all of this took place in the context of the Cold War and the very real threat which we were facing from the Soviet Union and its allies.[55]

Charles Powell contends that the Belizean question was:

just one of those inconvenient little problems that get left over from history. We had an obligation to defend Belize as a British overseas territory. It was a pretty expensive exercise maintaining the Harriers. Did we want to do it? You bet we didn't. It was a diversion of resources, a diversion of expenditure and so on. But we had a proud record of standing by our obligations. Had the Americans been able to solve it sooner, then no-one would have been happier. We had a burden of debt to history as it were, where the Americans had a strategic interest.[56]

Cecil Parkinson suggests that Guatemalan threats were not of huge importance to the UK during the Thatcher government. He recalls: 'I have to be truthful, we never really took Guatemalan threats very seriously . . . I don't think it ever really impinged on the conscience.'[57] Peter Carrington confirms this view as he suggests: 'I don't think it was considerably important.' He argues that Guatemalan threats to invade were 'all very trying but not very serious'.[58] These comments, while illuminating, are at odds with the build-up in British strategic defence capabilities in Belize at the time.

Thatcher's first working visit to Washington on 26 February 1981, apart from consolidating close Anglo-American relations, allowed the Prime Minister to discuss the question of Belize with Reagan. This was particularly important in the light of the forthcoming Heads of Agreement talks on the future of Belize in London on 11 March. According to Reagan's briefing papers for his meeting with Thatcher, the US was to: 'urge Mrs Thatcher to advise the Belizeans to seriously consider ceding some minor cays to Guatemala if that is what is required to reach a successful overall settlement of the dispute, and encourage the British to provide a post-independence security guarantee in Belize'.[59] The suggestion of land cession to Guatemala did not sit well with Thatcher. Having expressed her displeasure at the suggestion, the US agreed to work closely with Britain to develop a regional structure for cooperation. In keeping with this policy, the US agreed to ensure the peaceful granting of independence to Belize and to act as a regional coast guard in the Caribbean. Furthermore, the Reagan administration was 'prepared to impress upon the Guatemalans the advantages of gracefully accepting Belizean independence, as well as the dangers to their own and regional security of a bellicose response'.[60] In return for this US pressing of Guatemala, the Reagan administration wanted the UK to urge the Belizeans to 'seize what may be the last chance for a peaceful resolution to this issue'.[61]

Indeed, a peaceful resolution to the territorial issue was vital given the escalating violence in Guatemala at the time. Extreme left-wing violence in the country had become widespread with significant increases in the number of violent clashes between guerrilla and military forces. All major groups within Guatemalan society were targeted, including military/police personnel, government officials, priests, religious lay people, opposition political leaders, businessmen, peasants, academics, students, trades union activists, doctors, journalists and lawyers. These people were subject to death, torture, degradation, arbitrary arrest or imprisonment or denial of a fair public trial. Freedom of speech, religion and press were denied and journalists, in particular, faced violence from both leftist insurgents and right-wing activists.[62] The military government of Lucas García failed to halt such indiscriminate violence and its military forces were largely responsible for an acute escalation in human rights violations. Nevertheless, the US disregarded reports on the worsening situation in Guatemala by organisations such as Amnesty International as 'biased and inaccurate'.[63] In fact, the so-called 'scorched earth campaign' in Guatemala was later estimated to have resulted in the death or disappearance of between 100,000 and 150,000 people during 1981–3.[64]

Despite the growing human rights violations in Guatemala, the US wanted closer bilateral relations. A report by the US Interagency

Group on Guatemala on 3 March 1981 suggested that a military sales relationship with Guatemala was 'a prerequisite to any new approach to the Guatemalans'.[65] Given the turbulent environment in Guatemala at the time, the report suggested that the US 'could probably not supply helicopter spares or other military equipment unless the President certifies that extraordinary circumstances exist'.[66] The report suggested that the US should sell US$3 million in jeeps and trucks to Guatemala, which would not require a legislative finding. These recommendations were to be in accordance with an improvement in US–Guatemalan relations, providing that Guatemala addressed its domestic human rights violations.[67] However, the Reagan administration's quest to improve its relations with Guatemala by supplying the Guatemalan military with jeeps and trucks was impeded by congressional opposition to any renewal of US military assistance to the country.[68]

The Heads of Agreement

The Heads of Agreement was signed in London on 11 March by Belize, Guatemala and the UK as a means of expediting Belizean independence. The agreement (largely penned by Ridley) stated that both the UK and Guatemala would recognise the independent state of Belize as an integral part of Central America. It also bound both countries to respect Belize's 'sovereignty and territorial integrity in accordance with its existing and traditional frontiers'.[69] It appeared that Guatemala had accepted that it would no longer have a territorial claim to Belize. In return for this, Guatemala was to have 'unimpeded access to the high seas', the use and employment of the Ranguana and Sapodilla cays, and free port facilities in Belize City and Punta Gorda. Belize, for its part, agreed to facilitate the construction of a pipeline between Guatemala and Belize City, Dangriga and Punta Gorda. More importantly, Belize and Guatemala agreed to sign a Treaty of Cooperation in matters of security and mutual concern. In accordance with this, both the UK and Guatemala agreed to normalise diplomatic relations.[70] The Heads of Agreement also proposed the establishment of a Joint Commission between the UK,

Guatemala and Belize to work together to clarify details and to prepare the relevant treaties. The final provision of the agreement stated that: 'The controversy between the UK and Guatemala over the territory of Belize shall therefore be honourably and finally terminated.'[71]

The US welcomed the signature of the Heads of Agreement. Haig contacted Carrington upon its signature to offer his 'heartiest congratulations' to Carrington and his colleagues in the FCO. In his reply to Haig, Carrington referred to the importance the UK attached to US involvement in events preceding the signature of the Heads of Agreement:

> We are well aware that the US administration played no small part in creating the atmosphere which made this possible. I should like to take this opportunity of expressing my gratitude for your help and understanding . . . I know that we can count on your continuing help through the relationship which you are developing with Guatemala.[72]

US Under Secretary of State for Political Affairs Walter J. Stoessel was equally as congratulatory and termed the agreement a 'remarkable achievement'. Stoessel was quick to point out US concerns regarding the future security of Belize and suggested that British troops should remain to train the BDF. Stoessel argued that 'a continued British military presence for this purpose would be a valuable contribution to regional stability'.[73] Conversely, in Belize there was a violent reaction to the Heads of Agreement. Opposition demonstrators argued that the agreement had failed to protect Belize's ongoing security interests. The demonstrators lit fires and civil disturbances erupted throughout Belize City in the week following the signature of the agreement. Both the BDF and the Police Tactical Services Unit were deployed in response.[74] Price declared a state of emergency in Belize on 2 April in an effort to restore calm. In the UK, it became clear that additional measures would have to be implemented to address Belizean concerns over its future security requirements.

Amid these developments, the Reagan administration continued to try to foster closer relations with Guatemala. The State Department began studying ways in which to increase the US' ability to better assist the Government of Guatemala (GOG) to counter the Marxist insurgency. However, the escalation in political violence in Guatemala, which was 'directly traceable' to the GOG, caused the US internal political and legal problems. This impeded the ability of the US to provide the military cooperation Guatemala felt it needed at the time (i.e., FMS sales).[75] Regarding Belize, the State Department recognised that the US was seen by Guatemala as 'playing a facilitative role in promoting a settlement which accommodates essential GOG interests'.[76] While the GOG perceived the US to be helping it to achieve a settlement that would best suit Guatemalan interests, so, too, did the UK and Belize. Clearly, there was a dualism in US interests in mediating the Anglo-Guatemalan dispute.

A Belize Constitutional Conference was held at Marlborough House, London, from 6 to 14 April, during which a White Paper on the 'Proposed Terms of a Constitution for the Independent Belize' was presented to Britain by the Government of Belize for its consideration. The Belizean proposals included a constitutional monarchy with the Queen as the head of state. The Queen was to be represented by a Governor General, whom she would select for the role after close consultation with the Belizean Prime Minister.[77] The constitution made comprehensive provisions for human rights and freedoms, and also included a National Assembly comprising of a House of Representatives and a Senate.[78] These proposals were seen as highly desirable to the UK and they were signed by Ridley and the Belizean Deputy Premier, Carl Lindberg Bernard 'C. L. B.' Rogers.

Meanwhile, Reagan sent Lucas García a letter on 14 April in which he referred to Guatemala's signature of the Heads of Agreement as 'an act of high personal courage on your part'. In addition, Reagan reaffirmed the US commitment to renewed US–Guatemalan relations: 'Again, Mr President, I wish to thank you for your efforts in regard to Belize. I look forward to a new dialogue between our two countries on our mutual concerns.'[79] It was around this time that the UK began to assess the possibility of an American contribution to the costs of maintaining Belizean security post-independence. A US contribution would enable the UK to reduce the quantity of funds to be transferred from the

UK's independence aid package for Belize.[80] This, in turn, would effectively minimise the British need for further reductions to its garrison in Belize. Britain's desire for US financial support in Belize was reiterated by Carrington in a ministerial minute to Thatcher on 23 April. Carrington suggested a visit by Ridley to Belize to speak with Price regarding Belize's future independence. Carrington also suggested a visit by Ridley to Washington to discuss the possibility of US assistance in financing the enhancement of the BDF, and to seek assurances from the Reagan administration that it was prepared to help underwrite Belizean security post-independence. Carrington also wished Ridley to ask the US to continue to exercise restraint in supplying arms to Guatemala.[81]

The US decided to try to proceed with the sale of helicopter spare parts to Guatemala and to provide physiological testing to Guatemalan pilots during a visit by General Vernon Walters (Reagan's personal emissary) with Lucas García in May 1981.[82] According to the US, Guatemala continued to show 'flexibility on Belize' as Lucas García was 'prepared to settle for guaranteed access to the sea and non-military use of the Ranguana and Sapodilla cays for fifteen years, with a promise of later renegotiation'.[83] US–Guatemalan relations were further strengthened following a meeting on 4 June between Thomas Enders and the Guatemalan Presidential adviser, Colonel Hector Israel Montalvan. Enders informed Colonel Montalvan that the US was in the process of issuing licences for the export of military trucks to Guatemala. During this meeting, Enders also outlined three necessary stages to help build congressional and public support for US–Guatemalan relations. The first stage included an arrangement for formal intelligence briefing for Lucas García on regional developments from the US perspective and an initiation of informal intelligence exchanges on selected topics. Within this framework Guatemalan officials would be invited to the US to participate in discussions with 'appropriate Pentagon personnel'.[84] The second stage was to include attempts to encourage Congress to provide helicopter spare parts to Guatemala. The third stage included additional measures to develop the US–Guatemalan relationship contingent upon 'continued Guatemalan Government progress in meeting our concerns about violence'.[85]

Belizean independence and greater US involvement

Full Belizean independence was preceded by the Belize Bill in June 1981, which ensured that the Belizean Constitution would come into effect on 21 September, Independence Day. The Belize Bill limited the responsibility of the UK in the legislative operation of an independent Belize. According to Schedule 1 of the Belize Bill: 'The Colonial Laws Validity Act 1865 shall not apply to any laws made on or after Independence Day by the Legislature of Belize.'[86] The bill was put before the House of Commons on 30 June 1981 by the then Lord Privy Seal, Sir Ian Gilmour, and was supported by Thatcher, Whitelaw, Nott, Ridley and the Minister of State at the FCO, Douglas Hurd.[87] Despite Guatemala's signature of the Heads of Agreement, Lucas García ultimately decided against ratification of the agreement. He made renewed claims to Belize during his annual speech to the Guatemalan Congress on 1 July 1981. During this speech, Lucas García made it clear that unless acceptable terms were offered to Guatemala and were in accordance with Guatemala's interpretation of the Heads of Agreement, there could be no settlement of the territorial dispute.[88] Trilateral talks between Guatemala, Belize and the UK took place shortly afterwards in New York on 6–10 July. The primary obstacle to progress during these talks was the definition of Guatemala's right to the 'use and enjoyment' of the Ranguana and Sapodilla cays. Notwithstanding such obstacles, the parties agreed to leave the door open for further talks.[89] A joint communiqué was issued stating that: 'Further study should be given to the many ideas discussed at recent meetings within the context of the Heads of Agreement.'[90] However, Guatemalan mulishness was again evident in mid-July when Castillo Valdez remarked to journalists that if the UK granted unilateral independence to Belize this would be considered as diverting from the Heads of Agreement. In these circumstances, Guatemala would declare such an act illegal.[91]

Such comments compounded US concerns with regard to a withdrawal of the British garrison in Belize. Both the UK and Belize used American concerns to their advantage. Thatcher and Price encouraged the Reagan administration to approach Guatemala regarding the possible resumption of talks on the question of

Belize.[92] The UK believed that the US would support them in their future dealings with Guatemala over the territorial issue. According to Henderson: 'The Americans are committed not to interfere in the detailed way we play our hand and are unlikely to press us too hard if we treat the Guatemalan proposals with proper caution.'[93] This belief was somewhat shaken when Enders informed Price during a meeting on 5 August that he believed the British were trying to rid themselves of the Belize problem too quickly. However, Enders tempered his approach by promising that he would do what he could to bring about the continuation of negotiations before Belizean independence.[94] Indeed, Enders, along with Senator Richard B. Stone and Chief of the Office of Central American Affairs Craig Johnstone, met with Castillo Valdez on 24 August in order to encourage Guatemala to resume talks with the UK on Belize.[95] According to the US, three specific areas divided the parties on the issue of Belize: 'Guatemala's desire to use the cays for military purpose; Belize's insistence that Guatemala's use of the cays be limited to a specific period of time; and the delimitation of maritime frontiers.'[96]

Anglo-Guatemalan relations suffered another blow when Guatemala broke consular relations with the UK on 7 September in protest over Belizean independence in the absence of a settlement of Guatemala's territorial claim. Guatemala subsequently closed its borders with Belize and issued a communiqué stating that all sea, air and surface traffic between Guatemala and Belize was to be halted from 7 September onwards. The communiqué outlined Guatemala's desire to pursue its territorial claim within the UNSC and stated its refusal to recognise Belizean independence.[97] In the interim, the Reagan administration decided to broaden its relations within Guatemalan political circles. To that end, it sent Ambassador Chapin and embassy officials to meet with a Guatemalan Christian Democrat delegation on 18 September, which resulted in improved relations between the US and the Christian Democrat leader, Marco Vinicio Cerezo Arévalo.[98] This visit was a follow-up visit to one made by the Director of the NSC's Latin American Affairs Directorate, Roger W. Fontaine, who met with Cerezo Arévalo in mid-May.[99] These visits were designed to improve broader US relations with Guatemalan political parties in anticipation of the scheduled Guatemalan presidential elections in March 1982. However, the US was not prepared to abandon its recently improved relations with the then Guatemalan government and sent General Walters to Guatemala on 20–22 September in a bid to 'renew his dialogue with General Lucas García on the bilateral relationship'.[100] This visit was also important in terms of mediating the Anglo-Guatemalan dispute as Belize was scheduled to achieve full independence from the UK, which it did on 21 September 1981.

Following Belize's independence, Reagan was urged by NSC staff to write to Lucas García in order to offer the government's good services in resuming talks between Guatemala and Belize. This would help to guarantee Belize's security, which was deemed as 'vital to prevent a significant Cuban presence in Belize'.[101] Reagan wrote to Lucas García on 15 October outlining his commitment to improving relations between both countries. Reagan outlined his 'deep appreciation' for the 'statesmanlike approach' Lucas García had taken towards the independence of Belize: 'I fully appreciate the difficulty your government faces domestically on an issue of such a long history and with so high an emotional content.'[102] Reagan wrote of the possibility of providing a US mediator in the dispute and referred to the 'positive evidence' that Belize was willing to look at 'creative solutions' to the territorial dispute. Reagan also sought a resolution that would satisfy the concerns of both Belize and Guatemala:

> In this regard the United States government wishes to be as helpful as possible to both sides as they search for a means of ending the dispute. If you desire, we could serve as a conduit for serious talks between your government and the government of Belize; or, as both sides believe appropriate, to put forth our own ideas on the dispute. I am prepared to have a senior US government official undertake this delicate task. I have every confidence that Ambassador Chapin, who has long experience in the practice of our diplomacy, can be of assistance to you in initiating this process.[103]

US involvement in mediating the dispute subsequently intensified, and Enders met with Price and Lucas García separately during a visit to Latin America in mid-November 1981. Following his meeting with Lucas García, Enders suggested that the Guatemalans appeared to be prepared to 'conclude treaties based on the Heads of Agreement'.[104] This was a hopeful sign to the British who welcomed such US initiatives. Carrington, in particular, believed that the UK should 'encourage the US to act in concert with us as intermediaries. It is likely, as we have long recognised, that the US will have far greater leverage in dealing with [the] Guatemalans.'[105]

Notwithstanding such positive signs, the UK decided to bolster Belize's security after independence against possible Guatemalan reprisals. In an exchange of notes between the UK and Belize, Price requested that British troops remain in Belize following its independence. Both countries agreed that British troops would remain 'to assist with the training of the Belize Defence Force and to perform such other functions as the two Governments may agree'.[106] According to this agreement, British forces would remain under UK command and the number, rank and composition of these troops would be determined by the British.[107] In a note from C. L. B. Rogers to the UK High Commissioner in Belmopan (Belize's capital city), Francis Sidney Trew, on 1 December 1981, the exchange of letters was deemed as constituting an agreement between Belize and the UK, which would continue until it was terminated by agreement by both parties.[108] The UK thereafter decided to increase its garrison to 1,800 troops in 1982.[109] A further £3 million was allocated by the UK for the enhancement of the BDF in 1982 with an additional £2 million for 1983.[110] This was a significant financial blow to the Thatcher government as a reduced financial commitment had been one of the main motivations underlying the UK's pursuit of Belizean independence. In the face of this ongoing and as yet indeterminate British financial and military commitment to Belize, the UK continued to monitor Guatemalan actions closely.

The UK continued to monitor Guatemala's deteriorating human rights situation, its worsening civil war and its intentions towards a newly independent Belize. Reports received by the UK at the time suggested that Guatemala was 'on the verge of plunging into a ruthless pool of blood'.[111] With reports outlining the growing instability in Guatemala, the question of the US supply of arms to Guatemala became an increasingly important consideration for the Thatcher government. During a meeting of the Foreign Affairs Select Committee on 7 December 1981, the Committee's Chairman, Sir Anthony Kershaw, questioned which countries supplied Guatemala with arms. D. M. Day replied: 'I am not absolutely certain . . . There has been, I think, a resupply of some spares from the United States but I am not aware of any recent, large-scale supply of arms to Guatemala.'[112]

Such comments highlight the distinct lack of knowledge in the UK with regard to the precise nature of the US relationship with Guatemala during this time. As the UK feared aggression against a member of the British Commonwealth, its so-called Special Relationship partner was willing to supply the prospective aggressor, Guatemala, with arms. This US intention to supply arms to Guatemala was borne of a desire to quash the leftist insurgents in Guatemala and to install a regime friendly to the US. This would provide the Reagan administration with a strategic ally in Latin America, but the weapons could also be used for other purposes, including hypothetical aggression against Belize. US objectives therefore, appeared to be increasingly at odds with those of its Special Relationship partner, the UK.

Nevertheless, the US continued to play an active role in mediating the dispute. Richard Stone visited Guatemala on 20 December in a bid to put forward yet more US and UK proposals.[113] Henderson wrote to the FCO on 24 December to apprise them of Stone's visit to Guatemala. Stone had found the Guatemalans to be 'generally helpful' during his visit. However, a Guatemalan signature of any revised proposals was deemed unlikely as Castillo Valdez had allegedly convinced Lucas García not to sign a treaty before the Guatemalan elections on 7 March 1982. Castillo Valdez believed that other parties could make Guatemala's signature of any revised proposals an election issue. The US, however, wanted a treaty signed before then as it was hoped that Guatemala's signature of an agreement with Belize could mollify those in Congress who opposed the sale of US military spare parts to Guatemala.[114] It is clear from Henderson's message that there was growing concern in British circles surrounding the possibility of US military supplies to Guatemala.

168

Notwithstanding such concerns, the UK began to look again at ways in which to reduce its financial commitment to Belize. A 'small but significant force adjustment' was made on 6 January 1982 with the return to the UK of four Blowpipe missiles, a four-man radar detachment and thirteen personnel.[115] However, Britain's small reduction in Belize was counterbalanced by the US and Belizean agreement of 14 January 1982 concerning the training requirements of the BDF. According to this agreement, training of the BDF would take place either on the US mainland or in Panama. In addition, US armed forces training teams would travel to Belize to help train the BDF.[116] This represented greater US involvement in the future safety requirements of a member of the British Commonwealth. It signalled to the British that the Reagan administration was prepared to help its ally, the UK, in defending her strategic interests in Latin America. At the same time that the US was committing itself to training the BDF, the US continued to encourage an open dialogue with Guatemala. Lucas García wrote to Reagan on 15 January: 'We feel that it would be unproductive to hold talks on Belize at this time, as long as Great Britain has difficulty complying strictly with the Heads of Agreement signed at London on March 11, 1981.'[117] Lucas García thanked Reagan for his cooperation in resolving the difficult situation, but stated that Guatemala would act only in accordance with the Republic's Constitution. He also stated that Reagan's assistance would be 'of great and incomparable value in the future'. The letter took a more ominous tone towards its end:

I believe that I would be remiss in my duty if I did not express my concern that a friendly Government and country such as the United States of America might be accused of participating in an effort to disregard Guatemala's rights with respect to Belize and to divide the Guatemalan territory.[118]

Lucas García wrote to Reagan again on 24 January and 13 February referring to the close relationship between the US and Guatemala, and inviting the Reagan administration to send observers to the 7 March elections. Reagan wrote to Lucas García in response to discuss the forthcoming elections and to urge a settlement of the Belizean issue:

> I would hope that in the last months of your presidency that you would be able to lead Guatemala and Belize into an era of prosperity and a secure and peaceful future for both sides that will result from the settlement of this dispute . . . I wish to reiterate to you the desire of the United States Government to be as helpful as possible to all sides as they search for the means to end this most serious problem.[119]

In Belize, a disgruntled Price wrote to Thatcher on 9 February requesting that the British garrison stay in Belize for at least the next three years or until a settlement could be reached with Guatemala. Price reminded the Prime Minister that the British presence in Belize was 'an essential factor of stability in Central America'.[120] Price's concerns were undoubtedly fuelled by Guatemala's pending elections.

Ríos Montt comes to power

The British initially hoped that the US would produce a settlement to the dispute with Guatemala prior to the Guatemalan elections.[121] With these hopes dashed, the UK monitored the Guatemalan elections closely. Both the Reagan and Thatcher governments believed that the presidential candidate General Ángel Aníbal Guevara Rodríguez was the most probable victor. As former Defence Minister he was chosen by Lucas García as his successor. Guevara Rodríguez was found to be the winner of the elections, but he did not assume power as expected on 1 July.[122] His comfortable plurality in the final unofficial vote count was disputed by the opposition, in particular, the Movimiento de Liberación Nacional (MLN, National Liberation Movement), who came in second place with its candidate, Mario Sandoval Alarcón. Nonetheless, Guevara Rodríguez called for a government of 'National Unity' and made overtures to all political sectors to participate in his government.[123] There were concerns in both Guatemala and the US over the legitimacy of the election results. On 23 March, a coup took place outside the National Palace in Guatemala City and a military junta was established under the leadership of General José Efraín Ríos Montt. The new military junta issued a decree on 26 March annulling the 7 March elections as a result of the perceived generalised 'manipulation' of the electoral process.[124]

The coming to power of Ríos Montt was initially considered a success by the US: 'Rios Montt represents the first Government that the US has been able to support in Guatemala in the last six years.'[125] With a new government in power the Reagan administration could again try to resume military sales to Guatemala. Moreover, Ríos Montt was seen by the US as making substantial progress against the leftist guerrillas in Guatemala through the provision of medical and economic aid to the poor.[126] The new Guatemalan leader sought to defeat the guerrillas by both economic and military means, otherwise known as the policy of 'rifles and beans'. He created Patrullas de Autodefensa Civil (PACs, Civilian Self-Defence Patrols) to try to recapture territory from guerrillas throughout Guatemala. The PACs were successful, but at an enormous cost to human life. However, the US refused to find the government of Ríos Montt culpable of any atrocities or human rights abuses. The Reagan administration believed that reports on these abuses were unjustified. According to the American embassy in Guatemala, it was a political strategy on behalf of the leftist guerrillas: 'Groups backing the guerrillas intend to win the war against the GOG by making the US Congress the battlefield. It is the old but effective strategy of divide and conquer.'[127] Despite increasing evidence of government-sanctioned atrocities, the Reagan administration remained convinced that Guatemala was 'the linchpin to all of Central America' for the US.[128]

The US was quick to raise the issue of Belize with the new Guatemalan President. In a meeting with Ríos Montt on 29 March Ambassador Chapin found the President to be vague when questioned about his intentions towards Belize. Chapin informed him that the US was 'interested as a friend in seeing the Belizean issue settled'. Chapin also suggested that settling the Belizean issue at that time (the junta had just suspended the constitution), might be easier for Guatemala as a constitutional convention would not be required.[129] He further stated that, for reasons of security, the US wanted to incorporate Belize into the Rio Treaty, the OAS and the Central American Defence Council (CADC). Ríos Montt's response was noncommittal and he stated that the matter would have to be studied. However, the new President agreed that 'for security reasons it was desirable to tie Belize into a broader system and that the absence of a constitutional framework in Guatemala simplified solution of the problem'.[130] During the meeting, US economic assistance to Guatemala was also discussed and Chapin warned Ríos Montt that Guatemala's negative international image could hinder congressional approval on US assistance.[131] Chapin informed the State Department of the substance of his talks with Ríos Montt and concluded: 'He was vague on the dispute with the UK over Belize and did not seem to have any real interest in an early solution.'[132]

As the US continued to broker close relations with Guatemala, the UK was preoccupied with the issue of its garrison in Belize. In his capacity as the UK's new Foreign Secretary, Pym wrote to Thatcher on 9 April. The Falkland Islands had just been invaded by Argentina and Pym was understandably reluctant to withdraw British commitments in the region. According to Pym, the situation in the Falklands had made it 'politically impossible' to announce the withdrawal of the British garrison in the near future (21 September). Pym was mindful of US considerations in the proposed withdrawal as he stated: 'Moreover, in this difficult situation we must keep our lines as clear as possible with the US Government.' Upon reading Pym's minute, Thatcher wrote the following handwritten notes on its heading: 'We are _expected_ to take decisions to support _them_ [the US]. I hope this expectation will be _fully_ reciprocated.'[133] Thatcher was adamant that any UK decision to retain the garrison would be responded in kind by the Reagan administration. British attempts to gain US political and material support in the Falklands War were undoubtedly a consideration here. Thatcher's Principal Private Secretary, Clive A. Whitmore, wrote to Pym's Principal Private Secretary, Brian Fall, on 11 March regarding the decision to defer the withdrawal date of the British garrison. Whitmore wrote: 'she [Thatcher] hopes that we shall use this decision with the Americans'.[134] The Prime Minister clearly wanted to use Belize as a way to gain leverage with the US over another important Latin American issue, the Falklands. The UK's new proposed withdrawal date was the subject of much discussion in the FCO and the MOD. Pym wrote again to Thatcher on 19 April to reiterate his views on the importance of a deferral in relation to Britain's relations with the US: 'The US are of course crucial in all this . . . I believe that our first need is to reassure the Americans that we would not wish to take the precipitate or unilateral decision on the garrison while so many uncertainties beset us.'[135] Nott, for his part, wrote to Thatcher on 26 April to suggest that the withdrawal should be deferred for a mere three-month period. The Secretary of State for Defence wrote:

> Belize is an independent country, to which we have no binding defence commitment . . . It is anomalous, therefore, that we should retain a permanent garrison in Belize for any longer than is necessary. Moreover, the longer we postpone the withdrawal of the garrison the greater will be the risk that we shall get drawn into the conflicts which are spreading in that highly volatile region.[136]

Thatcher agreed with Nott's suggestion and informed Price on 4 May that the garrison would be extended for a three-month period beyond 21 September. The Prime Minister specified that no official announcement would be made on the duration of the extension. Such a brief extension was not what Price had hoped for and Thatcher cushioned her words with an assurance that the UK would continue to watch developments in Guatemala closely and would remain in touch with the US regarding the Belizean issue.[137]

In early May 1982, Guatemala requested the cost-price lease of six Huey UH-1H helicopters from the US. Guatemala wanted a six-month lease with the option to renew the lease for an additional six months if required. These helicopters were to provide logistical support for the army in its fight against the leftist guerrillas.[138] The Senate Foreign Relations Committee was informed that the sale of the helicopter parts was necessary to protect Ríos

Montt 'against a coup that would make even more difficult an improvement in human rights and a return to democracy in that country'.[139] Ríos Montt declared a state of siege in Guatemala on 1 July thereby restricting civil liberties. Cracks in US–Guatemalan relations began to appear in mid-1982 as Guatemala believed that the US was becoming more aligned with Belize in the territorial dispute. Guatemala saw 'US generosity towards Belize particularly in security assistance'.[140] In all likelihood, this was in reference to the 14 January US–Belizean agreement on the training of the BDF. In the light of such views, the American embassy in Guatemala recommended that it was not the time for the US to 'abandon a conciliatory approach to Belize negotiations in favor of trying to strongarm Guatemala into a particular outcome'.[141]

In a meeting between the UK's new Minister of State at the FCO, Cranley Onslow, and Thomas Enders on 6 August, Belize was discussed in great detail. Enders assured Onslow that the US hoped to get Belize included in the Rio Treaty in order to provide 'automatic collective security' for Belize. Enders also assured him that the US would try again to point out the risks to Guatemala of the possibility of Cuban subversion in Belize if a settlement was not reached.[142] The pair discussed the possibility of the US transferring intelligence-gathering aircraft from its base in Honduras to Belize. Enders said that a final decision had yet to be made and that it would involve no more than a dozen personnel and the 'occasional stop-over by US aircraft in Belize'.[143] This possibility had previously been discussed in a meeting between Ambassador Henderson and US Deputy Secretary of State for Inter-American Affairs Stephen Bosworth in June 1982. Henderson was then somewhat sceptical of US intentions as he commented:

> It is pretty clear that in pursuit of their general policy in Central America; the Americans will want to try to establish some sort of facility in Belize . . . A US presence would have considerably more attraction from a Belizean point of view if it formed part of an increased effort to help the Belizean Defence Force.[144]

The Thatcher government continued to face significant financial difficulties at the time due largely to the financial toll of the

Falklands War. As a result, it briefly contemplated the complete removal of the British garrison from Belize. The UK ultimately decided against this during a Heads of Mission Conference in Mexico, 22–24 September. However, the duration of the garrison remained unspecified.[145] Meanwhile, the American embassy in Guatemala was inundated with reports of growing human rights atrocities linked to the government of Ríos Montt. Having analysed reports from Amnesty International and the Guatemalan Human Rights Commission in October 1982, the embassy determined that 'a concerted disinformation campaign' was being waged in the US against Guatemala. It concluded that this campaign assigned responsibility for atrocities to the GOG 'without verifiable evidence'.[146]

Anglo-American consultation on the British garrison in Belize continued in late 1982. During a meeting between Nott and Weinberger on 30 November at the US Mission to NATO, Nott reminded Weinberger of the limits of Britain's support of an independent Belize. Nott said that he hoped the US appreciated that the garrison 'could not remain there indefinitely', and he reminded Weinberger that the UK had small armed forces and a large number of commitments. He also reminded Weinberger that the UK did not normally maintain British forces in an independent country.[147] In the US, Reagan was scheduled to make a presidential visit to Latin America in early December to meet with various heads of state, including Ríos Montt, President Roberto Suazo Córdova of Honduras and President Álvaro Alfredo Magaña Borja of El Salvador. Reagan's objective in meeting Ríos Montt was to convince him that the US government supported his efforts to defeat the guerrillas in Guatemala while 'cleaning up the human rights situation'.[148] In addition, Reagan wished to raise the issue of Belize. Reagan and Ríos Montt held a bilateral meeting at Armando Escalon Air Force Base in San Pedro Sula, Honduras, on 4 December. During this meeting Ríos Montt produced a map detailing Guatemala's preferred delineations with regard to Belize. The areas highlighted on the map went north of the Monkey River, up its tributaries to the west and went from the Headwaters to the Rio Bladen, west of the existing border. Ríos Montt referred to the existing border as the lines recognised by the UK. He reaffirmed Guatemala's desire to negotiate with the UK further on the matter, but referred to his country as being 'hemmed in between Belize and Honduras'. He argued that Guatemala required access to the Caribbean as without this the country could not participate legitimately in the US' CBI.[149] It was during this meeting that Ríos Montt requested significant US military assistance for Guatemala, including 40,000 M-1 rifles, 10,000 M-2 carbines, 5,000,000 cartridges, 600 M-79 grenade launchers, 60,000 grenades, five helicopters, spare parts and communication equipment.[150] The proposed resumption of commercial arms sales to Guatemala by the US would be under the FMS credit scheme, which did not require congressional approval or notification.[151] This US strategy of selling arms to Guatemala was congruent with its objective of establishing regimes friendly to the US in Latin America. It was not, however, in harmony with the policy of mutual understanding and security supposedly inherent in its Special Relationship with the UK. Following his meeting with Ríos Montt, Reagan described the Guatemalan President as 'a man of great personal integrity and commitment' and pledged that the US would do all that it could to support Montt's 'progressive efforts'.[152] George Shultz authorised the sale of the helicopter spare parts to Guatemala on 6 January 1983 and made the announcement the following day. The US$1.2 million in spare parts for the Guatemalan Air Force's A-37B Dragonfly counter-insurgency aircraft along with vital communications equipment was worth an estimated US$6.3 million.[153] The US also lifted a five-year arms embargo against Guatemala on 7 January. However, shortly afterwards Ríos Montt announced that Guatemala could not afford to purchase these items. Thereafter, the US focused more intently on financial help to Guatemala. In the meantime, the Belize issue required further discussion.

Ríos Montt agreed to meet with Belizean and British officials in New York on 24 January to 'explore the possibility' of finding a solution to the dispute.[154] Guatemala proposed a redefinition of the borders of Belize in order that the area in the south of Belize should be included in Guatemalan territory. This proposal was rejected by Belizean officials, who suggested that the maritime borders could be adjusted and that an area of two square miles either side of the southern border between Belize and Guatemala should undergo joint development. The meeting ended on a sombre note when Guatemala rejected the Belizean proposal and reaffirmed its claim to the entire territory of Belize.[155] Guatemala's intransigence greatly worried the US, and it was decided to broach the subject of the withdrawal of the British garrison during a meeting between Defence Secretaries Weinberger and Heseltine in Vilamoura, Portugal, on 21 March. General Vessey, who also attended the meeting, raised the issue of US concerns surrounding the British garrison. Heseltine reaffirmed the UK's intention to withdraw the garrison and suggested that perhaps the US could interest other countries such as Canada in helping to provide for future Belizean security. Heseltine's suggestion 'provoked some amusement on the American side'.[156]

Conversely, as the US sought to maintain the security of Belize, it also continued to establish closer ties with Guatemala during this time. In April 1983, the NSC activated an 'interagency effort' to determine what 'immediate steps' could be taken to assist Guatemala in terms of overcoming congressional constraints on funding for military assistance to the country.[157] This was at a time when the US claimed that it was seeking to reduce ongoing tensions between Guatemala and Belize. This polarity in US objectives was exemplified during a meeting in Washington on 4 May between Reagan and Ríos Montt's special emissary, Jorge Antonio Serrano Elías. During this meeting the focus was placed squarely on Guatemala's economic concerns; the Belize issue was not even raised.[158]

The Belizean question was raised when Reagan met Price on 13 May in Washington. During this meeting Reagan found Premier Price 'a sincere and dedicated leader' who was 'working diligently in the best interests of his country'.[159] Reagan was seemingly keen to resolve the territorial dispute and wrote to Price on 1 June outlining US objectives towards Belize and the Central American region:

You know of the deep interest which I take in Belize – an interest we shared in our meeting on May 13. It is one of the major goals of my administration to assist the countries of the region to find peace and strengthen democracy.[160]

Reagan informed Price of his intention to send Richard Stone as his personal representative to the region to meet with Central American leaders to see how the US could 'best facilitate the search for peace'.[161] Indeed, by this stage the US was deeply involved in mediating the Belize dispute. A foreign policy adviser and member of the Senate Foreign Relations Committee, John Carbaugh, presented a proposed solution to the dispute to the FCO on 27 June. Carbaugh presented his paper (undertaken with the knowledge and support of William P. Clark and US Under-Secretary of Defense Fred Iklé) to Heseltine and A. J. Coles.[162] Carbaugh's paper included a proposal to address Guatemala's territorial aspirations, which had previously included territory south of the Monkey River amounting to between one-sixth and one-fifth of Belizean territory. Following conversations with Guatemalan officials, Carbaugh suggested that Belize should cede to its neighbour enough 'territorial waters for unimpeded access to the Gulf of Honduras'. The area was displayed on a map and was roughly fifty square miles in its entirety. Carbaugh championed the Guatemalan wish to build a naval base on this territory. Guatemala, in turn, would offer space to the US to build a similar base in Guatemala.[163] This would undoubtedly have benefited US strategic aspirations in Guatemala and the surrounding region, and was an important factor in the US attempts to solve the Belize issue in 1983. This represented a more unilateral and self-interested approach to the dispute on behalf of the US. In return for the stated Belizean territory, Guatemala offered to sponsor Belizean membership in the OAS which it had previously blocked. In addition to this, the Carbaugh proposals included treaties of non-aggression, mutual defence, economic cooperation, setting out national borders and the economic development of Belize.[164] These proposals were seen as highly desirable by the Reagan administration. The same could not be said for Belize and the UK.

Carbaugh's proposals were put forward at around the same time that Price and an adviser to Ríos Montt, Harrison Whitbeck, were due to meet in Miami to discuss the ongoing territorial problem.[165] According to FCO Assistant Under-Secretary John B. Ure, Whitbeck sought a Belizean agreement to sell a strip of land to Guatemala. British officials doubted that Belize would agree to such a suggestion. Nevertheless, the FCO sent a legal adviser to Belize to help Price prepare for the Miami meeting. The US, for its part, began to question the sense in trying to make 'painful compromises with the erratic and insecure regime of Ríos Montt'.[166] Despite these reservations, the US continued to act as an unofficial mediator with self-interested motivations in the territorial dispute.

The question of the British garrison

In Belize, the importance of the British garrison was a point of increasing concern for Price. With the appointment of a new Foreign Secretary in the UK, Price wanted Reagan's help in persuading the Thatcher government to maintain the garrison. To that end, Price contacted his Chargé in Washington prior to a scheduled meeting between Reagan and Howe in the White House on 14 July 1983. Price asked that a message be relayed to Reagan to ask the British to keep their troops in Belize 'for as long as necessary'.[167] During Reagan's and Howe's meeting the issue of the British garrison was raised by the President. The US doubted whether Howe as the new Foreign Secretary would 'unduly focus' upon Central America and thus the US wanted to reiterate its belief in the necessity of the garrison. William P. Clark suggested in briefing notes for the President's meeting with Howe that Reagan should 'encourage continued British military presence in Belize, both as a contributor to regional stability, and as an important symbol of Britain's sharing of what in NATO terminology is called out of area defence'.[168] The US increasingly saw the British garrison as a bulwark against Marxist influence and possible guerrilla activity in Belize. Howe also met with Shultz during his visit to Washington. During that meeting Howe explained that it would be difficult to maintain a military presence in Belize as such a presence was 'inconsistent with the objective of giving independence to former colonies'.[169] Clearly, the US would have to work hard to persuade the UK to retain the British garrison. Following Howe's trip to Washington, Shultz' Executive Secretary, Charles Hill, wrote to Clark stating that US interests dictated that it continued 'to seek a way to preserve the British military presence in Belize. We believe HMG will be responsive to firm US pressure on this issue and defer any withdrawal plans' if the US re-emphasised its concerns.[170] Clark subsequently wrote to Reagan urging the President to write to Thatcher regarding British withdrawal plans: 'While we are not sanguine that we can bring a complete halt to British withdrawal plans, both George Shultz and I believe a personal appeal from you to Mrs Thatcher would at a minimum slow down the withdrawal.'[171]

Reagan wrote to Thatcher on 4 August and acknowledged that much of Belize's good fortune was attributed to British efforts in guiding Belize to self-government and complete independence. The President reaffirmed the importance he attached to the British garrison in Belize and warned that should the garrison be withdrawn it 'could heighten insecurity' and 'create a power vacuum in this strategic area with serious regional consequences'.[172] Reagan also acknowledged the financial implications of maintaining the garrison and pledged to 'make every effort' to work with all parties to find a peaceful settlement to this territorial issue. In order to achieve this, Reagan had asked Shultz to maintain 'especially close contact' with Howe.[173] (Reagan and Thatcher often capitalised on the close consultative relationship that existed between both governments when seeking to address issues of individual or joint concern. Howe recalls that his working relationship with Shultz was 'very close' and agrees that this relationship helped to facilitate close Anglo-American relations at the time.[174]) In his letter to the Prime Minister, Reagan also thanked Thatcher for the support she had shown in Parliament regarding US policies in Central America.[175] However, Reagan warned the Prime Minister that: 'the problems which plague the region may more directly threaten Belize if it loses the security that your military garrison presents'.[176] The President then moderated the tone of his letter by pledging his support to Thatcher in her efforts to resolve the territorial dispute. He concluded his letter by stating: 'I believe we can pursue a path that will resolve the territorial dispute and preserve stability, allowing for the orderly departure of British forces.'[177]

The establishment of a new and unfamiliar government in Guatemala a few days later on 8 August, following the military overthrow of Ríos Montt by his Minister of Defence, General Óscar Humberto Mejía Victores, reinforced Reagan's desire to find a peaceful settlement to the Belizean issue. In the UK, Thatcher responded to Reagan's letter on 11 August in which she promised that 'no irrevocable steps' would be taken by Britain with regard to the withdrawal of the British garrison from Belize. In an effort to appease Reagan's concerns, Thatcher indicated that she hoped to be able to inform the Reagan administration of British intentions towards the garrison during their scheduled bilateral meeting in Washington on 29 September. This response was seen as 'mildly encouraging' to the NSC.[178] From Britain's perspective, Thatcher's response provided the Prime Minister with an opportunity to discuss the matter in greater depth at the September meeting and try to gain some valuable strategic and, perhaps, financial support from the US. According to a confidential source, the Thatcher government decided in early September to keep the garrison in Belize for a further two to three years. The source advised the NSC that 'the blood was ankle deep in Whitehall on this one', and that it was Howe who had carried the motion in the House of Commons despite the Prime Minister's apparent opposition.[179] It was clear in US political circles that, given Thatcher's opposition to retaining the garrison, the US would have to work hard to convince the Prime Minister of the ongoing necessity of Britain's contribution to the BDF. Notwithstanding this, the US interpreted Howe's success in the House of Commons as a 'hopeful sign' that US efforts with its European ally were 'paying off'.[180]

Thatcher and Reagan continued to strengthen close bilateral relations during their 29 September meeting in Washington. The formal agenda for their meeting included the East–West relationship, the Middle East, economic issues, and Central and South America. One of the primary objectives of the US during this meeting was to secure a long-term commitment of British forces in Belize. The State Department anticipated that Thatcher would be reluctant to make such a commitment. Therefore, Shultz wrote to Reagan suggesting that the President should make clear to Thatcher the importance Reagan attached to British forces remaining in Belize in order 'to protect the stability of the area' as there was 'no adequate substitute' for the British garrison.[181] A briefing paper for the President prior to the meeting outlined the difficulties involved in Anglo-Guatemalan negotiations over Belize. According to this paper, bilateral talks between Guatemala and Britain were deemed 'likely to remain intractable'. The briefing paper acknowledged US limitations in encouraging Guatemala to settle the Belizean dispute: 'we neither have the carrot nor the stick needed to attract the Guatemalans to a settlement'.[182] It also acknowledged Thatcher's unwillingness to risk British involvement in a Central American war through the British presence in Belize. Furthermore, it referred to the financial burden of the garrison for the UK, but argued that the garrison served US objectives by reinforcing:

> [the] domestic tranquility and political order in Belize; by undercutting the arguments of the leftist members of the GOB [Government of Belize] for close-ties with Nicaragua and Cuba to counter the Guatemalan threat, and by deterring Guatemalan insurgents from becoming more active in Belize.[183]

In order to encourage the UK to keep its garrison, the briefing paper suggested that the Reagan administration indicate its willingness to work with the UK 'to identify ways to lessen the burden of their presence' in Belize.[184] Thatcher's briefing notes for the meeting outlined the importance of 'seeking to establish implicit linkage between the retention of the garrison (if decided) and the US role in finding a long-term solution to the problems of Belize'.[185] During the meeting itself, Reagan was pleased to hear of Thatcher's decision to leave the garrison in Belize for a further eighteen months. He voiced his gratitude with the words 'Bless you!'[186] But Thatcher confided in Reagan that she did not believe that Price was serious in his negotiations with Guatemala due 'at least in part' to the continued presence of British forces. Thus, the Prime Minister reiterated that British troops could not stay

Figure 5 Deep in discussion in the White House Red Room, 29 September 1983

indefinitely in Belize and she requested further talks between US and UK officials to 'ensure the future security of Belize after British withdrawal'.[187] Anglo-American consultation over Belize was set to continue in the future, albeit not at such regular intervals. Two fundamental objectives had already been achieved: the British desire for Belizean independence within the Commonwealth; and the US desire for an extended British commitment to defend Belize against external aggression and communist influence.

The Thatcher government's commitment to maintain the garrison in Belize was strengthened in late October 1983 following the US invasion of Grenada. The garrison became a symbol of British interests in Latin America in the face of regional instability and US unilateralism. However, this view was not shared by all in the UK. Some feared that recent US actions in the Caribbean could be

repeated elsewhere in the region. As Anthony Parsons wrote to
A. J. Coles in the aftermath of the invasion:

> Grenada strengthens my view that we should get out of Belize at the
> earliest practicable opportunity before we find ourselves in another
> false position. While accepting American primacy throughout the
> area, we should do some plain speaking about the need for full con-
> sultation before the Americans decide to take military actions against
> another Commonwealth country.[188]

While US military action was unlikely in Belize, Parsons' letter
reveals the impact US actions in Grenada had upon remaining
British interests in Latin America. In fact, the UK maintained its
garrison in Belize and the territorial question remained throughout Thatcher's and Reagan's terms in office. The matter was
addressed intermittently by the US, UK and Belize as consecutive
Guatemalan leaders afforded the territorial issue less and less
attention.[189]

When examining the Anglo-Guatemalan dispute over Belize
it is clear that the US had its own objectives in unofficially
mediating the dispute. The US desire to prevent Cuban infiltration of Belize, the wish to acquire a strategically beneficial
ally in a newly independent Belize, and a desire to retain the
British garrison were certainly important US considerations. So,
too, was the establishment of closer US–Guatemalan relations,
the possibility of resuming arms sales to Guatemala, the possibility of cementing the proposed 'Intermares Trans-Guatemala
Pipeline' deal, along with the possible establishment of a US
naval base in Guatemala and a similar facility in Belize. The more
US-centric objectives clashed with the Reagan administration's
alleged commitment to the Anglo-American Special Relationship.
The dispute, therefore, was potentially a contentious issue in the
sphere of Anglo-American relations. And yet the UK chose to
encourage US participation in mediating the territorial dispute.
The Thatcher government needed an influential ally in the region
in the face of possible Guatemalan aggression. As a result, the
Reagan administration played a key role in defusing a potentially
volatile situation. Regardless of whether or not the US was safe-

guarding its own interests in the process, it was also safeguarding British interests in Latin America. Moreover, the US and the UK sought closer consultation on the issue throughout this time, thereby enhancing the bonds of political and personal diplomacy between their respective governments. Such consultation proved to be an invaluable resource to both countries when dealing with Latin American crises, not least in the case of the US involvement in Nicaragua under the Reagan administration.

Notes

1. During the early 1980s the US established a military presence in Honduras as a means to counter leftist activity in the country and as a base to support both the contras in Nicaragua (see Chapter 5) and the US-supported government in neighbouring El Salvador. For more information on the US military presence in Honduras at the time, see Thomas Carothers, *In the Name of Democracy: US Policy toward Latin America in the Reagan Years* (Berkeley, CA: University of California Press, 1991), pp. 47–58. More generally, see Jack R. Binns, *The United States in Honduras, 1980–1981: An Ambassador's Memoir* (Jefferson, NC: McFarland, 2000); George W. Liebmann, *The Last American Diplomat: John D. Negroponte and the Changing Face of US Diplomacy* (London: I. B. Tauris, 2012). For further readings on US interests in El Salvador, see Chapter 5, n. 1.
2. See Assad Shoman, *Belize's Independence and Decolonization in Latin America: Guatemala, Britain and the UN* (New York: Palgrave Macmillan, 2010); C. H. Grant, *The Making of Modern Belize: Politics, Society and British Colonialism in Central America* (Cambridge: Cambridge University Press, 1976); P. K. Menon, 'The Anglo-Guatemalan territorial dispute over the colony of Belize (British Honduras)', *Journal of Latin American Studies*, 11(2) (November 1979): 343–71.
3. Menon, 'Anglo-Guatemalan territorial dispute', p. 346.
4. Grant, *Making of Modern Belize*, pp. 31–3.
5. TNA, FCO 58/1983, Select Committee on Foreign Affairs report on Belize, 28 November 1980, p. 4.
6. TNA, FO 973/101, FCO background brief, 'Belize: The Need for Independence', July 1980, p. 2.

7. HCPP, 1981/82, HC 47, Foreign Affairs Select Committee, 'Caribbean and Central America, British approach to security, stability and development', fifth report (3 parts) with proceedings and evidence (previously HC 47 i–xiv) and appendices (received 17/12/82), p. 48.

8. D. A. G. Waddell, 'Developments in the Belize question 1946–1960', *American Journal of International Law*, 55(2) (April 1961): 459–69, at p. 468.

9. HCPP, 1981/82, HC 47 (i), Foreign Affairs Select Committee, 'Caribbean and Central America, British approaches to stability, security and development', Minutes of evidence, 23 November 1982 (received 20/01/82), p. 9.

10. TNA, FCO 58/1983, Select Committee report, p. 6. For more on Webster's various proposals, see Shoman, *Belize's Independence*, pp. 54–65.

11. Shoman, *Belize's Independence*, p. 108.

12. TNA, DEFE 11/890, Secretary of State cable regarding the reinforcement of Belizean garrison, 3 November 1977.

13. Shoman, *Belize's Independence*, p, 150.

14. *Ibid.*, p. 153.

15. TNA, DEFE 71/198, FCO to Belmopan, 14 July 1978.

16. Department of State background notes on Guatemala, December 1986, pp. 3–4, file: Guatemala (1/4), box 91173, Latin American Affairs Directorate NSC Records, Ronald Reagan Library.

17. TNA, FCO 99/347, record of Ridley–Habib conversation, 5 July 1979, p. 2.

18. TNA, FCO 99/631, Carrington to British embassies, 20 February 1980, p. 1.

19. TNA, FCO 99/623, record of US–UK talks on Belize/Guatemala and the Caribbean, 18 January 1980, p. 1.

20. TNA, PREM 19/383, briefing notes for Pym, 20 February 1980, p. 1.

21. TNA, FCO 99/631, draft paper for OD Committee, p. 5 (Ridley initialled these comments 'NR'. The draft paper was attached to a letter written by F. S. Trew on Belize, dated 28 November 1980).

22. TNA, PREM 19/959, Armstrong briefing for Thatcher, 1 April 1980.

23. TNA, FCO 99/642, extracts from Carrington's interview with Harold Briley of the BBC, 31 July 1980.

24. TNA, PREM 19/959, UK embassy in Mexico City to FCO, 8 August 1980.

25. TNA, FCO 99/626, Castillo Valdez statement at the UNGA, 6 October 1980.
26. TNA, FCO 99/623, record of Ridley–Bushnell meeting, 15 October 1980, p. 2.
27. *Ibid.*, Henderson to FCO, 20 October 1980, p. 1.
28. TNA, FCO 99/624, Telno. 389, Belize/Guatemala, 19 December 1980, p. 1.
29. TNA, PREM 19/959, Carrington to UK embassy in Washington, 23 December 1980.
30. TNA, FCO 46/2848, OD Committee report on Anglo-Guatemalan negotiations over Belize, 5 February 1981, p. 3.
31. TNA, PREM 19/959, Henderson to FCO, 27 January 1981.
32. TNA, FCO 46/2848, D. M. Day letter, 28 January 1981, p. 1.
33. TNA, PREM 19/959, UK Mission in New York to FCO, 6 February 1981.
34. Department of State briefing paper on Central America, 11 February 1981, p. 1, file: Guatemala (7), RAC box 8, Roger W. Fontaine Files, Ronald Reagan Library.
35. TNA, PREM 19/959, UK Mission in New York to FCO, 13 February 1981; UK Mission in New York to FCO, 14 February 1981.
36. Fontaine to Allen, 17 February 1981, p. 1, file: Guatemala (7), RAC box 8, Roger W. Fontaine Files, Ronald Reagan Library.
37. TNA, PREM 19/959, Hennessy to FCO, 19 February 1981.
38. *Ibid.*, Hennessy to FCO, 24 February 1981.
39. Cable No. 202322, Guatemala policy review, 23 February 1981, p. 3, file: Guatemala (7), RAC box 8, Roger W. Fontaine Files, Ronald Reagan Library.
40. Briefing materials for Thatcher's visit attached to Bremer–Allen memo, 25 February 1981, pp. 3–4, file: Official Working Visit of Prime Minister Thatcher of the UK (2/26/81) (7/8), box 4, Charles P. Tyson Files, Ronald Reagan Library.
41. McFarlane to Reagan, 8 December 1983, p. 1, file: Grenada (11/5/1983–2/21/1984) (Too Late to File), box 30, Executive Secretariat NSC Country Files, Latin America, Grenada, Ronald Reagan Library.
42. Interview with Gloria Hooper.
43. TNA, PREM 19/383, briefing notes for Pym, pp. 1–2, n.d.
44. Churchill Archives Centre, THCR 1/10/18, Carrington to UK embassy in Washington, 24 February 1981, p. 1.
45. Reagan to Lucas García, 15 October 1981, pp. 1–2, file: Guatemala (6), RAC box 8, Roger W. Fontaine Files, Ronald Reagan Library.

46. HCPP, 1981/2, HC 47, p. 52.
47. *Ibid.*, p. 53.
48. *Ibid.* Appendix 30, British Policy in the Central America Region (29/81–82 FM) memo by Dr David Stephen, p. 510.
49. HCPP, 1981/82, HC 47, p. 14.
50. *Ibid.*, p. 77.
51. HCPP, 1979/80, Cmnd. 7826, MOD: Defence in the 1980s, Statement on the Defence Estimates 1980 (in two volumes), p. 43.
52. Margaret Thatcher, *In Defence of Freedom: Speeches on Britain's Relations with the World, 1976–1986* (London: Aurum Press, 1986), p. 113. Excerpt from Thatcher speech to the Joint Houses of Congress, 20 February 1985.
53. HCPP, 1979/80, Cmnd. 7987, Home Office: British Nationality Law, Outline of proposed legislation 1979/80, pp. 34–7.
54. HCPP, 1981/82, HC 214, Treasury: Supply estimates 1982/3 for the year ending 31 March 1983, p. 15.
55. Interview with John Nott.
56. Interview with Charles Powell.
57. Interview with Cecil Parkinson.
58. Interview with Peter Carrington.
59. Briefing paper on the Caribbean and Central America, 26 February 1981, p. 1, file: Official Working Visit of Prime Minister Thatcher of the UK (2/26/81) (7/8), box 4, Charles P. Tyson Files, Ronald Reagan Library.
60. *Ibid.*, p. 2.
61. *Ibid.*, p. 2.
62. Overview of situation in Guatemala, pp. 1–4, file: Guatemala Human Rights, box 90505, Jacqueline Tillman Files, Ronald Reagan Library.
63. *Ibid.*, pp. 5–6.
64. Susanne Jonas, 'Democratization through peace: the difficult case of Guatemala', *Journal of Interamerican Studies and World Affairs*, 42(4) (Special Issue: Globalization and Democratization in Guatemala) (Winter 2000): v–38, at p. 11.
65. Chairman of the Interagency Group to Bushnell, 5 March 1981, p. 1, file: Guatemala (7), RAC box 8, Roger W. Fontaine Files, Ronald Reagan Library.
66. Jonas, 'Democratization through peace', p. 2.
67. *Ibid.*, p. 2.
68. Carothers, *In the Name of Democracy*, p. 61.
69. HCPP, 1980/81, HC 47, Annex C, Heads of Agreement, p. 126.

70. *Ibid.*, p. 126.
71. *Ibid.*, p. 126.
72. TNA, PREM 19/959, Carrington to Haig, 13 March 1981.
73. TNA, FCO 46/2850, Telegram No. 425, Belize/Guatemala, 13 March 1981, p. 1.
74. TNA, PREM 19/959, Hennessy to FCO, 28 March 1981.
75. Cable No. 0980326, Initiative on Guatemala, 8 April 1981, p. 2, file: Guatemala, vol. 1 (1/20/81–7/31/84) (3/5), box 30, Executive Secretariat NSC Country Files, Latin America, Grenada, Guatemala, Ronald Reagan Library.
76. *Ibid.*, p. 3.
77. HCPP, 1980/81, Cmnd. 8245, FCO: report of the Belize Constitutional Conference, April 1981, p. 3.
78. *Ibid.*, pp. 8–9.
79. Reagan to Lucas García, 14 April 1981, p. 1, file: Guatemala (6), RAC box 8, Roger W. Fontaine Files, Ronald Reagan Library.
80. TNA, FCO 46/2879, Roderic Michael John 'R. M. J.' Lyne (Assistant Private Secretary to Carrington) to B. Watkins in the MOD, 14 April 1981, p. 1.
81. TNA, PREM 19/959, Carrington to Thatcher, 23 April 1981.
82. Haig to Reagan, addendum, 11 August 1981, p. 1, file: NSC00020 17 August 1981(East–West Trade, Central American Strategic Forces), box 91282, Executive Secretariat NSC Meeting Files, Ronald Reagan Library.
83. *Ibid.*, p. 3.
84. Secretary of State to the American embassy in Guatemala, 16 June 1981, pp. 1–2, file: Guatemala, vol. 1 (1/20/81–7/31/84) (1/5), box 30, Executive Secretariat NSC Country Files, Latin America, Grenada, Guatemala, Ronald Reagan Library.
85. *Ibid.*, p. 3.
86. HCPP, 1980/81, Bill 162 Belize Bill, A bill to make provision for and in connection with; the attainment by Belize of Independence within the Commonwealth, p. 8.
87. *Ibid.*, p. 10.
88. TNA, PREM 19/959, UK embassy in Guatemala City to FCO, 2 July 1981.
89. TNA, FO 973/188, Chronology of Belize/Guatemala developments since 1969, p. 3, n.d.
90. TNA, PREM 19/959, UK Mission in New York to FCO, 10 July 1981.

91. *Ibid.*, UK embassy in Guatemala City to FCO, 16 July 1981.
92. 'Talking Points', p. 4, n.d., file: Guatemala (4), RAC box 8, Roger W. Fontaine Files, Ronald Reagan Library.
93. TNA, PREM 19/959, Henderson to FCO, 4 August 1981.
94. *Ibid.*, UK embassy in Panama City to FCO, 5 August 1981.
95. Johnstone to Enders, 21 August 1981, p. 1, file: Guatemala (4), RAC box 8, Roger W. Fontaine Files, Ronald Reagan Library.
96. *Ibid.*, 'Talking Points', p. 3, n.d.
97. Briefing notes on Guatemala, p. 1, n.d., file: Guatemala (3), RAC box 8, Roger W. Fontaine Files, Ronald Reagan Library.
98. Cable No. 3016312, Ambassador's meeting with Christian Democrats, September 1981, p. 2, file: Guatemala 1981 of interest, box 90502, Jacqueline Tillman Files, Ronald Reagan Library.
99. Fontaine to Allen, 19 May 1981, file: Guatemala (5), RAC box 8, Roger W. Fontaine Files, Ronald Reagan Library.
100. Situation listing on Walters' visit to Guatemala and El Salvador, 16 September 1981, p. 1, file: Guatemala, vol. 1 (1/20/81–7/31/84) (1/5), box 30, Executive Secretariat NSC Country Files, Latin America, Grenada, Guatemala, Ronald Reagan Library.
101. Fontaine to Allen, 7 October 1981, 1, file: Guatemala (3), RAC box 8, Roger W. Fontaine Files, Ronald Reagan Library.
102. *Ibid.*, Reagan to Lucas García, 15 October 1981, p. 1, file: Guatemala (6), RAC box 8.
103. *Ibid.*, pp. 1–2.
104. TNA, FCO 46/2879, Henderson cable regarding Belize/Guatemala, 23 November 1981, p. 1.
105. *Ibid.* Carrington cable regarding Belize/Guatemala, 24 November 1981, p. 1.
106. HCPP, 1981/82, Cmnd. 8520, FCO: Exchange of notes with Belize on the continuing presence in Belize after independence of UK armed forces (Belmopan 1981), p. 3.
107. *Ibid.*, Annex to letter, p. 5.
108. *Ibid.*, p. 14.
109. HCPP, 1982/83, HC 154, Third report from the Defence Committee, p. 75.
110. HCPP, 1981/82, Cmnd. 8494, Treasury: Government's expenditure plans 1982/1983 to 1984/1985 (in two volumes), p. 36.
111. HCPP, 1981/82, HC 47(ii), Foreign Affairs Select Committee: Caribbean and Central America, Minutes of evidence 7 December 1981 (received 20/01/82), p. 9.
112. *Ibid.*, p. 10.

113. Memcon. of Fontaine–Stone discussion, 15 December 1981, p. 1, file: Guatemala (1), RAC box 8, Roger W. Fontaine Files, Ronald Reagan Library.
114. TNA, PREM 19/959, Henderson to FCO, 24 December 1981.
115. TNA, DEFE 25/417, Belize report 1980–2, 31 August 1982, p. 2.
116. TNA, DEFE 25/414, Telno. 43, US military aid to BDF, 22 January 1982, p. 1.
117. Cable No. 017508, regarding Lucas García to Reagan on 15 January 1982, 25 February 1982, p. 2, file: Guatemala President Lucas Cables, box 14, Executive Secretariat NSC Head of State Files, Ronald Reagan Library.
118. *Ibid.*, p. 2.
119. Reagan to Lucas García, n.d., file: Guatemala 1982 (5), RAC box 8, Roger W. Fontaine Files, Ronald Reagan Library.
120. Churchill Archives Centre, THCR 3/1/18, Price to Thatcher, 9 February 1982, p. 1.
121. TNA, DEFE 25/416, Notes on MOD meeting on Belize, 18 February 1982, p. 1.
122. Department of State background notes on Guatemala, December 1986, p. 4, file: Guatemala (1/4), box 91173, Latin American Affairs Directorate NSC Records, Ronald Reagan Library.
123. Cable regarding Guatemalan elections, March 1982, p. 2, file: Guatemala 1982 Elections (1/2), box 90502, Jacqueline Tillman Files, Ronald Reagan Library.
124. Department of State cable regarding Guatemala coup developments, March 1982, p. 1, file: Guatemala Coup, box 90502, Jacqueline Tillman Files, Ronald Reagan Library.
125. Briefing paper, 'Supplementary Issues and Objectives for the President's Visit to Central America', p. 1, n.d., file: NSC 00067 23 November 1982 (President's Trip to Latin America), box 91284, Executive Secretariat NSC Meeting Files, Ronald Reagan Library.
126. McFarlane to Reagan, 8 December 1983, p. 1, file: Guatemala (2), box 90378, Constantine C. Menges Files, Ronald Reagan Library.
127. Cable No. 029037, Analysis of human rights reports, October 1982, p. 1, file: Guatemala 1982 (1), RAC box 8, Roger W. Fontaine Files, Ronald Reagan Library.
128. *Ibid.*, Department of State document on Guatemala, p. 3, n.d.
129. Cable No. 018472, Ríos Montt meeting, pp. 1–4, n.d., file: Guatemala, vol. 1 (1/20/81–7/31/84) (2/5), box 30, Executive Secretariat NSC Country Files, Latin America, Grenada, Guatemala, Ronald Reagan Library.

130. *Ibid.*, pp. 4–5.
131. *Ibid.*, pp. 6–7.
132. Summary of Chapin–Ríos Montt meeting, 31 March 1982, file: Guatemala 1982 (3), RAC box 8, Roger W. Fontaine Files, Ronald Reagan Library.
133. TNA, PREM 19/959, Pym to Thatcher, 9 April 1982 (underlining in original Thatcher response).
134. *Ibid.*, Whitmore to Fall, 11 April 1982.
135. *Ibid.*, Pym to Thatcher, 19 April 1982.
136. *Ibid.*, Nott to Thatcher, 26 April 1982.
137. *Ibid.*, Thatcher to Price, 4 May 1982.
138. Cable No. 011025, Junta President requests no-cost lease of helicopters, 3 May 1982, p. 1, file: Guatemala (2), box 90328, Robert H. Lilac Files, Ronald Reagan Library.
139. John M. Goshko, 'Guatemala likely will get US helicopter spare parts', *Washington Post*, 6 November 1982, p. 8, file: Guatemala 1982 (1), RAC box 8, Roger W. Fontaine Files, Ronald Reagan Library.
140. American embassy in Guatemala to Secretary of State in Washington, 5 August 1982, file: AT: Guatemala (2), box 3, Robert H. Lilac Files, Ronald Reagan Library.
141. *Ibid.*
142. TNA, DEFE 25/417, Summary of Onslow–Enders meeting, 6 August 1982, p. 1.
143. *Ibid.*, p. 1.
144. *Ibid.*, Henderson to FCO, 7 July 1982, p. 2.
145. *Ibid.*, cable regarding Heads of Mission Conference, 25 September 1982, p. 1.
146. American embassy in Guatemala to Washington, 22 October 1982, p. 1, file: Guatemala 1982 (1), RAC box 8, Roger W. Fontaine Files, Ronald Reagan Library.
147. TNA, PREM 19/979, record of Nott–Weinberger meeting, 30 November 1982, p. 2.
148. Briefing paper 'Supplementary Issues and Objectives for the President's Visit to Central America', n.d., file: NSC 00067, 23 November 1982 (President's Trip to Latin America), box 91284, Executive Secretariat NSC Meeting Files, Ronald Reagan Library.
149. Cable No. 039465, draft memcon. of Reagan–Ríos Montt meeting on 4 December 1982, 10 December 1982, pp. 1–2, file: Guatemala, vol. 1 (1/20/81–7/31/84) (2/5), box 30, Executive Secretariat

NSC Country Files, Latin America, Grenada, Guatemala, Ronald Reagan Library.

150. Cable No. 073548, GOG request for military equipment, April 1983, p. 1, file: Guatemala (1), box 90328, Robert H. Lilac Files, Ronald Reagan Library.

151. *Ibid.*, Secretary of Defense memo, 20 December 1982, p. 1.

152. Reagan remarks following meeting with Ríos Montt, 4 December 1982, file: Guatemala, Oliver L. North, NSC Staff (1/3), OLN Middle Upstairs Office Vertical File, box 62, Oliver L. North Files, Ronald Reagan Library.

153. Black *et al.*, *Garrison Guatemala*, p. 161.

154. HCPP, 1982/83, Cmnd. 8819, FCO: Caribbean and Central America, ministerial observations on the fifth report of the Foreign Affairs Select Committee, p. 4.

155. *Ibid.*, p. 4.

156. TNA, PREM 19/979, record of Heseltine–Weinberger meeting, 21 March 1983, pp. 4–5.

157. Oliver North and Alfonso Sapia-Bosch (NSC officials) to Clark, 19 April 1983, p. 1, file: Guatemala (2), box 005 (90244), Alfonso Sapia-Bosch Files, Ronald Reagan Library.

158. Hill to Shultz, 28 May 1983, p. 1, file: Guatemala, Oliver L. North NSC Staff (2/3), OLN Middle Upstairs Office Vertical File, box 62, Oliver L. North Files, Ronald Reagan Library.

159. Reagan to Thatcher, 4 August 1983, p. 1, file: United Kingdom PM Thatcher Cables (3/4), box 35, Executive Secretariat NSC Head of State Files, Ronald Reagan Library.

160. Reagan to Price, 1 June 1983, p. 1, file: Belize PM George Price (8303789), box 4, Executive Secretariat NSC Head of State Files, Ronald Reagan Library.

161. *Ibid.*, p. 1.

162. Cable No. 027791, Belize/Guatemala: FCO query about US initiative, June 1983, p. 1, file: Guatemala, vol. 1 (1/20/81–7/31/84) (5/5), box 30, Executive Secretariat NSC Country Files, Latin America, Grenada, Guatemala, Ronald Reagan Library.

163. *Ibid.*, pp. 2–3.

164. *Ibid.*, p. 3.

165. *Ibid.*, p. 2.

166. *Ibid.*, p. 2.

167. Sapia-Bosch to Clark, 14 July 1983, p. 1, file: United Kingdom 1983 (07/12/1983–07/21/1983), box 90424, Peter R. Sommer Files, Ronald Reagan Library.

168. Briefing paper for Reagan–Howe meeting, 13 July 1983, pp. 1–2, file: United Kingdom (8/1/82–10/31/83) (4/5), box 20, Executive Secretariat NSC Country Files, Europe and the Soviet Union, Ronald Reagan Library.

169. Cable No. 057639, Secretary's bilateral with Foreign Secretary Howe, 21 July 1983, p. 2, file: United Kingdom 1983 (07/12/1983–07/21/1983), box 90424, Peter R. Sommer Files, Ronald Reagan Library.

170. *Ibid.*, Hill to Clark, 29 July 1983, p. 1, file: United Kingdom 1983 (07/22/1983–08/08/1983), box 90424.

171. *Ibid.*, Clark to Reagan, 4 August 1983.

172. Reagan to Thatcher, 4 August 1983, p. 2, file: United Kingdom PM Thatcher Cables (3/4), box 35, Executive Secretariat NSC Head of State Files, Ronald Reagan Library.

173. *Ibid.*, p. 2.

174. Interview with Geoffrey Howe.

175. The Prime Minister had publicly supported US initiatives in seeking democracy in Central America, in particular, in El Salvador and Nicaragua. This public show of support was important to the Reagan administration given international condemnation of US involvement in Latin America. It also allowed Thatcher to consolidate her position as a staunch ally to Reagan. See Chapter 5.

176. Reagan to Thatcher, 4 August 1983, p. 2, file: United Kingdom PM Thatcher Cables (3/4), box 35, Executive Secretariat NSC Head of State Files, Ronald Reagan Library.

177. *Ibid.*, p. 2.

178. Poindexter to Sommer, 16 August 1983, p. 1, file: United Kingdom, PM Thatcher (8305659–8306168), Executive Secretariat NSC Head of State Files, Ronald Reagan Library.

179. Clark to North, 16 September 1983, p. 1, file: (8/1/82–10/31/83) (4/5), box 20, Executive Secretariat NSC Country Files, Europe and the Soviet Union, Ronald Reagan Library.

180. *Ibid.*, p. 1.

181. Shultz to Reagan, 20 September 1983, pp. 1–2, file: Thatcher visit 29 September 1983, box 90902, European and Soviet Affairs Directorate NSC Records, Ronald Reagan Library.

182. Briefing paper on Belize, p. 1, n.d., file: 187 Meeting with PM Thatcher of the UK (9/29/83) (2/3), box 18, Charles P. Tyson Files, Ronald Reagan Library.

183. *Ibid.*, p. 1.

184. *Ibid.*, p. 1.

185. TNA, PREM 19/1153, Confidential 'Game Plan' for Prime Minister's visit to Washington on 29 September 1983, p. 1.
186. *Ibid.*, record of Reagan–Thatcher meeting, 29 September 1983, p. 8.
187. Memcon. of Reagan–Thatcher meeting, 29 September 1983, pp. 5–6, file: United Kingdom 1983 (09/24/1983–10/10/1983), box 90424, Peter R. Sommer Files, Ronald Reagan Library.
188. TNA, PREM 19/1048, Parsons to Coles, 26 October 1983.
189. Mejía Victores, for example, promised a quick return to democracy in Guatemala, but the country continued to suffer increasing levels of violence and repression. As a result of considerable US pressure, Mejía Victores agreed to presidential elections in November 1985. Following these elections, Cerezo Arévalo came to power as Guatemala's first elected Christian Democratic President on 14 January 1986. Cerezo Arévalo made numerous attempts to create a lasting peace in Guatemala in the face of an increasingly repressive civil war. In fact, under him the potential of conflict between the UK and Guatemala over Belize was minimised. The Guatemalan President even hinted at his willingness to recognise Belizean independence during a visit to Europe in October 1986 and full diplomatic relations between the UK and Guatemala were restored shortly thereafter in December 1986. Cerezo Arévalo was succeeded by Jorge Antonio Serrano Elías on 14 January 1991. Guatemala finally recognised Belizean independence on 11 September 1991. See James Ferguson *et al.*, 'Under attack: Central America and the Caribbean', in Latin American Bureau, *The Thatcher Years: Britain and Latin America* (London: Latin America Bureau, 1988), p. 47.

5 Nicaragua: The Allies Stand Together

US involvement in Nicaragua during the Reagan administration became synonymous with subterfuge, illegal and covert operations, a disregard for congressional and public approval, and the infamous Iran–Contra scandal. Nicaragua was a country of significant strategic geographical importance to the US due to its central location in Latin America. It provided the Reagan administration with a chance to quash the perceived communist threat in the form of the Sandinista government. Thus, US involvement in Nicaragua was characterised by deep-rooted Cold War suppositions. Removing the Sandinistas from power became one of the foremost foreign policy objectives of the Reagan administration. US hegemony in the region was threatened by what the Americans saw as a Marxist proxy in Latin America in the guise of the Sandinistas. Nicaragua's close association with Cuba and the Eastern bloc fuelled US fears of Marxist expansionism in the region. Reagan could not, nor would not, allow the US to be further isolated in its own backyard.

Nicaragua posed a number of additional challenges for the US, namely, the Sandinista's alleged provision of arms to insurgents in neighbouring El Salvador, a country in which the US had considerable interests.[1] Salvadoran guerrillas armed by Nicaragua and Cuba could potentially uproot the US-supported Salvadoran government. As a result, El Salvador and Nicaragua were inextricably linked for the Reagan administration. Therefore, immediate and unequivocal US action had to be taken. US involvement in Nicaragua evolved from initial financial assistance to the role of training proxy 'freedom fighters', or more commonly termed 'contras' after the Spanish word 'contrarevolucionarios'.

The Reagan administration began to supply, train and organise the contras both at home and in Honduras, where the contras established base camps along its southern border with Nicaragua.

US involvement in Nicaragua took an ominous turn in 1985 when NSC officials, such as Colonel Oliver L. North, John Poindexter and Robert McFarlane, agreed to sell US arms to Iran in return for the release of seven American hostages held captive in Beirut. The proceeds from these arm sales were thereafter redistributed to the contra forces in Nicaragua and Honduras, in violation of US federal law. This plan allowed the US to override congressional orders to halt all US assistance to the contras and to break a pre-existing US embargo on arms sales to Iran. US actions came to light during the mid-1980s and, more notably, following a report by the Lebanese *Al Shiraa* magazine in November 1986. The 'Irangate' affair, or Iran–Contra scandal as it was otherwise known, shook the foundations of the Reagan administration to its core and exposed the unilateral tendencies of the US in Latin America. A political firestorm ensued and the extent of the NSC's and the President's involvement in such illegal and covert activities was called into question. Reagan needed a strong ally in the face of possible impeachment and widespread international condemnation.

This chapter will examine Britain, in particular, Thatcher's support of US policies in Nicaragua under the Reagan administration. By examining a host of US documents and those more recently released by the TNA in January 2014 (CAB 128/78/13 and CAB 128/79/13 file series) and August 2013 (PREM 19/1152 and PREM 19/1153 file series), the chapter will assess the differences in US and UK policies towards Nicaragua in the 1980s, thereby highlighting the importance of British support. It will show that Thatcher's many attempts to support Reagan's Nicaraguan policies were largely unwelcome at home in the UK. The Prime Minister's support reinforced the idea of a Special Relationship between the US and the UK, and consolidated her position as a valuable ally to one of the world's most important leaders.

US–Nicaraguan relations in the 1970s

The US had long-standing interests in Nicaragua prior to the involvement of the Reagan administration in the 1980s. From the establishment of a US military presence in Nicaragua in the 1890s to safeguard US property interests, to its monitoring of the various dictatorships of Somoza García and his successors from 1936 onwards, the US maintained a keen interest in the political and economic future of Nicaragua.[2] The 1970s saw the US become more overtly interested in Nicaragua's political orientation under the leadership of Anastasio Somoza Debayle. Throughout this time Nicaragua endured a turbulent period of violence, censorship and human rights abuses by Somoza Debayle's government which sought to quash leftist opposition in the form of the Frente Sandinista de Liberación Nacional (FSLN, Sandinista National Liberation Front).[3] A state of emergency was imposed by Somoza Debayle in 1974, and Nicaragua's National Guard intensified its crackdown against the FSLN and those suspected of supporting it.

A split in the FSLN in 1975 resulted in the emergence of three factions – the Proletarian Tendency, the Prolonged People's War and the Insurrectionals – all of which maintained the aim of ousting Somoza Debayle. In 1977, the Carter administration began to press Nicaragua for improvements in the country's deteriorating human rights situation. The US announced that it would suspend US$12 million in US aid to Nicaragua unless steps were taken to improve matters. On 5 September, Somoza Debayle lifted the state of emergency and US$2.5 million in US military aid to Nicaragua resumed. The FSLN's resistance to Somoza Debayle was strengthened with the establishment of Los Doce (the Group of Twelve), founded by Sergio Ramírez Mercado in October 1977.[4] The desire to oust Somoza Debayle increased following the assassination of the editor of *La Prensa* newspaper and leader of the opposition alliance, Unión Democrática de Liberación (UDEL, Democratic Union of Liberation), Pedro Joaquín Chamorro Cardenal, on 10 January 1978.[5] His murder resulted in rioting and a general strike in Nicaragua, and marked the beginning of a bloody civil war. The National Guard became increasingly violent in its attempts to quash the opposition. In the light of such events, the US suspended its military assistance to Nicaragua in February 1978. In August, the State Department recommended that Somoza Debayle should be removed from power and a more moderate government be put in place. The Carter administration was reluctant to be so bold and decided instead to try to mediate the ongoing dispute between Somoza Debayle and the opposition.

Political opposition continued to grow in Nicaragua with the formation of groups such as Edén Pastora Gómez' the Third Way, the Movimiento Democrático Nicaragüense (MDN, Nicaraguan Democratic Movement), the Frente Amplio de Oposición (FAO, Broad Opposition Front) and the Movimiento Pueblo Unido (MPU, United People's Movement). US attempts to mediate and support negotiations between Somoza and the various opposition groups came to an end in January 1979. The Carter administration imposed sanctions against Nicaragua on 8 February, thereby suspending all US economic aid to the country.[6] The FSLN reunified on 7 March and established a joint National Directorate with three men from each faction.

This reunification led to an escalation in clashes between the FSLN and the increasingly repressive and violent National Guard. The FSLN's 'final offensive', led by the party's Southern Front under the leadership of General Humberto Ortega Saavedra, began in late May 1979 with a number of coordinated attacks against the National Guard. By mid-June the National Guard had abandoned many of its posts and the FSLN was in control of much of the country.[7] In the US, it became increasingly evident that Somoza Debayle would be forced from power by the FSLN. US fears thereafter centred on the necessity of containing the Soviet Union's perceived influence on the FSLN in the likely event of the party taking power in Nicaragua. The Carter administration began to look at ways in which to remove Somoza Debayle and replace him with a more democratic government. It looked towards the OAS as a forum in which to pursue US mediation with the warring parties in Nicaragua. US mediation efforts failed and the FSLN made significant advances in Nicaragua culminating in a march by FSLN guerrillas on the country's capital, Managua, on 17 July. Somoza Debayle was forced to resign.

A worried Carter administration watched as the Sandinista Junta del Gobierno de Reconstrucción Nacional (GRN, Provisional Government of National Reconstruction), under the leadership of Daniel Ortega Saavedra, Alfonso Robelo Callejas, Sergio Ramírez Mercado, Moisés Hassan Morales and Violeta Barrios de Chamorro, assumed power on 19 July. The GRN promised to reconstruct the national economy following the devastating effects of the civil war by nationalising banks and enforcing the Agrarian Law Reform.[8] The junta proclaimed the Fundamental Statute of the Republic of Nicaragua on 22 August, thereby abolishing the pre-existing Constitution, Congress and the Presidency. To the US, this was further proof that the junta was Marxist-orientated. The creation of the Ejército Popular Sandinista (EPS, Sandinista People's Army), which replaced Somoza's National Guard, further fuelled US fears. The EPS were allegedly trained by personnel from the Soviet Union and its proxies in Latin America and Eastern Europe. The US feared that the Sandinistas would look towards the Soviet Union and its proxies to obtain arms for the EPS.[9]

Carter initially tried to foster improved relations with the GRN in order to maintain an open dialogue with the Sandinistas. To that end, he proposed an aid package of US$75 million for Nicaragua in November 1979 subject to congressional approval. Congress approved the package in July 1980 on condition that Nicaragua was not 'aiding, abetting, or supporting acts of violence or terrorism in other countries'.[10] However, US–Nicaraguan relations deteriorated with rumours that Nicaragua was providing arms to insurgents in El Salvador. This, combined with Sandinista censorship of the press and an announcement on 19 September 1980 that national elections were to be suspended until 1985, made the US increasingly wary of the GRN.[11]

Reagan and the Sandinistas

Upon Reagan's inauguration, the Sandinista government confirmed that it wanted 'friendly relations' with the US.[12] This was not a feeling reciprocated by the Reagan administration. Within two days of taking office Reagan suspended all aid to Nicaragua, with the exception of US$51.6 million in NGO funds for assisting the Nicaraguan people.[13] The US based its policies towards Nicaragua upon intelligence that indicated a pattern of Cuban, Soviet and Nicaraguan involvement in the training and arming of guerrillas in El Salvador. The termination of US aid was made despite protests from the US Ambassador to Nicaragua, Lawrence Pezzullo, who stated that any transfer of arms to El Salvador had already diminished or had stopped since January 1981. However, it was believed in the NSC that while some arms trafficking routes from Nicaragua had been closed, the Sandinistas were seeking new ones at the time.[14] The Reagan administration cited intelligence reports of arms transfers by land via Honduras, by air from the Papalonal airstrip and by sea across the Gulf of Fonseca to the insurgents in El Salvador. The administration therefore decided to 'persuade the Sandinistas to halt the weapons deliveries by escalating the political and economic costs to Nicaragua'.[15] The US implemented a propaganda campaign to highlight Nicaragua's alleged support for the Salvadoran guerrillas. It sought to impede financial assistance to the Sandinistas by trying to block international loans to Nicaragua, requesting countries such as Venezuela and West Germany to restrict aid to Nicaragua, encouraging the postponement of short-term trade credits by US banks and encouraging the liquidation of US investors' assets in Nicaragua.[16]

In February 1981, the State Department issued a White Paper on El Salvador titled 'Communist Interference in El Salvador', which claimed an incontrovertible link between the Sandinistas and the insurgents in El Salvador. The White Paper was widely discredited by the national press with claims that it was inconsistent and that some of the evidence lacked authenticity.[17] McFarlane, who was then an assistant to Haig, proposed a coordinated economic, military and political approach to Nicaragua in February 1981. This plan was built upon by the National Security Planning Group (NSPG) under the direction of Director of the CIA William Casey, Haig, Allen, Weinberger and Kirkpatrick.[18] McFarlane's paper, titled 'Taking the War to Nicaragua', proposed a naval blockade and the use of open force against Cuban ships in the region believed to be supplying arms to Salvadoran guerrillas.[19] This paper was not accepted as the NSPG position.

Casey put forward a plan in early March on countering Cuban subversion in Central America. Casey's plan outlined a paramilitary operation to interdict arms supplies from Nicaragua and Honduras into El Salvador and detailed plans to provide assistance to opponents of the Sandinistas. Reagan signed a 'Presidential Finding on Nicaragua' on 9 March that effectively authorised Casey's plan. This finding authorised the CIA to engage in covert activities in Central America in order to counter foreign-sponsored subversion and terrorism.[20] CIA operatives were dispatched to the region to establish close ties with subversive groups who could help the US to topple communism in Latin America.

In spring 1981, Vernon Walters was sent to enlist further support from Honduras, Argentina and other governments in the region to help the CIA with the 'freedom fighters'. Argentina's involvement with the contras was beneficial to the US as the Reagan administration also wanted to foster close relations with Argentina as a powerful non-communist ally in Latin America. The CIA provided US$50,000 to Argentine military intelligence officials as an 'incentive to unite under one anti-Sandinista banner'.[21] Thus, Argentine advisers essentially acted as a cut-out for the CIA in its initial contra dealings, in particular in Honduras.[22] Argentine advisers in Honduras, with US financial assistance, trained the contras in a variety of skills, including intelligence, counter-intelligence, weapons, ground combat, terrorism, light artillery and explosives. These techniques were also taught to contra forces in locations around the US, such as camps in the Mojave Desert, the Florida Everglades, Texas and southern Louisiana. Ex-Vietnam veterans, Cuban exiles and Green Berets trained the contras in these camps.[23] The Argentine trainers later withdrew in 1983 largely as a result of US support of the British during the Falklands War of 1982, leaving the CIA with a more active role in training the contras in Honduras.[24] Reports of contra training camps began to emerge in the US press in March 1981, beginning with *Parade* magazine and the *New York Times*.[25]

During this time, Nicaragua began to receive shipments of arms from sources associated with the Soviet Union. In April, an Algerian merchant ship delivered four Soviet tank ferries, a patrol boat and twelve BM-21 missiles to Nicaragua. This ship was believed to have acquired its cargo from the Soviet Union.[26] Daniel Ortega replied that such reports by the State Department were 'totally unfounded'. A further deterioration in US–Nicaraguan relations was evident a few weeks later when Enders alleged that Cuba had between 600 and 800 military advisers in Nicaragua, and was trying to establish a Cuban operations base in the country.[27] As 1981 progressed, the Reagan administration continued to monitor events in Nicaragua. Enders produced an ill-fated five-point peace plan on Nicaragua in August 1981.[28] Enders' non-aggression treaty called for the renewal of economic assistance to the contras on condition that the Sandinistas should 'stop training and supplying Salvadoran guerrillas, to give pluralism a chance in their country … and to limit their military build-up'. Enders' plan failed because Nicaragua rejected it, as did Casey, Kirkpatrick, Clark and Weinberger.[29]

Following the failure of Enders' plan, a more cohesive strategy was put in place to deal with US policy towards Latin America. An Interagency Core Group was established and contained officials from the principal agencies dealing with Latin America (the group was referred to as the RIG after 1983). The Core Group oversaw US policy towards Latin America, particularly Nicaragua, and included Enders, Langhorne Motley, the Department of Defense's (DOD), Nestor Sanchez, and the head of the CIA's Directorate of Operations for Latin America, Duane 'Dewey' R. Clarridge. Colonel North joined the Core Group later in 1983.[30]

The Reagan administration corresponded with the Thatcher government at this time in order to keep the UK informed on US objectives in the region. Haig sent Carrington a letter outlining US–Nicaraguan relations on 31 August 1981 in which he outlined possible US proposals for Nicaragua, including arms controls, the resumption of certain types of economic and technical assistance, and the improved monitoring of exile groups. Haig wrote: 'However this turns out, I believe we must go through the current process in a serious fashion, and ensure that others understand that we are willing to exhaust all possibilities of reaching an understanding.' Haig concluded his letter to Carrington with an assurance: 'I will keep you informed of developments.'[31] Indeed, Haig was one of the key proponents of countering the Soviet threat in Latin America. As Ambassador Henderson reported to the FCO in 1981:

> Carter's policy on human rights has been turned on its head by Haig . . . This change of emphasis removes an obstacle to support of authoritarian regimes, particularly in Latin America . . . Haig has said that the Americans aim to tackle the problems of Cuban subversion at source (meaning Cuba).[32]

Meanwhile, the CIA's involvement with the contras intensified in September 1981 with the establishment of the Fuerza Democrática Nicaragüense (FDN, Nicaraguan Democratic Force), which was established in southern Honduras under CIA supervision. Enrique Bermúdez was installed as the commander of the military wing of the FDN and a former CIA source, Adolfo Calero Portocarrero, was installed as the FDN's nominal head in the US.[33] The FDN was comprised of ex-National Guardsmen and those who disapproved of Sandinista rule. The FDN would go on to play a vital role in US attempts to subvert the Sandinistas. US support of the contras strengthened on 17 November when Reagan approved a US$19 million programme of covert assistance to the contras. The President was convinced that Nicaragua was building a large army that was 'disproportionate to its size or its needs', and that the contras therefore needed US help.[34] A further Presidential Finding was signed by Reagan on 1 December to 'support and conduct paramilitary operations against Nicaragua'.[35] This finding built on the Presidential Finding of 9 March and authorised the CIA to oversee covert operations against the Sandinistas. The CIA was authorised to create a force of up to 500 Latin Americans to conduct sorties against the Sandinistas in Nicaragua from bases in Honduras.[36] This finding was closely followed by Executive Order 12333 on 4 December, under which covert activities were described as 'special activities' which would be the direct responsibility of the CIA.[37] The CIA was essentially provided with a carte blanche for its activities in Nicaragua.

The UK and Nicaragua, 1979–82

The UK's relationship with Nicaragua in early 1979 was not particularly close. Britain maintained a similar stance to that of the US in that it promoted democracy in Latin America. Thus, the UK monitored events closely as they unfolded in Nicaragua. However, this proved to be somewhat problematical as British representation in Nicaragua had previously been withdrawn in 1975.[38] The UK was aware of the potential for further unrest in the region should developments in Nicaragua continue to deteriorate. More importantly, it was mindful of its own interests in the region, in particular, Belize's quest for independence and corresponding Guatemalan threats of aggression. As both countries were in close proximity to Nicaragua, the UK monitored events in Nicaragua with interest. When Thatcher assumed power in the UK, Nicaragua seized the opportunity to improve its relations with Britain. To that end, Somoza Debayle wrote to Thatcher indicating that he was keen to 'consolidate and increase the traditional ties of friendship' between both countries.[39] However, the Thatcher government was reluctant to respond to such proposals as it seemed unlikely that stability would return to Nicaragua as long as Somoza Debayle remained in power.[40] Notwithstanding this, the British government was mindful that closer bilateral relations with Nicaragua could potentially be of benefit to the UK in the event of Guatemalan aggression against Belize. UK–Nicaraguan relations therefore required careful review by the Thatcher government. Indeed, the UK, in contrast to the US, did not see a need to discontinue its bilateral aid to Nicaragua throughout the Thatcher premiership. This, according to Hazel Smith, indicated a degree of British 'independence from US tutelage' regarding Nicaragua.[41]

When the GRN approached the British government on 12 July 1979 requesting that the UK sever its relations with Somoza Debayle and recognise the junta instead, the UK was placed in a difficult position.[42] While the UK wanted to support US efforts to promote democracy in Nicaragua, it also wished to establish 'friendly relations' with the new GRN.[43] However, friendly relations with Nicaragua could potentially damage Britain's reliance upon the US for support in Belize. Michael Perceval in the FCO's Mexico and Caribbean Department wrote to Anthony Parsons on 23 July outlining the difficulties inherent in Britain's refusal to recognise the GRN. Perceval suggested that this could have:

> possible repercussions for Belize. If we are to achieve an independent Belize, we need to persuade the US to be tough on Guatemala. But with a hostile government in Nicaragua the US would be reluctant to damage its relations with Guatemala which would be the US's strongest remaining ally in the region. It is therefore important that we support the efforts to encourage democracy in Nicaragua.[44]

Despite these reservations, the UK established relations with the new regime in Nicaragua on 7 August 1979.[45] In fact, throughout 1980 the UK looked at ways in which to improve its relations with Nicaragua. To that end, Nicholas Ridley, who had reluctantly been assigned to dealing with Latin American matters in the FCO by Thatcher, visited Nicaragua during a Central American trip in May 1980. Following this visit, Ridley determined that the UK should keep 'close and friendly' relations with Nicaragua.[46] In addition to this visit, on 8 September 1980 Ridley met with Alfonso Robelo, who had recently left the GRN and was then leader of the MDN, to discuss the situation in Nicaragua.[47] UK–Nicaraguan relations began to receive more attention in the FCO in late 1980 when Assistant Under-Secretary of State, G. W. Harding, met with the Nicaraguan Ambassador to the EEC, Gonzalo Murillo-Romero, in the FCO on 11 December. During this meeting, Harding stated that HMG wished to maintain closer contact with Nicaragua. Ambassador Murillo-Romero stated that while Nicaragua was satisfied with the development of relations with the UK, it would like relations to be given 'more substance'.[48]

The UK continued to monitor events closely in Nicaragua throughout 1981. However, the lack of formal diplomatic ties between the UK and Nicaragua made success in improved bilateral relations difficult to achieve. As a result, the House of Commons Foreign Affairs Committee recommended in a 1981 report that the UK should re-establish a British mission in Nicaragua at the 'earliest opportunity'.[49] This would afford the UK more influence in the Latin American region as whole. Greater British influence was desirable given that the US under Reagan was becoming increasingly preoccupied with the region, in particular, with the Sandinistas in Nicaragua. As the Committee opined:

> The current aim of the US is to place pressure on Nicaragua which will 'destabilise' the FSLN to the point where it will be replaced by a different regime by supplying, or at least tolerating, the activities of those Nicaraguan exiles who seek to harass and overturn the government in Nicaragua; by obstructing and reducing the flow of economic aid to Nicaragua; by attempting to isolate Nicaragua within the region by promoting encircling alliances such as the recent Central American Democratic Community; and by other measures designed to coerce change of policy or of leadership within Nicaragua.[50]

Clearly, the Foreign Affairs Committee did not want the UK to align itself too closely with the US with regard to Nicaragua. Indeed, an independent British policy towards Nicaragua was required. The Thatcher government would have to formulate a policy that was not as belligerent as the policies the Reagan administration appeared to have adopted towards Nicaragua. This would be a difficult task for the UK as Thatcher, in theory, agreed with many of the Reagan administration's policies in the Latin American region. Notwithstanding this difficulty, the UK re-established diplomatic ties with Nicaragua later that year.

In the US, Reagan signed NSDD 17, 'National Security Decision Directive on Cuba and Central America', on 4 January 1982. NSDD 17 defined US policy as:

> to assist in defeating the insurgency in El Salvador, and to oppose actions by Cuba, Nicaragua, or others to introduce into Central America heavy weapons, troops from outside the region, trained subversives, or arms and military supplies for insurgents.[51]

NSDD 17 authorised the US to provide 'military training for indigenous units' and to support 'democratic forces' in Nicaragua.[52] It is estimated that following NSDD 17 around 1,500 additional paramilitary experts were hired by the CIA to work with the contras and Argentine advisers in Honduras.[53] 'The Project', as it became known in the intelligence community, allocated under NSDD 17 US$19.5 million to the CIA for covert military operations in the region.[54] The FDN subsequently used part of these proceeds to purchase weapons such as machine guns, FAL rifles, M-79 grenade launchers and 60-mm mortars.[55]

In the UK, during a meeting between the Foreign Affairs Committee and the Nicaraguan Ambassador to London, Licenciado Francisco d'Escoto, on 8 February, shocking claims against the US and its support of the contras were made by the Ambassador:

> The Americans are sending weapons and money to those people on the Atlantic coast to start a revolution, to start a separation from the English-speaking Nicaraguans and their brothers, the Spanish-speaking Nicaraguans. It is one of many schemes that you will see fermenting in Central America against Nicaragua to isolate us.[56]

Despite such claims, the UK was not prepared to openly condemn the Reagan administration. Indeed, when questioned in a House of Commons debate on 31 March regarding the possibility of a direct US invasion in Nicaragua, Richard Luce, who had recently retired as Minister of State in the FCO, confirmed that the British government had: 'noticed that on a *Panorama* programme earlier this week Ambassador Bosworth of the United States denied that the United States had any intention of military intervention, or the use of troops'.[57] In US and UK political circles such responses were interpreted as unofficial British support of the Reagan administration. So, too, was the British decision to reduce UK economic aid to Nicaragua in 1982 to a mere £49,000.[58] This reduction in aid was inconsistent with the Thatcher government's provision of aid to other Latin American countries such as El Salvador in 1982. Such actions could be interpreted as the UK following the US policy of economic destabilisation of the Sandinistas while continuing to provide aid to more democratic governments in Latin America such as the US-supported Salvadoran government.

In Nicaragua, contra military attacks increased against the Sandinistas in March 1982, resulting in the declaration of a state of emergency by the GRN. Constitutional rights were suspended, including the right of assembly, the right to strike and the freedom of the press.[59] The scale of these attacks led the Sandinistas increasingly to believe that a US invasion of Nicaragua was imminent. As the situation deteriorated, many of Nicaragua's neighbours became concerned about its possible impact on the wider Latin American region. The President of Mexico, José López Portillo, made continued suggestions for US–Nicaraguan bilateral talks. In response to these suggestions and wider regional concerns, the US formulated an eight-point plan towards Nicaragua, which was delivered on 8 April to the GRN by the US Ambassador to Nicaragua, Anthony Quainton. The plan included proposals for Nicaragua to end its destabilisation activities in the region; an offer by the US to reaffirm its intention of neutrality; a joint US–GRN statement on friendly relations; a ban on the importation of heavy weapons into the region; the re-establishment of US economic aid to Nicaragua; and a call for the GRN to respect its original promises with respect to pluralism, elections and a mixed economy.[60] The Reagan administration did not believe that the proposals would be accepted by the GRN, but they would demonstrate to critics of US policies in Latin America that the Reagan administration was prepared to foster 'friendly' relations with the Sandinistas. The proposals were not well received by the GRN. In fact, it aligned itself more closely with the Soviet Union in the wake of Quainton's visit. On 10 May, the GRN announced a five-year US$166.8 million aid agreement with the Soviet Union.[61]

As US assistance to the contras continued to grow, Reagan intensified the propaganda campaign to secure both domestic and international support for the contras. During a stirring speech to British MPs in the Houses of Parliament on 8 June, Reagan spoke of the communist threat to the wider international community: 'If the rest of this century is to witness the gradual growth of freedom and democratic ideas, we must take actions to assist the campaign for democracy.'[62] This propaganda campaign continued on 4 October with a US-organised forum in Costa Rica, which was attended by many heads of Central American countries. During this forum the San José Principles were put forward, including a call for each country in the region to create and maintain democratic governmental institutions. There was also a call to 'prevent the use of their territory for the purpose of supporting, supplying, training terrorist or subversive elements in other states'.[63] Claims of US involvement in Honduras and Nicaragua continued to abound, such as stories in *Newsweek* on 8 November that claimed that the US Ambassador in Honduras, John Negroponte, was involved in training and arming the contras.[64] These claims resulted in widespread alarm, which influenced congressional attitudes towards US funding of the 'freedom fighters'.

Meanwhile, the Sandinistas continued to receive more shipments of Soviet weapons. Twenty-five T-54/55 tanks were delivered to Nicaragua in November. The Reagan administration saw the deliveries as being a direct result of Daniel Ortega's visit to Moscow earlier in the year. The delivery was supplemented in December by the delivery of Soviet electronic high-frequency detectors 'of a type previously seen in Cuba'. These detectors would allow the Sandinistas to intercept signals throughout Central America, which would allow them to locate strategic military communication sites in Honduras.[65] To the US, this was further proof that the Sandinistas were becoming increasingly militant and therefore constituted a greater risk to the US pursuit of liberal democracy in Latin America.

The Boland Amendments and Contadora initiatives

Congress began to reassess US aid to the contras in December 1982, with Democrat Senator for Massachusetts Edward Boland as the principal voice of opposition. As Chairman of the House Intelligence Committee, Senator Boland orchestrated an amendment, known as the Boland Amendment, to be attached the House Defense Appropriations Bill for FY 1983. The amendment restricted US humanitarian aid to the contras and prohibited the use of American funds 'for the purpose of overthrowing the government of Nicaragua'.[66] The amendment was passed by the US House of Representatives on 8 December by a vote of 411 to 0. It was in effect from 21 December 1983 to 8 December 1984. This was a foreign policy defeat for the Reagan administration.

However, the amendment was somewhat overshadowed by the Congress Intelligence Committee's subsequent decision to allow the CIA to use contingency funding to support the contras.[67] Despite the Boland Amendment, the contras began to make deeper and more successful incursions into Nicaragua. As 1983 dawned, the contras increased their operations along the northern and southern borders of Nicaragua. These operations began to put additional pressure on already strained US allocated resources for the 'freedom fighters'.

Given these advances, the Reagan administration needed to garner political and financial support for the contras. Thus, it was opportune that the FDN announced a twelve-point peace initiative on 13 January 1983, which referred to Nicaragua as a 'Soviet base for aggression' and described the contras as 'Nicaraguan Patriots'.[68] At the same time, the heads of government of Mexico, Colombia, Panama and Venezuela met on the Panamanian island of Contadora to work out a settlement to the ongoing crisis in Central America, including Nicaragua. The so-called Contadora group was augmented in 1985 with the creation of a Contadora Support Group, which included Uruguay, Brazil, Peru and Argentina. The purpose of Contadora was to find a peaceful solution to the regional crisis in Latin America and to ensure peaceful coexistence between the US and Central American countries, including Nicaragua.[69] The US was unenthusiastic about pursuing the various initiatives as championed by the Contadora Group in the coming years. Indeed, the Reagan administration increasingly disengaged itself from the Contadora initiatives as they ran counter to US unilateral policies in Latin America.[70]

On 22 March 1983, Nicaragua requested an urgent meeting of the UNSC to deal with the 'alleged massive infiltration of insurgent followers of former President Somoza into Nicaragua with heavy US and Honduran support'.[71] During a press conference on the same day, Nicaragua's Deputy Foreign Minister, Victor Tinoco, alleged that there was an imminent threat of a large-scale, US-backed invasion of Nicaragua by Honduran forces. In order to counter such allegations, Kirkpatrick delivered a speech in the UNSC on 23 March placing the situation in Nicaragua in historical perspective. In preparation for the debate, the US looked for 'friendly states' to make statements in its support. The UK headed the list of potential speakers and a memo sent by Shultz to various embassies stated: 'addressees have been selected for approach on the basis of our friendly relations with them and our belief that they may be interested in supporting the moderate position in the council against Nicaragua'.[72] Moreover, according to Shultz' memo, Nicaraguan claims were 'utterly false'.[73]

The Thatcher government, for its part, continued to monitor the situation in Nicaragua, but was circumspect when questioned about British views on US policies in Latin America. When the matter arose in a House of Commons debate on 11 May, Francis Pym gave a guarded response: 'We support the objectives that President Reagan is pursuing. They are in support of democracy, reform, human freedom, attention to human rights, continued help for economic development and other matters.'[74] The US was happy to have such support from the UK. British support was re-emphasised by Geoffrey Howe during a meeting with Reagan in Washington on 14 July. The Foreign Secretary assured the President that the UK shared US concerns and objectives in the region and emphasised: 'we all need to do a much better job of getting across to the public what is actually happening in the area'.[75] Such declarations of support served to enhance the bonds of political diplomacy between the Reagan and Thatcher governments.

In the US, there was mounting pressure in Congress to develop a more cohesive US strategy towards Latin America. Democrat Senator Henry Jackson thereby encouraged the establishment of a bipartisan commission to visit Central America. As a result, Reagan signed Executive Order 12433 on 19 July to formally establish the National Bipartisan Commission on Central America (NBCCA), also known as the Kissinger Commission, with Henry Kissinger as its head. NBCCA was established 'to study the nature of United States interests in the Central American region and the threat posed to those interests', and was to present its findings to Reagan by 1 December 1983.[76] It was hoped that the creation of the NBCCA would help to ease the tensions between the Reagan administration and Congress, which might lead to a resumption of congressional aid to the contras.

In the UK, Thatcher came under considerable pressure from her peers to outline British views on US policy in Latin America, in particular, Nicaragua, during a House of Commons debate on 26 July 1983. The Prime Minister was quick to reaffirm the UK's commitment to the Contadora group and to praise the 'immense amount of non-military aid that the United States is putting into the area'. Thatcher defended the US presence in the region by pointing to the communist influence there: 'Cuba has ten times the number of military advisers in Central America as the United States.'[77] Thatcher's comments were measured as the FCO had just denied claims by the FDN that it was engaging in talks with the UK, and one of Thatcher's advisers, Sir Alfred Sherman, had denied reports that he was planning to visit Honduras and El Salvador to meet FDN representatives.[78]

In general terms, the Thatcher government tempered its support of the US position with its adherence to the EEC position on Central America. This position was formulated in 1983 and argued that the problems of the region could be resolved only through peaceful diplomacy. As a result, the UK consistently supported the Contadora peace process and participated in many of the San José meetings of EEC foreign ministers to discuss a negotiated settlement to the many political and socio-economic problems that plagued Central America in the 1980s.[79] In line with the general EEC position on Contadora, the Thatcher government supported the Contadora Group's 'Document of 21 Points' presented on 9 September as a framework for a regional peace treaty in Latin America. The document outlined various political, security and socioeconomic objectives for the region. It effectively criticised the US presence in the region and looked for a reduction in the amount of foreign military advisers with a view to their full withdrawal in Latin America.[80]

The 'Document of 21 Points' was unacceptable to the US, and the Reagan administration effectively responded by proposing a military solution to the Central American peace crisis. On 12 September, Fred Iklé spoke of the need to prevent a consolidation of the Sandinista regime and argued that if the US could not prevent this from happening it would be forced to 'man a new military front-line of the East–West conflict, right here on our continent'.[81] This hard-line attitude did not go unnoticed in the UK, and most likely contributed to the British general public's disdain of US involvement in Latin America at the time. An opinion poll conducted by the US in mid-September indicated that 40 per cent of the British public disapproved of US assistance to the contras as opposed to 23 per cent who approved. According to this poll, 72 per cent of Britons pleaded ignorance of the alleged supply of arms to Salvadoran guerrillas by Nicaragua and Cuba.[82] Thatcher, however, was committed to supporting US policy in Latin America; a fact she outlined during her visit to Washington on 28–30 September. During a breakfast meeting with the Senate Foreign Relations Committee in Washington on 29 September, the Prime Minister conveyed her impression that US policy in Central America was not fully understood in Europe. She informed the Committee that Britain would do what it could to help in this regard.[83] Thatcher reiterated this support in a meeting with Reagan later that morning. The Prime Minister stated that the UK 'had consistently tried to support the Administration's policy' in Central America, and had frequently quoted Reagan's speech on Central America before a Joint Session of Congress on 27 April which had set out US objectives in the region.[84]

1984: a year of uncertainty and change

The Kissinger Commission report was released on 10 January 1984, and determined that: 'The US has fundamental security interests at stake: a Soviet–Cuba success and resulting collapse of Central America would compel a substantial increase in our security burden or redeployment of forces to the detriment of vital interests elsewhere.'[85] Along with a recommendation for US$8 billion in economic assistance to the region during FYs 1985–9, the report recommended that the US provide significantly increased levels of military assistance for greater mobility, more training, higher force levels and more equipment. Based on this recommendation, Reagan proposed the Central America Democracy and Development Initiative Act to Congress on 3 February. This included the US$8 billion as recommended in the

Kissinger report, with an additional US$259.5 million in military assistance grants for FY 1984 and $255.9 million for FY 1985.[86] While the US wanted to increase funding to the contras, it also wanted to dispel the Vietnam analogy that was widely associated with its commitment to the Central American region. Enders later remarked to the Council of the Americas: 'all the talk about a Vietnam analogy is rather misleading. The more appropriate analogy is to past US policy in the area. Until recently we either ignored Central America . . . or when things got out of hand, sent the troops.'[87]

On 7 February 1984, Reagan signed NSDD 124, 'Central America: Promoting Democracy, Economic Improvement and Peace'. According to this, the NBCCA and the internal strategy review conducted by the NSPG agreed that vital US interests were 'jeopardized by the continuing crisis in Central America'. It defined US objectives in Nicaragua as, among others, terminating Nicaragua's support of Marxist/Leninist subversion and guerrilla activity in any foreign country; removing Soviet bloc/Cuban personnel and intensifying efforts in the Contadora forum; and reviewing economic sanctions against Nicaragua. An action plan on such sanctions was to be put before the NSPG for review by 1 March 1984.[88] In fact, economic sanctions had been considered as early as January 1983 when the administration estimated that a US trade embargo would deny the GRN of a maximum of US$17 million in the first six months of its implementation.[89]

February to April 1984 saw the CIA conduct some of its most contentious covert activities in Nicaragua. US-backed contra forces placed in excess of 600 aquatic mines in the Nicaraguan harbours of Sandino and Corinto on the Pacific coast and in the harbour of El Bluff on the Atlantic coast. The mines were designed by the CIA Weapons Group in Langley, Virginia, and the Marine Warfare Division of the Naval Surface Weapons Center in Maryland. The mines were placed in order to prevent further military supplies from reaching the Sandinistas and to prove the growing abilities of the contras under CIA tutelage. This was the first such mining carried out by the US since the Vietnam War.[90] The mining resulted in damage to both Nicaraguan and internationally owned vessels, and received widespread international condemnation. A British merchant vessel was struck by one of the mines in late February. However, the damage was minimal and the Thatcher government simply conveyed its concern to the US and was seemingly satisfied by the CIA's expression of regret that a British ship had been damaged.[91] Nicaragua, on the other hand, was outraged by such actions and initiated proceedings against the US in the International Court of Justice (ICJ) on 9 April, accusing the US of violating the UN Charter, the OAS Charter and the Treaty of Friendship, Commerce and Navigation between Nicaragua and the US. The Reagan administration had anticipated Nicaragua's reaction and just three days earlier, on 6 April, it had revoked its long-standing acceptance of the ICJ's compulsory jurisdiction which had been in place since 1946. According to the US, the ICJ's compulsory jurisdiction did not apply to 'to disputes with any Central American State arising out of or related to events in Central America' for a period of two years.[92]

In the House of Commons, on 10 April, Thatcher was questioned on British views towards the mining of Nicaragua's harbours. The Prime Minister was emphatic in her response: 'We have previously made it clear to the United States government that we are against mining the ports in Nicaragua because, of course, it is very dangerous to international traffic on the high seas.'[93] While it was not an open denunciation of the US, Thatcher's comments implied a certain level of discontent. The ICJ responded to Nicaraguan requests in May 1984 with an order for the US to cease all aggression towards Nicaragua. The Reagan administration again argued that the ICJ did not have the legal authority to act upon Nicaragua's claims. Such US unilateralism angered many in the international community. Howe raised the matter of US involvement in the mining of the harbours during a ministerial visit to Washington on 29 May. In a meeting with Vice-President Bush, Howe 'not wanting to sound critical', noted that the mining of Nicaraguan harbours had been a 'setback with public opinion, having been viewed as the wrong approach to the problem'.[94] The Foreign Secretary's comments, although mild-mannered, conveyed British concerns on the matter.

It was around this time that Casey advised McFarlane that the contras could run out of funds by mid-May. Casey proposed the acquisition of funds through private citizens. These funds could then be made available to the FDN, thereby sidestepping the need for congressional approval.[95] McFarlane briefed Reagan on the contra situation in late May and was encouraged by the President's words: 'I want you to do whatever you have to do to help these people keep body and soul together. Do everything you can.'[96] McFarlane began to approach individuals such as the Saudi Arabian Ambassador, Prince Bandar bin Sultan, in June 1984, who agreed to provide US$1 million per month to the contra effort for the rest of the year.[97] When McFarlane informed the President of the Saudi contribution Reagan was extremely pleased, but offered the admonition 'Mum's the Word'.[98] The US continued to fund the contras, and the CIA established psychological operations units, troops trained in jungle and night-time operations (TESONs), tactical operations commands and special operations commands.[99] This augmented CIA involvement was revealed in October 1984 when a CIA manual for the contras titled 'Psychological Operations in Guerrilla Warfare' surfaced in the media and detailed ways in which to neutralise Nicaraguan government officials and use seemingly indiscriminate violence to undermine the Sandinistas.

Congress remained convinced of the need to prohibit the allocation of US financial assistance to the contras and a Boland II Amendment was enacted from 3 October 1984 to 3 December 1985. Boland II was a blow for the Reagan administration and Shultz argued strongly that the contras needed to be supported in order to keep pressure on the Sandinistas given the ongoing Contadora talks and US–Nicaraguan talks in Manzanillo, Mexico. Senator Boland rejected this assertion.[100] Disappointed, but undeterred, the Reagan administration was preoccupied with the forthcoming Nicaraguan general elections on 4 November. This date was significant as it was selected by the GRN in order that the Sandinistas would be seen as a democratically elected government prior to the anticipated re-election of Reagan on 6 November.[101] The results of the Nicaraguan elections were denounced by both the Reagan administration and the Thatcher government despite the protestations of many of the 400 international observers who believed the elections to have been free and fair, including Lord Pratap C. Chitnis, an independent political observer and a Liberal member of the House of Lords.[102] In fact, the UK was the only European government not to send official observers to the Nicaraguan elections. Howe informed the Cabinet on 8 November that, although the electoral mechanisms appeared to have functioned 'reasonably well' in Nicaragua, the picture did not take into account events in the period leading up to the elections. He pointed to the non-participation of the main conservative and liberal opposition groups in the elections.[103] The Thatcher government's rejection of the results was seen in British and American circles as evidence of Thatcher's sympathy with US views on the Sandinistas. The Sandinistas won almost 67 per cent of the votes in the election, which had an estimated turnout of 75.4 per cent of all registered voters in Nicaragua.[104] These landslide results invariably helped to increase the legitimacy of Nicaraguan claims against the US in both the ICJ and the UN.

The UK and Blowpipe missiles

Shortly after the Nicaraguan elections, US officials approached a British national, Major David Walker, for help in Nicaragua. In a memo sent from North to McFarlane dated 4 December 1984, North informed McFarlane that he had met with Walker at the request of the US Secretary of the Navy, John Lehman. Walker was a former SAS commander and then head of the Keenie Meenie Services (KMS) and Saladin security companies, which provided security assistance to foreign governments around the world. During this meeting Walker offered his services (via KMS) to help the FDN in special operations, in particular, operations designed to destroy Soviet HIND helicopters, which were detrimental to the contra efforts in Nicaragua. Following this meeting, North sent McFarlane a note advising him that: 'Unless otherwise directed, Walker will be introduced to Calero and efforts will be made to defray the cost of Walker's operations from other than Calero's limited assets.'[105] By using Walker and his team of mercenaries the US hoped to prove to the Sandinistas that the contras had both the contacts and funds to perform dangerous operations in Nicaragua. The attack on the Soviet helicopters was later cancelled as Walker allegedly believed the operation to be too dangerous.[106] Nevertheless, the Jersey-based KMS played a substantive role in training some of the contras and in delivering military equipment into Nicaragua. North and Walker worked closely together over a two-year period in organising contra-led attacks on various Nicaraguan installations, including airports and arms depots.[107]

Both McFarlane and North considered approaching Thatcher for help with the contras in late December 1984. The documents do not bear the hand-written initials 'RR' which denoted that the President had read and approved them. Therefore, it is difficult to determine if the President was aware of such considerations. However, the documents imply that Thatcher was considered to be a viable person of interest in terms of providing help to the contras. The Prime Minister's name is redacted in the documents and is replaced by the words 'a European Country Leader'. It is probable that this refers to Thatcher as the memo also refers to HMG. A memo from McFarlane to Reagan stated that the US: 'have been apprised that the Chilean Government is prepared to provide up to 48 Blowpipe surface-to-air missiles to the freedom fighters' (Blowpipes were manufactured by the then UK government-owned Short Brothers Company in Belfast, Northern Ireland).[108] It further stated:

> The Chileans indicate that they need to have permission from HMG to transfer these missiles which apparently were staged in Chile during the Falklands War. These weapons; or something similar (e.g. SA-7's) are essential if the resistance is to stay in the fight now that the Sandinistas are employing their Soviet-provided MI-24 HIND-D helicopters.[109]

Although it was noted that the Chilean government had not yet approached the 'European Country Leader' at that point, it was suggested that: 'we should very privately express approbation for any that (the European Country Leader) is willing to do in support of their cause'.[110] The memo also stated that the US was willing to offer the European Country Leader 'a very discrete briefing' on the Soviet bloc build-up in Nicaragua and the relevant consequences should the resistance be forced to 'go it alone'.[111]

In a similar memo sent by North to McFarlane on 20 December 1984, it was suggested that the President might wish to raise such 'sensitive issues' during the European Country Leader's forthcoming visit to Washington. Thatcher was scheduled to visit Washington two days later on 22 December. According to this memo, the person behind the idea of giving Chilean Blowpipe missiles to the contras was Major Walker, who had agreed to assist in special mission planning and training for the Nicaraguan resistance. The memo claimed that Walker informed the US that the missiles 'may be available in Chile for use by the FDN in dealing with HIND helicopters'.[112] This information was then passed to Calero, who, in turn, visited Santiago, Chile. Following Calero's visit, it was confirmed that, along with the Blowpipe missiles, Chile was willing to provide between five to eight missile launchers. The Chilean government would charge US$15,000 for each of the launchers, but would provide the missiles free of charge.[113]

It was noted that the Chileans required 'British permission for the transfer' (for such a deal to move forward the British government would have to issue a re-export licence) and that they were also willing to provide training on the weapons systems for up to ten three-man teams from the FDN. The memo suggested that the US had been planning to approach the Thatcher government for some time regarding the possibility of providing aid to the resistance in Nicaragua: 'You will recall that before the June Summit we discussed the matter of (the European Country's) aid to the resistance'.[114] (Reagan and Thatcher both attended the London G7 Economic Summit on 7–9 June). The memo concluded that approaching the leader during the forthcoming visit 'may be the best opportunity we have to obtain such support for the resistance. Given recent actions in Nicaragua, we may not have another chance if we wait.'[115]

During Thatcher's visit to Camp David the subject of Central America was discussed at length. This was an important meeting for the President as he wished to convey his appreciation for Thatcher's support of the US, particularly in Central America. According to briefing notes provided prior to this meeting, the UK

Figure 6 Speaking during a break in meetings at Camp David, 22 December 1984

was the Reagan administration's 'strongest supporter on Central America', and had a 'sympathetic understanding' of US concerns and policy. However, the briefing notes stated that some reassurance was required as 'not even the British are immune to concern that we are opposing any Contadora agreement and that we might resort to direct use of force against Nicaragua'.[116] The briefing paper also stated that the UK regularly sought in-depth briefings on the issue to avoid being 'blindsided' in Parliament. The notes also stated that Howe conveyed such concerns to the US in a letter dated 2 October 1984.[117] During the meeting itself, Thatcher observed that the Soviets seemed to be sending additional shipments of arms to Nicaragua. She was particularly concerned when Reagan confirmed the presence of MIG aircraft aboard ships destined for Nicaragua. The Prime Minister agreed that the situation was 'very worrying' as it was difficult for the Americans to determine the cargoes that the ships were carrying due to poor visibility.[118] There is, however, no record of the Blowpipe missiles being discussed at this meeting. The Blowpipe matter appears to have been temporarily shelved by the US. It would resurface again in 1986 and 1987 (see sections below).

Throughout this time the US continued to engage in perfunctory bilateral talks with Nicaragua in Manzanillo. The US called for the removal of Cuban and Soviet military advisers from Nicaragua within a ninety-day period, and called for a 'redesigning of Nicaragua's internal political system' in return for a rethinking of US policy in Nicaragua.[119] The talks reached an inevitable stalemate on 18 January 1985 when the US officially suspended talks, thereby abandoning its part in the Contadora peace process. Shortly after the failure of these talks, the newly appointed Vice-President of Nicaragua, Sergio Ramírez Mercado, made a visit to the UK.

Sergio Ramírez visits the UK

In early February 1985, Sergio Ramírez met with both Thatcher and Howe in London. The Vice-President was in the capital to meet the Foreign Affairs Committee, opposition party leaders and to attend a debate at the Oxford Union on US policy in Central America. For Thatcher and Howe, the visit was the perfect opportunity for 'some plain speaking and to counter any misleading impressions which he might obtain from his other contacts about British attitudes'.[120] Meetings were held on 6 and 8 February, during which Howe made British concerns known to Sergio Ramírez regarding the size of the Nicaraguan army and the build-up of Soviet arms in the country, which the UK believed had a 'destabilising effect' on neighbouring countries.[121] Howe also explained the reasons why the UK had concluded that conditions for fair elections in Nicaragua in 1984 had not been upheld, that is, censorship of the press and mob attacks on opposition party leaders. The Vice-President, for his part, asked the UK in its capacity as a close friend to the US to convey to the Americans Nicaragua's wish to urgently renew bilateral negotiations. In return for such negotiations Nicaragua was willing to make a 'formal commitment within Contadora that the USSR [Union of Soviet Socialist Republics] would be given no military or communications facilities of any kind'.[122]

222

Sergio Ramírez spoke of a strengthening of provisions for the verification and implementation of a Contadora Treaty, which would include a definitive timetable for freezing arms levels, an end to cross-border arms smuggling and a withdrawal of all foreign advisers from Nicaragua. He also stated that the verification could involve outside countries, including those of Western Europe, Latin America and Canada. The Vice-President dismissed allegations of fraudulent elections and asserted that all political parties in Nicaragua would have the opportunity to express their views on the new constitution through the establishment of a Joint Commission. Howe later informed Langhorne Motley, who was visiting London at the time, of the substance of the visit. Motley was quick to argue that pressure from the contras was 'a necessary incentive to make the Nicaraguans negotiate seriously on Contadora'.[123] According to Motley, the US had postponed further bilateral talks as Nicaragua tried to use these talks as an alternative to the Contadora process. Motley asserted that without 'positive movement from Nicaragua on Contadora it would be difficult to resume Manzanillo talks'.[124]

Thatcher used her meeting with the Vice-President to express her concern over the substantial build-up of Soviet arms, troops and foreign military advisers in Nicaragua, and the Nicaraguan support for attempts made in Central America to destabilise democratic governments.[125] According to the Prime Minister: 'I made clear that the Government's future relations with Nicaragua would be determined by progress towards establishing genuine democracy there, scaling down of armaments and the cessation of support for subversion.'[126] Thatcher's and Howe's meetings with Sergio Ramírez highlighted a similarity in Anglo-American views towards the Sandinista government in Nicaragua. This did not go unnoticed in the US.

Thatcher was scheduled to visit Washington for bilateral talks with Reagan shortly afterwards on 20 February. In anticipation of this visit, Shultz sent a memo to Reagan stating that the Prime Minister was a 'staunch supporter' of US Central American policy, but admitted that this posed a number of difficulties for Thatcher on the domestic front:

She faces frequent criticism from an opposition Labor Party which is quite sympathetic to the Sandinistas ... Mrs Thatcher met with Nicaraguan Vice President during his recent visit to London. Thatcher will want to know whether we will continue to support Contadora and that we do not intend to use force directly against Nicaragua. You may wish to reassure her on these points.[127]

According to another memo sent by McFarlane to Reagan before the visit, Anglo-American relations remained 'close and special', and Thatcher was praised as among Reagan's 'strongest and most vocal supporters'. McFarlane referred to the Prime Minister's meeting with Sergio Ramírez and stated that she was 'very firm and critical of the Sandinistas in this meeting. You sent her a cable of thanks.'[128] Clearly, Thatcher's support was much appreciated by the US. However, it is also clear that Thatcher was not prepared to support the US on such a contentious matter as US policy in Latin America without regular briefing at the highest levels. Such a focus on US objectives in Latin America appears to contradict the perception in British circles that Latin America, with the exception of the Falkland Islands, was of little interest or importance to the Thatcher government.

Ingham suggests that apart from the Falklands, Latin American policy scarcely crossed his desk.[129] Powell supports this assertion as he argues: 'Latin America was of no importance to the Thatcher government outside of the context of the Falklands War'.[130] Hooper opines that the UK's position in general towards Latin America in the 1980s was 'not close enough'.[131] For his part, Carrington laughingly suggests that Thatcher had 'enough problems with Europe without bothering with Latin America'.[132] Kinnock, too, believes that Central and Latin America was overlooked by the Thatcher government. He suggests that the region 'virtually disappeared off the British map which, of course was a huge mistake. That predated the Falklands and it followed from the Falklands.'[133]

In Nicaragua, the contra forces declared unity among the resistance forces with the San José Declaration on 2 March 1985. The declaration was signed by contra leaders Adolfo Calero, Alfonso Robelo and Arturo Cruz Porras, and marked a renewed impetus in the contra fight against the Sandinistas.[134] In response, the Reagan administration unsuccessfully lobbied Congress on 23 April for additional funding for the contras. On 1 May 1985, Reagan signed Executive Order 12513 prohibiting trade between the US and Nicaragua. According to this, Nicaragua constituted 'an unusual and extraordinary threat to the national security and foreign policy of the United States'. Reagan declared a 'national emergency' to deal with this threat and prohibited all Nicaraguan imports into the US and all US exports to Nicaragua except those destined for the 'organized democratic resistance'.[135] This represented another way for the US to destabilise the Nicaraguan economy whilst safeguarding the contras. Despite the international condemnation surrounding the trade embargo, Congress passed a bill on 12 June approving US$27 million in humanitarian assistance to the contras. The Reagan administration was ecstatic. The DOD subsequently established a Nicaraguan Humanitarian Assistance Office to distribute the funds.

'The Enterprise', Blowpipes and the Iran–Contra scandal

During 1985, the US became more actively involved in the illegal funding of the 'freedom fighters'. Following the first Boland Amendment, North began a secret operation in order to supply military equipment and money to the contras. 'The Enterprise', as the operation was otherwise known, was a highly successful venture with aircraft, airfields, ships, Swiss bank accounts and secure communications at its disposal.[136] The operation functioned well under the guidance of McFarlane, Casey, Poindexter and North. McFarlane travelled to Honduras in early 1985, along with North, Nestor Sanchez and Negroponte, to meet Calero to see how the contras were progressing. This was part of a visit to many Central American countries by the US delegation, and provided an excellent opportunity for McFarlane to urge Calero and the contras to improve their military performance. He reminded Calero that there were a lot of people in Congress who were sympathetic to the contra cause, but were hesitant to vote for funding until the contras could demonstrate that they were capable of military victories.[137]

It was also during 1985 that Israeli officials approached McFarlane with a proposal to sell arms to Iran in return for the release of US hostages held captive in Beirut. The hope in US circles was that such a deal would help to improve strained US–Iranian relations. This was a perilous venture as such a deal would not only be in violation of the Arms Export Control Act, it would also be morally questionable given that Iran was deemed to be a sponsor of terrorism at the time. Nonetheless, the plan was considered a viable option by McFarlane as the Israeli officials offered to act as broker between Iran and the US. The plan was discussed on 6 August in a meeting between Reagan, McFarlane and Shultz in the White House. However, this was not an easy decision for Reagan to make given the illegality of the actions and Shultz' inherent opposition to the idea. Shultz stated emphatically during the meeting that the idea 'had to be stopped'.[138] On 30 August, Israel shipped 508 US tube-launched, optically-tracked, wire-guided (TOW) antitank missiles to Iran. Reagan subsequently authorised the sale of US arms to Israel to replenish their stockpiles.[139] On 15 September, one of the US hostages, Reverend Benjamin Weir, was released in Lebanon.

The US–Israeli plan was expanded upon following a meeting in London on 8 December between North, McFarlane, the British-born Director General of the Israeli Foreign Ministry, David Kimche, Israeli arms dealers Yaacov Nimrodi and Adolph Schwimmer, and retired US Air Force General Richard Secord. The group was brought together by an Iranian contact of the Reagan administration, Manucher Ghorbanifar. The purpose of the meeting was for McFarlane (then a private citizen) to try to secure the release of the remaining US hostages and to try to broker improved US relations with pro-Western moderates in Iran. According to a note written by North to Ghorbanifar following the meeting, no further deliveries of arms would be made by the US to Iran until all US hostages were released.[140] It was during this visit to London that the UK became aware of the arms for hostages deal. The meeting with Ghorbanifar was not bugged, but a meeting between North, McFarlane and Kimche in the hotel suite in which the Americans were staying was bugged by Britain's MI5 intelligence services. MI5 informed MI6, the intelligence services responsible for foreign intelligence, who then informed the CIA.[141] It seems inconceivable that Thatcher and relevant high-ranking government officials would not have been informed of the events. Thus, it is probable that the Thatcher government knew of such illegal US activities a year before the *Al Shiraa* magazine revelations.

On 7 January 1986, a meeting was held in the Oval Office with Reagan, Casey, Bush, Shultz, Weinberger, McFarlane and Poindexter in attendance. US Attorney General Edwin 'Ed' Meese also attended the meeting to give his legal opinion on the possibility of the arms for hostages deal. While Weinberger and Shultz steadfastly opposed the idea, Reagan was noncommittal. Poindexter sent Reagan a memo on 17 January recommending that the President sign a Covert Action Finding on Iran. It detailed the possibilities for such a deal and recommended that due to the 'extreme sensitivity' of the project, the President should exercise his 'statutory prerogative' to withhold notification of the Finding to Congress until such time as Reagan deemed appropriate.[142] On the same day, Reagan signed an Intelligence Finding which authorised the sale of US arms to Iran. The finding was for the purpose of:

(1) establishing a more moderate government in Iran, (2) obtaining from them significant intelligence not otherwise attainable, to determine the current Iranian government's intentions with respect to its neighbors and with respect to terrorist acts, and (3) furthering the release of the American hostages held in Beirut and preventing additional terrorist acts by these groups.[143]

The suggestion that certain officials in the Thatcher government knew of the arms for hostages deal is strengthened by a visit to Washington on 20 February by two of Thatcher's most trusted advisers, Antony Acland and Chairman of the JIC Sir Percy Cradock. During this visit Acland and Cradock met with Poindexter and allegedly discussed reports of a US arms for hostages deal in the Middle East. British concerns were heightened by Poindexter's evasive response to the British line of questioning.[144] Little did the British know, but the US had just begun to bypass

Israeli mediators by selling arms directly to Iran. The US charged inflated prices for the weapons and partial profits of these sales were subsequently funnelled to the contras. It is estimated that of the US$48 million in profits made from such arms deals, US$16.5 million went to support the contras, US$1.2 million was lodged to Swiss bank accounts and the rest was used for various other operations.[145] The US shipped an additional 1,000 TOWs to Iran during the month of February.

The question of US acquisition of Blowpipe missiles resurfaced in March 1986. North had continued in his efforts to acquire the missiles for the contras and informed McFarlane of his efforts on 26 March:

> We are trying to find a way to get 10 BLOWPIPE [sic] launchers and 20 missiles from (a South American Country) thru the Short Bros. Rep ... Short Bros ... is willing to arrange the deal, conduct the training and even send U.K. 'tech reps' fwd [sic] if we can close the arrangement.[146]

McFarlane replied to North on 4 April: 'I've been thinking about the blowpipe problem and the Contras. Could you ask the CIA to identify which countries the Brits have sold them to. I ought to have a contact in at least one of them.'[147] This correspondence further suggests that the UK was considered a conduit for the provision of Blowpipe missiles to the contras.

McFarlane and NSC staff member, Howard Teicher, travelled to Iran on 25 May to participate in talks with Iranian spokespersons. They stopped in Israel en route to pick up North and Secord. The group were met in Tehran's Mehrabad airport on board a private American jet that contained missile spare parts and weaponry along with gifts to the Iranians, including a Bible with a handwritten verse by Reagan (a fact that would later cause much embarrassment for the White House) and a key-shaped chocolate cake symbolising improved US–Iranian relations.[148]

North wrote to Poindexter on 10 June regarding the Blowpipe issue: 'We should look to going back to a head of an allied government on the blowpipes if we are going to do anything at all about outside support in the next few days, and I wd [sic] love to carry the letter from RR.'[149] The UK was the only allied government which manufactured Blowpipes. This would strongly suggest that the Thatcher government knew, and was possibly involved in, a deal with the US to supply Blowpipes to the contras.

Meanwhile, the Reagan administration continued to champion the cause of the contras in the US. In his Address to the Nation on 24 June Reagan stated: 'The Sandinistas call these freedom fighters contras for counterrevolutionaries. But the real counter-revolutionaries are the Sandinista commandantes, who betrayed the hopes of the Nicaraguan revolution and sold out their country to the Soviet empire.'[150] The timing of this speech was propitious; the following day CBS aired a programme on the private aid network to the contras. On 27 June, the ICJ, following an appeal from Nicaragua, again denounced US aggression in Nicaragua and upheld Nicaragua's claim for reparations for damages caused by the US. The amount of reparations was unspecified, but was estimated to be in the region of between US$17 and $18 billion.[151] This verdict gave the Sandinistas political leverage against the US on the international stage. However, the US refused, yet again, to comply with the ICJ ruling.

On 31 July, the UNSC voted for full compliance with the ICJ rulings of 26 November 1984 and 27 June 1986 against US activi-ties in Nicaragua. The US vetoed the resolution and found an ally in the UK, who chose to abstain from the vote. The decision to abstain from voting was not popular within UK political circles. Howe, in particular, believed that the UK should uphold interna-tional judgments as a matter of principle. He later wrote in his memoirs: 'I had no doubt that we should support that proposition ... This was yet another occasion on which Margaret insisted on carrying the "special" relationship perhaps one bridge too far.'[152] Howe further suggests: 'we had agreed in principle that we would endorse ICJ judgments routinely. Margaret didn't like us doing that, so there was a dissent between us. Not a matter of great seri-ousness, but a matter of irritation and principle.'[153] Thatcher later defended the UK's abstention from the UNSC vote: 'Although we had no legal objection to the resolution, we were not prepared to support the attempt by Nicaragua to exploit a legal judgment for its own [interruption] political ends.'[154]

The US again found British support in a UNGA vote on 3 November, which called for the US government to comply with the ICJ ruling of 27 June. The UK, France and West Germany abstained from the vote much to the delight of the Reagan administration. However, this delight was short-lived when the clandestine nature of US actions in Nicaragua was revealed by the *Al Shiraa* revelations on the same day. Reagan and the NSC were unceremoniously thrust into a political quagmire that threatened the credibility and possible future of the Reagan administration. The scandal rocked the White House as the media questioned the extent of Reagan's participation in the illegal operations. There were talks on Capitol Hill of the President's possible impeachment and criminal indictments for those who orchestrated the plan. However, Reagan vehemently denied all knowledge of the arms for hostages deal and resisted calls from members of Congress for his 'scalp'. The President was ultimately spared impeachment proceedings, but his approval ratings dropped sharply in the weeks following the revelations.[155] On 13 November, Reagan addressed the issue in a nationally televised address during which he admitted authorising a small shipment of arms to Iran, but denied that he knew it was part of a trade for hostages. The President tried to allay the nation's concerns as he stated:

> Our government has a firm policy not to capitulate to terrorist demands. That no concessions policy remains in force, in spite of the wildly speculative and false stories about arms for hostages and alleged ransom payments. We did not – repeat – did not trade weapons or anything else for hostages, nor will we.[156]

Incredibly, despite the mounting domestic and international condemnation of US actions, the Reagan administration continued in its quest to secure arms for the contras. On 14 November, the Blowpipe matter resurfaced when Poindexter received a memo from Special Assistant to the President for National Security Affairs Raymond F. Burghardt regarding British concurrence for the use of Blowpipe missiles in Nicaragua. The memo was received the day before a scheduled visit by Thatcher to the US. It included suggested talking points for the President for use during his meeting with Thatcher, including a suggestion that Reagan should outline his appreciation for Britain's abstention from the UN vote on Nicaragua. The memo (most of which is redacted) also stated: 'There is another Central American issue of which you could help us. Nicaraguan freedom fighters must be able to deal with Soviet helicopters. Our experts say your Blowpipe missiles would be ideal.'[157] Clearly, the Blowpipe issue remained an important matter for the US. However, there is no documentary evidence to suggest that Reagan raised the issue directly with Thatcher during her visit to the US.

Thatcher's support

Thatcher travelled to Camp David on 15 November 1986 and proved to be a valuable ally to the President. When questioned during a press conference on the Iran–Contra revelations she replied: 'I believe implicitly in the President's integrity on that subject.'[158] In his diary entry on 15 November, Reagan wrote of Thatcher's support: 'Later in Wash. [sic] she did a press conf. [sic] & went to bat for us. Most helpful.'[159] US media coverage of the scandal did not abate and Reagan was forced to address the issue again on 25 November during a White House press conference. The President announced that he had directed Meese and White House Chief of Staff Donald T. Regan, to review NSC conduct in the arms for hostages deal. Reagan stated: 'This report led me to conclude that I was not fully informed on the nature of one of the activities undertaken in connection with this initiative. This action raises serious questions of propriety.'[160] Reagan announced that North had been relieved of his duties and that Poindexter had returned to another assignment in the Navy.[161] He also announced that a Special Review Board would be established to conduct a comprehensive review of the NSC's involvement in Iran–Contra. On 26 November, a presidential commission known as the Tower Commission was established under the guidance of former Republican Senator John Tower at its head along with former US Secretary of State Edmund Muskie and former National Security Advisor to President Ford Brent Scowcroft.

Figure 7 Welcoming a friend before their Camp David meetings, 15 November 1986

Figure 8 The pair walking at Camp David, 15 November 1986

Reagan spoke before the Tower Commission on 2 December and denied any role in authorising the arms deal with Iran.

In the UK, Thatcher was keen to provide moral support to her friend as the media feasted on the scandal. In a warm handwritten letter to Reagan on 4 December, Thatcher offered the following words of comfort:

> you and Nancy are in my thoughts at this difficult time. The press and the media are always so ready to criticise and get people down. I know what it's like . . . Whatever happened over Iran is in the past . . . Denis joins me in sending you and Nancy our affectionate good wishes and support.[162]

This support was welcomed by Reagan as official investigations into the scandal were gathering pace in Washington. A House Select Committee to Investigate Covert Arms Transactions with Iran and a Senate Select Committee on Secret Military Assistance to Iran and the Nicaraguan Opposition were formed in January 1987 to investigate the affair (their so-called 'Iran–Contra hearings' would last from 5 May 1987 to 6 August 1987). Meanwhile, the Tower Commission report was released on 26 February, and although critical of Reagan's lack of control over his NSC staff, it concluded that the President did not know about the diversion of funds to the contras via the arms for hostages deal. While this was welcomed by the White House, the Iran–Contra scandal continued to plague the Reagan administration. On 4 March, Reagan addressed the nation and admitted that he had authorised the arms for hostages deal. The President stated:

> A few months ago I told the American people I did not trade arms for hostages. My heart and my best intentions still tell me that's true, but the facts and the evidence tell me it is not . . . It was a mistake . . . I let my personal concern for the hostages spill over into the geopolitical strategy of reaching out to Iran.[163]

Reagan denied any knowledge of the diversion of funds to the contras. The Iran–Contra scandal continued, but it did not derail US plans to acquire Blowpipe missiles from the UK.

Confidential US sources claimed in late February 1987 that the Thatcher government had given preliminary approval for the sale of Blowpipe missiles to the US. Sources claimed that 150 missiles were to be sold along with thirty shoulder-held launchers. If true, this was a significant increase in number as initially discussed between North, McFarlane and Poindexter. The Thatcher government denied supplying arms to North, but refused to comment on any future possible sales of Blowpipe missiles.[164] As a result, Thatcher faced increasing demands at home to address Britain's alleged supply of Blowpipes to the US. In a House of Commons session on 12 May, the Prime Minister's response was unambiguous: 'I can say categorically that we have not agreed to supply Blowpipe and we have not supplied Blowpipe to the Contras.'[165] The allegations did not affect the newly re-elected Prime Minister's commitment to close Anglo-American relations. Thatcher wrote to Reagan on 15 June: 'I want to assure you that my resolve to maintain the special relationship which exists between Britain and the United States is as strong as ever.'[166]

Two weeks later, Thatcher was again questioned on the Blowpipe issue in a debate in the House of Commons, where she stated: 'I am advised that there is no evidence of the presence or use of Blowpipe missiles in Nicaragua. The United States Government assured us that there are no Blowpipe missiles in Contra hands and that they have no intention to supply them.'[167] The Prime Minister proved her unwavering loyalty to Reagan during a press conference for American correspondents in Downing Street on 3 July. When questioned about the negative effect of the Iran–Contra crisis on Reagan's political vitality Thatcher replied: 'I do not think that it has had that effect on America's international standing.'[168] Thatcher's loyalty to Reagan was reinforced during a brief visit to Washington on 16–17 July. During a meeting with Shultz on 17 July, the Prime Minister expressed her 'consternation and dismay' over congressional and media handling of the Iran–Contra affair. Thatcher said that she had used her interviews in Washington to support Reagan and to emphasise 'the importance to the western world of continued strong US leadership'.[169]

One of the many interviews the Prime Minister gave during her visit was an interview to the CBS programme *Face the Nation* on

Figure 9 The closest of allies. Speaking on the patio outside the Oval Office, 17 July 1987

the morning of her arrival. The programme's presenter, Lesley Stahl, sought to press the Prime Minister on the scandal, but Thatcher refused to be drawn into any negative press. Instead, Thatcher referred to her friendship with the US and admonished Stahl for 'taking far too downbeat a view'.[170] The Prime Minister defended the US and its leader: 'America is a strong country with a great president, a great people and a great future.'[171] The programme aired on 19 July and was considered a resounding success by the Reagan administration. In his diary entry of the same day Reagan wrote: 'Watched Sun. talk show – Margaret Thatcher on Face the Nation was absolutely magnificent & left Lady Stahl a little limp.'[172] This was a very public display of loyalty to Reagan by Thatcher, who later wrote in her memoirs: 'I was determined to do what I could to help President Reagan ride out the storm.'[173]

Reagan was quick to telephone his friend to thank her for her valued support. In the middle of a Cabinet meeting the President put down the telephone for the Prime Minister to hear the rapturous applause of his Cabinet in appreciation of her support on *Face the Nation*. This was a unique and touching tribute to the Prime Minister. Thatcher had firmly ingratiated herself to both Reagan and his administration. As Powell recalls:

> when President Reagan was under attack for sending arms to Nicaragua, to combat the Sandinistas, she came out strongly in support, publicly, on television, of the US . . . it really was unique . . . It was an act of friendship and she was ready to deploy her political capital in the US, which was quite considerable. She helped her friend.[174]

In the US, the Iran–Contra hearings continued to divulge shocking revelations as key figures, including North and Poindexter, gave evidence regarding the extent of their complicity in the illegal arms deal with Iran. However, upon their completion all three investigating committees failed to implicate Reagan in the illegal operations. The President, although bruised from the affair, emerged relatively unscathed (with the exception of a temporary, but notable, drop in approval ratings). Reagan's inability to monitor the activities of his own administration was criticised by the investigating committees, but he was ultimately exonerated. In fact, the Senate Select Committee concluded that the scandal had 'resulted from the failure of individuals to observe the law, not from any deficiencies in existing law or in our system of government'.[175]

Thatcher's unwavering support during the Iran–Contra crisis demonstrated that the Special Relationship was very much alive and well between both leaders. The Prime Minister's refusal to criticise Reagan and her many words of comfort were much welcomed by the beleaguered President. Indeed, Thatcher proved herself a valuable ally in the face of both domestic and international criticism regarding US activities in Latin America, in particular, in Nicaragua. This staunch support helped the Prime Minister to consolidate a position of greater strength within the Anglo-

American alliance. Thatcher's political capital was thereafter forti-fied in Washington. Writing in his memoirs, Shultz opined: 'The president had immense confidence in her, and her views carried great weight.'[176] This was a fitting depiction of the Prime Minister, who had resisted domestic pressure to condemn US foreign policy objectives in Latin America and had faced potentially damaging allegations concerning possible British involvement in the provision of Blowpipe missiles for use by the contras.

Notes

1. Reagan saw El Salvador as a key component in stabilising the Latin American region. Thus, the Reagan administration supported various Salvadoran governments in the fight against leftist rebel groups, in particular, the Frente Farabundo Martí para la Liberación Nacional (FMLN, National Liberation Front), throughout the 1980s. For more information on US–Salvadoran relations under the Reagan administration, see: Lester D. Langley, *America and the Americas: The United States in the Western Hemisphere*, 2nd edn (Athens, GA: University of Georgia Press, 2010), pp. 260–5; C. William Walldorf, Jr, *Just Politics: Human Rights and the Foreign Policy of Great Powers* (New York: Cornell University Press, 2008), pp. 155–63. More generally, see Michael McClintock, *The American Connection, vol. 1: State Terror and Popular Resistance in El Salvador* (London: Zed Books, 1985); Edward A. Lynch, *The Cold War's Last Battlefield: Reagan, the Soviets and Central America* (Albany, NY: State University of New York Press, 2011).
2. For more information on the development of US–Nicaraguan relations prior to the Reagan administration, see Thomas W. Walker and Christine J. Wade, *Nicaragua: Living in the Shadow of the Eagle* (Boulder, CO: Westview Press, 2011); Bernard Diederich, *Somoza and the Legacy of US Involvement in Central America* (Princeton, NJ: Markus Wiener, 2007).
3. Anastasio Somoza Debayle was first sworn in as President of Nicaragua from 1 May 1967 to 1 May 1972. For a two-year period following his rule, Nicaragua was run by a junta under the de facto influence of Somoza Debayle, who maintained his position as leader of the National Guard (Nicaragua's national army). During this time Nicaragua's constitution was rewritten

to allow Somoza Debayle to run again for the presidency in 1974. He assumed the office of President of Nicaragua for the second time on 1 December 1974. The FSLN was created in 1961 by Tomás Borge Martínez, Silvio Mayorga and José Carlos Fonseca Amador as a revolutionary group committed to the overthrow of the Somoza dynasty in Nicaragua. The FSLN's popularity grew steadily and by the 1970s it appealed to both student and peasant groups across Nicaragua.

4. For more on the formation of Los Doce, see Kenneth E. Morris, *Unfinished Revolution: Daniel Ortega and Nicaragua's Struggle for Liberation* (Chicago, IL: Lawrence Hill Books, 2010), p. 80; Matilde Zimmermann, *Sandinista: Carlos Fonseca and the Nicaraguan Revolution* (Durham, NC: Duke University Press, 2004), p. 212.

5. Hazel Smith, *Nicaragua: Self-determination and Survival* (London: Pluto Press, 1993), pp. 124–5.

6. Martha L. Cottam, *Images and Intervention: US Policies in Latin America* (Pittsburgh, PA: University of Pittsburgh Press, 1994), p. 98.

7. For more information on the 'final offensive', see Holly Sklar, *Washington's War on Nicaragua* (Boston, MA: South End Press, 1988), pp. 25–7.

8. These reforms worried the US as the agricultural ownership laws in Nicaragua were altered to create cooperatives and state-owned farms. In the US, this was seen as being consistent with the Soviet system of state ownership, collective farming and a command economy.

9. Directorate of Intelligence report, 'Nicaragua: Arms Build-up', 1982, p. 1, file: Central America 1982, box 1, William P. Clark Files, Africa–Central American Commission, Ronald Reagan Library.

10. Carothers, *In the Name of Democracy*, p. 81.

11. Daniel K. Inouye *et al.* (eds), *Report of the Congressional Committees Investigating the Iran–Contra Affair: With Minority Views* (New York: Random House, 1988), p. 37.

12. Sklar, *Washington's War*, p. 63.

13. Haig, *Caveat*, p. 109.

14. Carothers, *In the Name of Democracy*, p. 82; Robert A. Pastor, *Condemned to Repetition: The United States and Nicaragua* (Princeton, NJ: Princeton University Press, 1987), p. 233.

15. Nicaragua Talking Points, 5 February 1981, pp. 1–2, file: NSC

00001, 6 February 1981, (Caribbean Basin and Poland) (1/2), box 91282, Executive Secretariat NSC Meeting Files, Ronald Reagan Library.

16. *Ibid.*, pp. 1–2.
17. Haig, *Caveat*, p. 140.
18. James M. Scott, 'Interbranch rivalry and the Reagan Doctrine in Nicaragua', *Political Science Quarterly*, 112(2) (Summer 1997): 237–60, at pp. 240–1.
19. Thomas W. Walker, *Reagan versus the Sandinistas: The Undeclared War on Nicaragua* (Boulder, CO: Westview Press, 1987), p. 22.
20. LeoGrande, *Our Own Backyard*, pp. 114–15; Morris, *Unfinished Revolution*, p. 138; Peter Schweizer, *Reagan's War: The Epic Story of His Forty-Year Struggle and Final Triumph over Communism* (New York: Anchor Books, 2003), pp. 204–5.
21. Walker, *Reagan versus the Sandinistas*, p. 24.
22. Binns, *United States in Honduras*, p. 195.
23. William I. Robinson and Kent Norsworthy, *David and Goliath: Washington's War against Nicaragua* (London: Zed Books, 1987), p. 46.
24. Lynn Horton, *Peasants in Arms: War and Peace in the Mountains of Nicaragua, 1979–1994* (Athens, OH: Ohio University Press, 1998), p. 124.
25. Sklar, *Washington's War*, pp. 75–6.
26. Briefing paper, 'Supporting Evidence on Nicaragua's Threatening Activities', p. 6, n.d., file: Nicaragua US Policy in Central America (2), box 4, William P. Clark Files, Ronald Reagan Library.
27. Roy Gutman, *Banana Diplomacy: The Making of American Policy in Nicaragua, 1981–1987* (New York: Simon & Schuster, 1988), p. 65.
28. Bill of Particulars, 'Nicaragua under the Sandinistas', p. 2, n.d., file: Nicaragua, US Policy in Central America (2), William P. Clark Files, Ronald Reagan Library.
29. Scott, 'Interbranch rivalry', p. 242.
30. Robinson and Norsworthy, *David and Goliath*, p. 85.
31. Haig to Carrington, 31 August 1981, p. 3, file: UK (1/20/81–8/31/81) (3/6), box 20, Executive Secretariat NSC Country Files, Europe and the Soviet Union, Ronald Reagan Library.
32. TNA, PREM 19/1152, Henderson to FCO, 21 March 1981.
33. Alexander Cockburn and Jeffrey St. Clair, *Whiteout: The CIA, Drugs and the Press* (London: Verso, 1998), p. 5.

34. Carothers, *In the Name of Democracy*, p. 83; Reagan, *The Reagan Diaries*, p. 48.
35. David Ryan, *US–Sandinista Diplomatic Relations: Voice of Intolerance* (Basingstoke: Macmillan, 1995), p. 21
36. Gail E. S. Yoshitani, *Reagan on War: A Reappraisal of the Weinberger Doctrine, 1980–1984* (College Station, TX: Texas A&M University Press, 2011), p. 56.
37. John Prados, *Safe for Democracy: The Secret Wars of the CIA* (Chicago, IL: Ivan R. Dee, 2006), p. 496.
38. TNA, OD 28/385, FCO memo regarding closure of embassies in Tegucigalpa and Managua, n.d. British representation in Nicaragua was withdrawn on 'economy grounds'.
39. TNA, FCO 99/350, Somoza to Thatcher, 1979.
40. *Ibid.*, notes for House of Commons debate on Foreign Affairs, n.d.
41. Hazel Smith, *European Union Foreign Policy and Central America* (Basingstoke: Macmillan, 1995), p. 118.
42. TNA, FCO 99/350, GRN to the UK government, 12 July 1979.
43. *Ibid.*, Lord Carrington memo regarding Nicaragua, 31 July 1979.
44. *Ibid.*, Perceval to Parsons, 23 July 1979.
45. TNA, FCO 99/625, Background brief on Nicaragua, May 1980.
46. TNA, FCO 99/561, Ridley memo regarding Nicaragua, 13 May 1980, p. 3. Ridley admitted in his memoirs that he was 'bitterly disappointed' at finding himself dealing with the problems of Latin America and the Caribbean in 1979 from the FCO. See Nicholas Ridley, *My Style of Government: The Thatcher Years* (London: Hutchinson, 1991), p. 25.
47. TNA, FCO 99/561, record of Ridley–Alfonso Robelo meeting, 8 September 1980.
48. *Ibid.*, record of Harding–Murillo-Romero meeting, 11 December 1980.
49. HCPP, 1981/82, HC 47, p. 16. The House of Commons Foreign Affairs Committee included both Labour and Conservative MPs.
50. *Ibid.*, p. 21.
51. NSDD 17, 'National Security Decision Directive on Cuba and Central America', 4 January 1982, file NSDD 17, box 91311, Executive Secretariat NSC NSDD Files, Ronald Reagan Library.
52. *Ibid.*
53. Robinson and Norsworthy, *David and Goliath*, p. 42.
54. Sklar, *Washington's War*, p. 71.
55. Horton, *Peasants in Arms*, p. 118.
56. HCPP, 1981/1982, HC 47 (vii), Foreign Affairs Select Committee:

Caribbean and Central America, British approaches to stability, security and development, Minutes of evidence 8 February 1982 (received 19/04/82), p. 37.

57. House of Commons debate, Nicaragua, 31 March 1982, available at: www.hansard.millbanksystems.com/commons/1982/mar/31/nicaragua, accessed 10 June 2010.

58. Will Podmore, *British Foreign Policy since 1870* (Bloomington, IN: Xlibris, 2008), p. 199.

59. Horton, *Peasants in Arms*, p. 161.

60. Briefing paper, 'Nicaragua and the US – An Overview', pp. 1–2, n.d., file: Nicaragua, US Policy in Central America (2), box 4, William P. Clark Files, Ronald Reagan Library. For more information on Ambassador Quainton's role as US Ambassador to Nicaragua, see Anthony C. E. Quainton, *'Five or One', Nicaragua and its Neighbors* (Miami, FL: Latin American and Caribbean Center, Florida International University, 1984), pp. 1–9.

61. Shultz, *Turmoil and Triumph*, p. 287.

62. Address to Members of the British Parliament, 8 June 1982, the Public Papers of President Ronald W. Reagan, Ronald Reagan Library, available at: www.reagan.utexas.edu/archives/speeches/1982/60882, accessed 4 June 2010.

63. Shultz, *Turmoil and Triumph*, pp. 287–8.

64. *Ibid.*, p. 288.

65. Briefing paper, 'Supporting Evidence on Nicaragua's Threatening Activities', pp. 6–7, n.d., file: Nicaragua US Policy in Central America (2), box 4, William P. Clark Files, Ronald Reagan Library.

66. Bob Woodward, *Veil: The Secret Wars of the CIA 1981–1987* (London: Simon & Schuster, 1987), p. 226. For more information on the Boland Amendment, see Peter Kornbluh, *Nicaragua: The Price of Intervention: Reagan's Wars Against the Sandinistas* (Washington, DC: Institute for Policy Studies, 1987), pp. 55–7; William C. Banks and Peter Raven-Hansen, *National Security Law and the Power of the Purse* (New York: Oxford University Press, 1994), pp. 137–54.

67. Inouye *et al.*, *Report of the Congressional Committees*, p. 40.

68. Pronouncement of the Nicaraguan Democratic Force, 13 January 1983, p. 1, file: Nicaragua US Policy in Central America (2), box 4, William P. Clark Files, Ronald Reagan Library. Prados, *Safe for Democracy*, p. 516.

69. Victor Bulmer-Thomas, *The Political Economy of Central America*

since 1920 (Cambridge: Cambridge University Press, 1987), p. 259.

70. For more information on the Contadora initiatives, see Bruce M. Bagley (ed.), *Contadora and the Diplomacy of Peace in Central America: vol. 1: The United States, Central America and Contadora* (Boulder, CO: Westview Press, 1987); Esperanza Durán, 'The Contadora approach to peace in Central America', *World Today*, 40(8/9) (August/September 1984): 347–54.

71. Situation listing sent by Shultz to various embassies, requesting speakers in UNSC debate on Nicaragua, March 1983, p. 2, file: UK (8/1/82–10/31/83) (3/5), box 20, Executive Secretariat NSC Country Files, United Kingdom, Ronald Reagan Library.

72. *Ibid.*, p. 2.

73. *Ibid.*, p. 2.

74. House of Commons debate, Nicaragua, 11 May 1983, available at: www.hansard.millbanksystems.com/commons/1983/may/11/nicaragua, accessed 10 June 2010.

75. Memcon. of Reagan–Howe meeting, 14 July 1983, p. 4, file: United Kingdom 1983 (07/12/1983–07/21/1983), box 90424, Peter R. Sommer Files, Ronald Reagan Library.

76. Executive Order 12433, 'National Bipartisan Commission on Central America', 19 July 1983, the Public Papers of President Ronald W. Reagan, Ronald Reagan Library, available at: www.reagan.utexas.edu/archives/speeches/1983/71983, accessed 5 June 2010.

77. House of Commons parliamentary questions, 26 July 1983, available at: www.margaretthatcher.org/document/05422, accessed 5 June 2010.

78. Ferguson *et al.*, 'Under attack', p. 52.

79. David Thomas, 'The United States factor in British relations with Latin America', in Victor Bulmer-Thomas, *Britain and Latin America: A Changing Relationship* (Cambridge: Cambridge University Press, 1989), p. 79. For more information on EEC–Latin American relations during the 1980s, see Esperanza Durán, *European Interests in Latin America* (London: Routledge & Kegan Paul, 1985); Wolf Grabendorff, 'European Community relations with Latin America', *Journal of Interamerican Studies and World Affairs*, 29(4) (Winter 1987/8): 69–87.

80. See Robert Kagan, *A Twilight Struggle: American Power and Nicaragua, 1977–1990* (New York: Free Press, 1996), pp. 259–60.

81. Sklar, *Washington's War*, p. 302.

82. Briefing paper, 'British public opinion on Central America', 14 September 1983, p. 1, file: 187 Meeting with PM Thatcher of the UK (9/29/83) (2/3), box 18, Charles P. Tyson Files, Ronald Reagan Library.

83. TNA, PREM 19/1153, Summary of breakfast meeting with Senate Foreign Relations Committee, 29 September 1983, p. 3.

84. *Ibid.*, record of Reagan–Thatcher meeting, 29 September 1983, p. 8. Reagan's speech before the Joint Session of Congress on 27 April 1983 is also discussed in Chapter 3, above.

85. 'Talking Points', 29 May 1984, p. 3, file: Central America (6/11), box 91782, Crisis Management Centre NSC Records, Ronald Reagan Library.

86. *Ibid.*, pp. 3–4.

87. Text of Enders' remarks to Council of the Americas, 2 June 1983, p. 9, file: Central America April–June 1983, box 1, William P. Clark Files, Ronald Reagan Library. The Vietnam analogy, or 'Vietnam syndrome' as it is otherwise known, refers to the negative impact the Vietnam War had on the American general public's perception of US foreign policy post-1975. Reagan regarded the Vietnam syndrome as a major obstacle to US efforts to combat communism and protect US national security interests, particularly in Latin America. Reagan first referred to the Vietnam syndrome in a campaign speech to American veterans on 18 August 1980. See Address to Veterans of Foreign Wars Convention, Chicago, Illinois, 'Peace: Restoring the Margin of Safety', 18 August 1980, the Public Papers of President Ronald W. Reagan, Ronald Reagan Library, available at: www.reagan. utexas.edu/archives/reference/8.18.80, accessed 2 June 2014. The Council of the Americas was a business organisation whose goal was to promote free trade and democracy throughout North and South America through open markets.

88. NSDD 124, 'Central America: Promoting Democracy, Economic Improvement and Peace', 7 February 1984, file: CA June 1984 (4), box 90524, Christopher M. Lehman Files, Ronald Reagan Library.

89. McFarlane memo regarding Nicaraguan economic sanctions, 10 January 1983, p. 3, file: NSDD 124 (Central America: Promoting Democracy, Economic Improvement and Peace), box 91292, Executive Secretariat NSC NSDD Files, Ronald Reagan Library.

90. Robinson and Norsworthy, *David and Goliath*, p. 100.

91. TNA, CAB 128/78/13, Conclusions of a meeting of the Cabinet, 29 March 1984, p. 1.

92. Wendell Gordon, *The United Nations at the Crossroads of Reform* (New York: M. E. Sharpe, 1994), p. 118.

93. House of Commons parliamentary questions, Mining of Nicaraguan harbours, 10 April 1984, available at: www.margaretthatcher.org/document/105656, accessed 2 June 2010.

94. Memcon. of Howe–Bush meeting, 29 May 1984, p. 3, file: United Kingdom 1984 (05/24/1984–06/03/1984), box 90549, Peter R. Sommer Files, Ronald Reagan Library.

95. Theodore Draper, *A Very Thin Line: The Iran–Contra Affairs* (New York: Simon & Schuster, 1991), pp. 54–5.

96. McFarlane and Smardz, *Special Trust*, p. 68.

97. Draper, *A Very Thin Line*, p. 80.

98. McFarlane and Smardz, *Special Trust*, p. 70.

99. Robinson and Norsworthy, *David and Goliath*, p. 99.

100. Kagan, *Twilight Struggle*, p. 322.

101. The US presidential elections on 6 November saw Reagan win his second term in office in a landslide victory against the Democrat candidate Walter Mondale. Reagan carried forty-nine of the fifty states and received 58.8 per cent of the electoral votes in comparison with Mondale's 40.6 per cent.

102. Lord Chitnis worked with the Catholic Institute for International Relations and the Parliamentary Human Rights Group in both Nicaragua and El Salvador observing elections and promoting peace and human rights.

103. TNA, CAB 128/79/13, Conclusions of a meeting of the Cabinet, 8 November 1984, p. 2.

104. Alexander Cockburn, *Corruptions of Empire: Life Studies and the Reagan Era* (London: Verso, London, 1987), p. 384. For more on the Nicaraguan elections of 1984, see Kagan, *Twilight Struggle*, pp. 318–36.

105. Draper, *A Very Thin Line*, p. 41.

106. *Ibid.*, p. 42.

107. Mark Curtis, *Web of Deceit: Britain's Real Role in the World* (London: Vintage, 2003), p. 108; Stephen Dorrill, *The Silent Conspiracy: Inside the Intelligence Services in the 1990s* (London: Mandarin, 1993), p. 271; Frederick Kempe, *Divorcing the Dictator: America's Bungled Affair with Noriega* (London: I. B. Tauris, 1990), pp. 159–60.

108. McFarlane–North briefings, McFarlane to Reagan, n.d., available

at: www.margaretthatcher.org/document/109443, accessed 4 June 2010.

109. *Ibid.*
110. *Ibid.*
111. *Ibid.*
112. *Ibid.*, North to McFarlane, 20 December 1984.
113. *Ibid.*
114. *Ibid.*
115. *Ibid.*
116. Department of State briefing paper on Central America, 1982, file: United Kingdom, Prime Minister Thatcher Official Visit (12/22/1984) (3/3), box 91440, Executive Secretariat NSC VIP Visit Files, Ronald Reagan Library.
117. *Ibid.*
118. Memcon. of Reagan–Thatcher meeting, 22 December 1984, available at: www.margaretthatcher.org/document/109185, accessed 5 June 2010.
119. Cottam, *Images and Intervention*, p. 126.
120. Howe to embassies, 7 February 1985, p. 1, available at: www.margaretthatcher.org/document/109445, accessed 29 June 2010.
121. *Ibid.*, p. 1.
122. *Ibid.*, p. 2.
123. *Ibid.*, p. 2.
124. *Ibid.*, p. 3.
125. House of Commons debate, Vice-President Sergio Ramírez, 14 February 1985, available at: www.hansard.millbanksystems. com/written-answers/1985/feb/14/vice-president-sergio-ramirez-of#S6CV0073P0-19850214-CWA-64, accessed 5 June 2010.
126. *Ibid.*
127. Shultz to Reagan, 15 February 1985, p. 2, file: United Kingdom: Prime Minister Thatcher Official Visit (02/20/1985) (1/2), box 91140, RAC box 6, Executive Secretariat NSC VIP Visit Files, Ronald Reagan Library.
128. *Ibid.*, McFarlane to Reagan, 19 February 1985, p. 1.
129. Interview with Bernard Ingham.
130. Interview with Charles Powell.
131. Interview with Gloria Hooper.
132. Interview with Peter Carrington.
133. Interview with Neil Kinnock.
134. Leslie Cockburn, *Out of Control: The Story of the Reagan Administration's Secret War in Nicaragua, the Illegal Arms*

Pipeline, and the Contra Drug Connection (London: Bloomsbury, 1988), p. 122.

135. Executive Order 12513, 'Prohibiting Trade and Certain other Transactions involving Nicaragua', 1 May 1985, the Public Papers of President Ronald W. Reagan, Ronald Reagan Library, available at: www.reagan.utexas.edu/archives/speeches/1985/50185a, accessed 3 March 2013.

136. Cheryl A. Rubenberg, 'US policy toward Nicaragua and Iran and the Iran–Contra affair: reflections on the continuity of American foreign policy', *Third World Quarterly*, 10(4) (October 1988): 1467–504, at p. 1478.

137. McFarlane and Smardz, *Special Trust*, pp. 72–3.

138. Summary of documentary record of Secretary of State, George P. Shultz, concerning Iran arms sales, 16 December 1986, p. 11, file: Iran/Arms Transactions: Secretary Shultz' 16 December closed session testimony to Senate Select Committee on Intelligence, CFOA 1130, Arthur B. Culvahouse Files, Ronald Reagan Library. The Culvahouse Files can also be accessed in the online document collections of the Reagan Files website, available at: www.thereaganfiles.com. Martin Anderson, *Revolution: The Reagan Legacy* (Stanford, CA: Hoover Institution Press, 1990), pp. 387–8.

139. Anderson, *Revolution*, pp. 387–8.

140. Smith, *Reagan and Thatcher*, p. 206.

141. *Ibid.*, p. 205.

142. Poindexter to Reagan, 17 January 1986, file: Iran/Arms Transactions: Chronologies (01/17/1986), Cover Memo and Finding, CFOA 1130, Arthur B. Culvahouse Files, Ronald Reagan Library.

143. *Ibid.*, Finding Pursuant to Section 662 of the Foreign Assistance Act of 1961, As Amended, Concerning Operations Undertaken by the Central Intelligence Agency in Foreign Countries, Other Than Those Intended for the Purpose of Intelligence Cooperation, 17 January 1986.

144. Smith, *Reagan and Thatcher*, pp. 204–5.

145. Rubenberg, 'US policy toward Nicaragua and Iran and the Iran–Contra affair', p. 1476.

146. John Tower *et al.*, *The Tower Commission Report: The Full Text of the President's Special Review Board* (New York: Bantam, 1987), p. 465.

147. *Ibid.*, p. 465.

148. Trita Parsi, *Treacherous Alliance: The Secret Dealings of Israel,*

Iran, and the US (New Haven, CT: Yale University Press, 2007), pp. 121–2. Larry Speakes later acknowledged that Reagan had written the verse at the behest of Poindexter. This was reported in a *Los Angeles Times* article, 'White House Verifies Reagan Did Write in Bible Sent to Iran', 30 January 1987.

149. Tower *et al.*, *Tower Commission Report*, p. 344.

150. Address to the Nation on United States Assistance for the Nicaraguan Democratic Resistance, 24 June 1986, the Public Papers of President Ronald W. Reagan, Ronald Reagan Library, available at: www.reagan.utexas.edu/archives/speeches/1986/62486, accessed 11 January 2014.

151. Noam Chomsky, *Hegemony or Survival: America's Quest for Global Dominance* (New York: Penguin, 2003), p. 100.

152. Howe, *Conflict of Loyalty*, p. 508.

153. Interview with Geoffrey Howe.

154. House of Commons parliamentary questions, Engagements, 6 November 1986, available at: www.hansard.millbanksystems.com/commons/1986/nov/06/engagements, accessed 3 June 2010.

155. Michael K. Deaver, *A Different Drummer: My Thirty Years with Ronald Reagan* (New York: HarperTorch, 2001), p. 189. Congress did not pursue calls for impeachment as there was little evidence to support claims that Reagan knew of the arms for hostages deal. According to a *New York Times* poll on 1 December 1986, Reagan's approval ratings dropped from 67 per cent in October 1986 to 46 per cent in November 1986. This was the largest one-month drop in presidential approval ratings ever recorded. For more information on Reagan's approval rating in the immediate aftermath of Iran–Contra, see: Ivo H. Daadler and I. M. Destler, *In the Shadow of the Oval Office: Profiles of the National Security Advisors and the Presidents they Served: From JFK to George W. Bush* (New York: Simon & Schuster, 2009), p. 162; Peter J. Wallison, *Ronald Reagan: The Power of Conviction and the Success of His Presidency* (Boulder, CO: Westview Press, 2004), p. 210; Sally-Ann Treharne, 'The Reagan presidency in retrospect: an assessment of Reagan's legacy', in Michael Patrick Cullinane and Clare Frances Elliott (eds), *Perspectives on Presidential Leadership: An International View of the White House* (New York: Routledge, 2014), pp. 172–3.

156. Address to the Nation on the Iran Arms and Contra Aid Controversy, 13 November 1986, the Public Papers of President Ronald W. Reagan, Ronald Reagan Library, available at: www.

reagan.utexas.edu/archives/speeches/1986/111386, accessed 12 January 2014.

157. Burghardt to Poindexter, 14 November 1986, p. 1, file: Thatcher Visit 15 November 1986 (2), box 90902, European and Soviet Affairs Directorate NSC Records, Ronald Reagan Library.

158. Smith, *Reagan and Thatcher*, p. 211.

159. Reagan, *The Reagan Diaries*, p. 451.

160. Remarks Announcing the Review of the National Security Council's Role in the Iran Arms and Contra Aid Controversy, 25 November 1986, the Public Papers of President Ronald W. Reagan, Ronald Reagan Library, available at: www.reagan.utexas.edu/archives/speeches/1986/112586, accessed 12 January 2014.

161. On 4 April 1986, North wrote the so-called 'diversion memo' to Poindexter, which detailed the transfer of funds from the arms deals to the contras. The memo was discovered by Ed Meese's investigating team in late November 1986. It proved North's implicit involvement in the arms for hostages deal and resulted in his immediate dismissal. See Edwin Meese III, *With Reagan: The Inside Story* (Washington, DC: Regnery, 1992), pp. 243–5.

162. Wapshott, *A Political Marriage*, pp. 255–6.

163. Address to the Nation on the Iran Arms and Contra Aid Controversy, 4 March 1987, the Public Papers of President Ronald W. Reagan, Ronald Reagan Library, available at: www.reagan.utexas.edu/archives/speeches/1987/030487h, accessed 14 January 2014.

164. Doyle McManus, 'Aftermath of the Tower Report: Britain oks missile sale for Contras: "Blowpipe" weapons would be nation's first aid to rebels', *Los Angeles Times*, 28 February 1987.

165. House of Commons Prime Minister's questions, 12 May 1987, available at: www.margaretthatcher.org/document/107239, accessed 3 June 2010.

166. Thatcher to Reagan, 15 June 1987, file: United Kingdom 1987, Memos, Letters (7/10), box 92082, Nelson C. Ledsky Files, Ronald Reagan Library. The UK general election on 11 June 1987 saw Thatcher win her third landslide election with 42.2 per cent of the votes and 375 seats in comparison with Labour's 229 seats.

167. House of Commons debate, Blowpipe, 29 June 1987, available at: www.hansard.millbanksystems.com/written-answers/1987/jun/29/blowpipe#S6CV00118P0-19870629-CWA-134, accessed 5 June 2010.

168. Press conference for American correspondents, 3 July 1987, avail-

able at: www.margaretthatcher.org/document/106907, accessed 6 June 2010.

169. Memcon of Shultz–Thatcher meeting, 17 July 1987, file: 17 July 1987 (Friday) OVW PM Margaret Thatcher UK (2), box 92082, Nelson C. Ledsky Files, Ronald Reagan Library.

170. Smith, *Reagan and Thatcher*, p. 212.

171. Thatcher, *Downing Street Years*, p. 771.

172. Reagan, *The Reagan Diaries*, p. 517.

173. Thatcher, *Downing Street Years*, p. 770.

174. Interview with Charles Powell.

175. Rubenberg, 'US policy toward Nicaragua and Iran and the Iran–Contra affair', pp. 1478–9.

176. Shultz, *Turmoil and Triumph*, p. 509.

Conclusion

Reagan and Thatcher forged a formidable alliance in a time of increasing Cold War tension and omnipresent fears of communist expansionism. Their close working, and indeed, personal, relationship was supported by a mutual respect and admiration, by shared fiscal and political ideologies and a strong anti-communist rhetoric. Despite the changing domestic and international realities of the UK and the US, both leaders were committed to a strengthening of bilateral relations between the two countries. Their relationship had an ease and level of familiarity that weathered their often diverging strategic interests, particularly in Latin America. Despite their often seemingly incompatible individual foreign policy objectives, the relationship continued to evolve and deepen. This strengthening in relations repaired the cleavages that emerged through challenges presented in the Latin American region during the 1980s.

As has been shown, the Falklands War had many implications for the Special Relationship. There was a discernible lack of US support of its transatlantic ally, the UK, in the early stages of the war, and US efforts to try to negotiate a settlement that would safeguard Argentine interests infuriated Thatcher and her supporters in the Cabinet. This was potentially damaging to the concept of a Special Relationship and threatened to invalidate the argument that such a relationship operated under Reagan and Thatcher. The initial US neutrality was seen as evidence in the UK of its desire for hegemony in the Latin American region. Thus, the conflict highlighted an asymmetry in strategic interests between both countries. The UK was ardent in its conviction that Argentina's occupation of South Georgia and later the Falkland

Islands was an act of calculated aggression. It believed that it was entitled to rely upon its transatlantic partner for swift and uncompromising support. The Prime Minister, in particular, was aghast at the US decision to remain neutral in the early stages of the conflict. This was an affront to British pride both at home and in the wider international community. There was an important lesson to be learned in that the British could not always depend upon the US for political support. Thatcher was forced to become more intransigent in her position when dealing with Reagan. The Prime Minister worked fervidly to change the President's stance. In fact, her use of personal diplomacy was a key feature in her dealings with Reagan. She spoke regularly with the President and kept him apprised of events in the South Atlantic. Thatcher was not inclined to appease American concerns in order to safeguard US strategic interests in Argentina as she had staked her prime ministership on the Falkland Islands. To that end, Thatcher made exacting demands on Reagan in her pursuit of US advocacy.

For its part, the US was placed in the unenviable position of having to choose between two influential allies, the UK and Argentina. This choice was made increasingly onerous by the Reagan administration's desire to forge closer US–Argentine relations in order to secure a powerful non-communist ally in Latin America. The US desire to safeguard its interests in Nicaragua, where Argentine officials were helping the CIA to train counter-revolutionaries against the Sandinista government, was also a decisive factor in the unusually reserved response of the US to the crisis. A distinctly pro-Latin American faction in the State Department disinclined Reagan to come out publicly in support of the UK. In the light of initial US neutrality, the ensuing US mediation efforts were tolerated by the British if only to bide time enough for the Task Force to reach the islands (as indicated by John Nott and Cecil Parkinson in their recent interviews). This was not an attempt by the British to gratify US concerns. It was a calculated decision on behalf of the UK to allow diplomacy to continue inconclusively until the Task Force could reach the Falklands. The research shows that Thatcher was not prepared to cede the Falklands to Argentina. The Haig mediation efforts merely provided the UK with a legitimate smoke-screen for its ongoing war preparations and military/naval movements. There were serious frictions in the Anglo-American relationship at this point that threatened to undermine the mutual respect, tolerance and admiration that were traditionally associated with the concept of a Special Relationship. Notwithstanding these, the Anglo-American sense of close association was able to overcome these challenges. The US and the UK engaged in unremitting consultation, allowing for a strengthening of the bonds of personal diplomacy. This endurance in a time of contention signified exceptionally close ties.

Anglo-American relations improved considerably following the US decision to end its mediation efforts and to publicly support the British in the Falklands War. Indeed, US support was seen as evidence that it was willing to forgo its own strategic interests in Latin America in deference to its Special Relationship partner. Recent interviews with key Cabinet members and advisers to the Thatcher government allude to the fact that Reagan was always believed by the British to be on their side, even prior to the end of the negotiating process. This British perception of Reagan's support of the UK in the war was bolstered by the provision of extensive material and intelligence support by the US. This allowed the friendship to regain a firm footing in the knowledge that the US had ultimately, albeit reluctantly, supported its transatlantic partner in a war between two US allies. Caspar Weinberger's assistance to the British war effort reaffirmed the Pentagon's and Reagan's commitment to the Special Relationship, in the eyes of the UK, and most probably Thatcher.

Argentina's rejection of the Peruvian peace plans and the failed attempts by Pérez de Cuéllar to achieve a negotiated settlement to the crisis meant that the Thatcher government was free to mount an offensive against Argentina. The Argentine government was proven to be intransigent in comparison with the apparently conciliatory attitude of the British. Thatcher mistakenly assumed at this point that any US attempts to negotiate a settlement were at an end. The Prime Minister was not prepared for further examples of US ambivalence. Therefore, UNSCR 505 was potentially very damaging to the Special Relationship in that it highlighted a re-emergence of pro-Latin American sentiment in the US. Notwithstanding this, the UK was prepared to forgive its alliance partner so as not to damage the Special Relationship any further. Reagan's five-point peace proposals, should they have been presented, would have revealed a residual US desire at the highest level to negotiate a settlement whilst affording the Argentines some dignity. Despite the contradictory viewpoints of Parkinson and Nott as to whether or not Reagan presented these proposals to Thatcher, it is clear that had the President chosen to present them, he would in all probability have faced the wrath of an incandescent Thatcher. Yet, despite the ill-fated US mediation efforts and offers to assist the British in the postwar decision-making on the future of the islands, the Reagan administration was ultimately a formidable ally to the British during the Falklands War. The US provision of substantial material and intelligence support bear witness to this. Furthermore, Reagan's and Thatcher's efforts to avoid a schism were ultimately successful.

The US invasion of Grenada in 1983 was yet another challenge to Anglo-American relations emanating from the Latin American region. It highlighted a disparity in the bilateral relationship and a distinct lack of trust that threatened to irrevocably damage the relationship had it not been for the joint commitment of Reagan and Thatcher to strengthen and improve interpersonal and diplomatic ties. The Anglo-American mismatch in relation to Grenada was arguably one of the greatest tests to the durability of the Special Relationship during the 1980s. It was a political and personal quagmire for both leaders. The relationship was of great importance to both leaders, yet it is clear that the US desire to serve its own strategic hemispheric interests over the needs of the UK was temporarily detrimental to Anglo-American relations. Moreover, the invasion highlighted a US disregard for Britain's colonial past and its existing commitment to the governing of the island. It was an affront to British interests in the region and represented a US desire to assert its own hegemonic interests regardless of the cost to the UK. It also represented a US propensity for unilateral action in Latin America despite the fact that it was allegedly responding to an OECS request. This unilateralism was indicative of Reagan's desire to assert US influence in response to the perceived attempts by the Soviet Union and its proxies to extend communist influence in the region.

The invasion was of dubious legal and moral legitimacy given that the US appears to have played a pivotal role in orchestrating a request from the OECS to intervene. This, coupled with the questionable origins of the Governor General's request for US help, serves to consolidate the view that the US, after it had decided to intervene, was determined to secure a formal request for intervention to legitimise its actions. The lack of American consultation with the British during discussions with the OECS suggests a disregard for British opinion. The US augmented its debateable legal justifications with allegations of a danger to American medical students studying on the island. This danger is arguable given that offers to remove the students and other US citizens from Grenada were refused by the Reagan administration. The improbability of such danger to US citizens highlights a determination to intervene in the affairs of a member of the British Commonwealth to pursue US objectives. The invasion helped to detract from the tragedy in Beirut and probably dampened the significant domestic recriminations against the Reagan administration for its involvement in the Middle East.

US actions caused a significant amount of tension on a personal level between both leaders, with the Prime Minister berating her American counterpart in the immediate aftermath. It also resulted in considerable embarrassment for her domestically. Thatcher and Geoffrey Howe endured domestic and party criticism for failing to denounce US activities as they made difficult presentations in the House of Commons to assuage concerns over the trustworthiness of the UK's 'ally'. Thatcher, in particular, had to suffer the ignominy of close identification with Reagan in the British media for the apparent US slight against British interests. Furthermore, the public denigration of Reagan and his administration in the aftermath of the invasion did little to improve Anglo-American relations. This was damaging to the cultivation of close bilateral relations and contributed to growing British concerns regarding the future deployment of Pershing II and Cruise missiles in the UK. Michael Heseltine's difficult encounter with Secretary Weinberger indicates the negative effect the US invasion had at an inter-ministerial level, at least in the short term. This embarrassment partially negated the collegial relationship that Reagan and Thatcher had worked so hard to achieve in the aftermath of the Falklands War. However, this embarrassment was counterbalanced by US efforts to restore close relations in recognition of the difficulties and embarrassment caused to the British government, and to Thatcher in particular, as a result of US actions. Reagan's telephone call to the Prime Minister on 26 October would not have been possible without a strong personal bond between both leaders. Similarly, it would not have been suggested by Robert McFarlane if the White House did not think that such a close relationship with Thatcher and her government was of considerable importance to the US.

This theory proved to be correct when the British government chose to abstain from the UN vote condemning US actions in late October 1983. This was a controversial decision as government members and the British press were likely to denounce the abstention. Moreover, this decision highlighted a British desire to repair the cleavages created in the Anglo-American alliance. This was clearly an indication of the UK's desire to normalise relations, but also it was, in all probability, an attempt by Thatcher to regain a strong US ally to reinforce her political status in the international community. Such motivations were commonplace in Thatcher's and Reagan's determination to cultivate the Special Relationship.

US efforts to improve relations were again evident in Kenneth Dam's visit to Chequers in November 1983, during which the Prime Minister was able to voice her many concerns. This allowed Thatcher to reassert her authority in the relationship and left the Reagan administration in little doubt of the need to placate her and restore Anglo-American relations. Britain's desire to improve relations in the aftermath of such a politically damaging situation, and US regret over the cleavages created, were indicative of the sustainability and adaptability of Anglo-American relations during this time. The concerted efforts made by both Reagan and Thatcher to normalise relations after the invasion reconfirmed their commitment to a renewal of close Anglo-American relations. This joint commitment to improve relations in spite of such obstacles emanating from Latin America is a unique feature of the Special Relationship under Reagan and Thatcher.

The Anglo-Guatemalan dispute over the territorial integrity of Belize was another obstacle in the path of a reinvigoration of US–UK special relations. The dispute was a contentious matter for the Thatcher government given Guatemala's sporadic threats to invade Belize. The UK believed that when the Reagan administration offered its services as an unofficial mediator in the dispute that this was in line with a US commitment to its transatlantic partner. In reality, US involvement was inspired by its own strategic hemispheric interests. During a time when the UK was actively seeking Belizean independence through the Heads of Agreement and protracted Anglo-Guatemalan negotiations, the UK hoped that US involvement might assist in gaining Guatemalan recognition of Belizean independence. This was a calculated decision by the Thatcher government, which hoped that limited US involvement would discourage Guatemalan aggression. The UK was, as such, using the US to secure vital British interests in Belize.

For its part, the US was interested in pursuing its own foreign policy objectives in the region via Belize. These objectives included, among others, the prevention of Cuban infiltration in Belize, the attainment of a beneficial democratic ally in a newly independent Belize and a wish to halt Marxist guerrilla activity in the region. The administration wanted to stop any potential Cuban influence in Belize post-independence. The US clearly hoped that fostering close relations with Guatemala would help to achieve these objectives. US involvement in the dispute afforded the Reagan administration an invaluable opportunity to forge a close relationship with Guatemala despite its appalling human rights record at the time. Additionally, the US had clear economic objectives in Guatemala, including the proposed 'Intermares Trans-Guatemala Pipeline' project. However, the primary reason behind a US wish to establish close relations with Guatemala was its desire to resume FMS sales to the country. It is ironic that, at a time when the US was drawing up proposals to resolve the Anglo-Guatemalan dispute with the help of John Carbaugh, it had already decided to try to reinstate US arms sales to Guatemala. This renewal of US–Guatemalan relations directly contravened the principle of solidarity traditionally associated with the concept of a Special Relationship.

US attempts to persuade Thatcher of the need to retain a British garrison in Belize as part of the BDF indicated an American desire to deter any possible Guatemalan incursion and/or potential Cuban infiltration of Belize. This US fear of Guatemalan aggression was possibly amplified by the knowledge that Guatemala potentially had access to more arms as result of the US decision to resume FMS sales to the country. Reagan made a concerted effort to persuade Thatcher to retain the garrison through written and spoken correspondence. The Prime Minister ultimately decided in favour of retaining a small garrison for various reasons, including a nominal desire to appease US concerns, but, more importantly, to suit British interests. Thatcher had faced domestic opposition in response to the possible withdrawal of the British contingent of the BDF and was forced to revise her position. This decision was helped by American assurances that it would look at ways to lessen the economic burden of the garrison for the UK. Thus, yet again, the Thatcher government stood to gain from US involvement in the dispute over Belize.

The US involvement in the Anglo-Guatemalan dispute could have had negative implications for Anglo-American relations resulting from its cultivation of close ties with Guatemala. It appears that the UK did not wish to come into conflict with the US regarding its policies in Guatemala as this could be detrimental to the health of the Special Relationship. However, the UK stood to make significant gains from US mediation efforts. The US played a vital role in defusing a volatile situation in which Guatemala made sporadic threats of invasion. This greatly benefited the UK as it allowed it to pursue its ongoing decolonisation efforts in the Latin American region. While the UK benefited from US leverage with Guatemala, the US was simultaneously able to cultivate improved diplomatic and trade relations with Guatemala. This dispute effectively allowed both the US and the UK to safeguard their individual interests in Latin America. It also afforded Belize continued security post-independence. By becoming increasingly involved in the dispute, the US was safeguarding both British and American interests.

The US involvement in Nicaragua throughout the Reagan presidency was an important factor in the administration's foreign policy objectives in the Latin American region. US support of the contras resulted in a scandal that threatened to topple the Reagan administration. The Iran–Contra scandal highlighted a US propensity for illegal and covert activities and a complete disregard for both domestic and international law. It was an example of unilateralism that was seen by the wider international community as undesirable in a region of great political uncertainty. The US used the tumultuous situation in Nicaragua to achieve its own strategic hemispheric interests, that is, to halt the perceived expansion of the Soviet threat in Nicaragua and to implement its own hegemonic influence in the wider region. US support of the contras prior to and after the Boland Amendments emphasised American commitment to the Reagan Doctrine in Latin America regardless of the domestic consequences. In the UK, these US activities were not generally supported by many MPs, but the Prime Minister refused to denounce them. This was an act of solidarity with her American counterpart. Despite frequent calls to outline British views on US activities in Latin America, the Prime Minister was guarded in her response that the UK supported the Contadora initiatives. Moreover, she consistently reaffirmed Reagan's commitment to democracy in the region.

The Reagan administration needed a close ally in the face of strong condemnation resulting from the ICJ ruling and UN vote against US activities in Nicaragua. The UK, in particular Thatcher, proved to be a staunch ally during this time. British abstention from a UN vote denouncing US/CIA participation in the mining of Nicaraguan harbours in 1984 consolidated Thatcher's position as a dependable ally. Thatcher's attempt to preserve the integrity of the Anglo-American alliance came at the cost of significant domestic opposition to Britain's abstention. As time progressed, Thatcher remained resolute in her conviction that Reagan was supporting democracy in Nicaragua by trying to oust the Sandinista government. The visit by Vice-President Sergio Ramírez to London in 1985 presented both Thatcher and Howe with an opportunity to condemn the perceived Soviet build-up in Nicaragua and the build-up of the Nicaraguan army. These concerns closely mirrored those of the Reagan administration and this could conceivably be seen as unofficial support by the British of US views towards Nicaragua.

The possibility that the UK and therefore, Thatcher, knew of the arms for hostages deal resulting from the MI5 bugging of the North/MacFarlane/Israeli meeting in London in late 1985 has yet to be proven. It is conceivable that given MI6 told the CIA of such a meeting that the British intelligence services would also have informed Thatcher. This would shed new light on the extent of British support of the US during this time. However, that supposition remains as yet to be proven or disproven by future releases of government records. The Iran–Contra scandal and ensuing investigations had a profound negative effect on the Reagan administration. The US was in clear need of strong support from an influential ally. But the Prime Minister came under increasing domestic pressure to denounce the Reagan administration's involvement in Nicaragua. Thatcher resisted this despite allegations of British involvement in Nicaragua through the activities of David Walker and his firm KMS. Ensuing allegations regarding the possible supply of British Blowpipe missiles to the contras via the Chilean government were also detrimental to the UK. Thatcher faced numerous parliamentary questions about these allegations. Nevertheless, the Prime Minister remained a staunch supporter of the President. She proved that the close relationship she had with Reagan was more important than short-lived domestic criticism. Thatcher's appearance on *Face the Nation* confirmed her position as a steadfast ally to Reagan. As such, it can be viewed as a pivotal moment in the cultivation of close interpersonal ties associated with the Special Relationship under Reagan and Thatcher. The Prime Minister's warm and encouraging correspondence with Reagan in the aftermath of the Iran–Contra scandal was much appreciated by the President. Thatcher's use of the bonds of personal diplomacy helped, yet again, to reinforce the Special Relationship between herself and Reagan. This allowed the Prime Minister to reaffirm and strengthen her position in the vaunted Special Relationship. It can be argued, therefore, that Thatcher was able to at least partially redress a political disparity between both leaders. This was undoubtedly beneficial to the Prime Minister and the continuing development of close bilateral relations. With both leaders on a more equal footing, Anglo-American relations would continue to strengthen in the years ahead, thereby reconfirming the idea that a Special Relationship operated under Reagan and Thatcher.

These challenges emanating from the Latin American region, coupled with long-standing geopolitical ties, contributed to the formation of enriched and strengthened bilateral relations between the governments of Reagan and Thatcher. Close inter-governmental relations were arguably overshadowed by the distinctive personal and working relationship cultivated by both leaders. Their relationship survived many challenges emanating from the turbulent Latin American region. While the Falklands War, the US invasion of Grenada, the Anglo-Guatemalan dispute over Belize and the US involvement in Nicaragua created many challenges for the relationship, they failed to overwhelm it. These Latin American crises answered the perennial question of whether or not a Special Relationship existed between Reagan and Thatcher. As a result of these crises, there was a resultant mutual commitment to improve bilateral relations, to strengthen communications and cooperation in the face of often competing foreign policy objectives, particularly in Latin America. This was inspired by an ardent desire to improve upon existing ties and to create a unique personal relationship that was to last well beyond their terms in office. Having assessed these potentially divisive Latin American case studies and subsequent British and American efforts to restore relations, particularly on a personal level, it can be strongly argued that Ronald Reagan and Margaret Thatcher did, in fact, enjoy a true 'Special Relationship'.

Appendix: Interviewees

Sir Adrian Beamish is a former member of the British Diplomatic Service. Beamish has served at missions in Tehran, Paris, New Delhi, Brussels and Bonn. He was head of the Falkland Islands Department in the FCO from 1985 to 1987. He left this position to become the British Ambassador to Peru from 1987 to 1989. Following this post, he returned as Assistant Under-Secretary of State for the Americas; a post whose responsibilities included, inter alia, the Falkland Islands and Argentina. He was appointed as British Ambassador to Mexico in 1994. He held this position until 1998. He was knighted in the Diplomatic Service and Overseas Honours List in 1999. Beamish is an assistant college lecturer in the School of History, UCC.

Lord Timothy Bell of Belgravia is a British communications and advertising executive. He is best known for his close working relationship with Thatcher as an executive for the Saatchi & Saatchi communications agency. He worked on all three of Thatcher's general election campaigns in 1979, 1983 and 1987. A staunch Conservative, he was a life-long friend and confidant to Thatcher. In 1989, he established his own communications agency, Lowe Bell Communications. He was knighted in 1990 after a nomination by Thatcher. Bell became chairman of Chime Communications in 1994 (which includes the Bell-Pottinger Group). He was a made a life peer as Lord Bell of Belgravia in 1998. Lord Bell still sits today as a Conservative peer in the House of Lords.

Lord Peter Carrington of Upton KG GCMG CH MC PC DL is a former British Conservative Party politician. Thatcher appointed him as Secretary of State for Foreign and Commonwealth Affairs in 1979. He held this position until he resigned as a result of the Falklands War in 1982. He was Secretary General of NATO from 1984 to 1988. Following the House of Lords Act 1999, which removed the automatic right of hereditary peers to sit in the House of Lords, Carrington was given a life peerage as Lord Carrington of Upton, Nottinghamshire. Lord Carrington still sits today as a Conservative peer and is the longest-serving member of the House of Lords.

Lord Michael Heseltine of Thenford CH PC is a former British Conservative Party politician. During the Shadow Cabinet of 1974–9, Heseltine was appointed Shadow Industry Secretary. Thatcher appointed him Secretary of State for the Environment upon her accession in 1979. Heseltine remained in this position until January 1983, when he was appointed Secretary of State for Defence following the resignation of his predecessor, John Nott. The Westland Affair resulted in Heseltine's resignation in January 1986. He returned to the backbenches and following Geoffrey Howe's resignation speech in November 1990, Heseltine announced his candidacy for the leadership of the Conservative Party. He later conceded defeat after John Major narrowly missed an outright majority in the second ballot of votes in the leadership contest. He was made a life peer as Lord Heseltine of Thenford, Northamptonshire, in 2001. Lord Heseltine still sits today as a Conservative peer in the House of Lords.

Baroness Gloria Hooper of Liverpool and St. James CMG is a former solicitor and Member of the European Parliament (MEP). As a party candidate for the Liverpool European Parliament elections in 1979, Hooper won a landslide victory and remained in that post until 1984. She was made a Companion of the Order of St. Michael and St. George. She entered the House of Lords as a life peer in June 1985 as Baroness Hooper of Liverpool and St. James in the City of Westminster. She was Government Whip in the House of Lords from 1985 to 1987. She became Parliamentary Under-Secretary of State in the Department of Education and Science from 1987 to 1988, the Department of Energy from

1988 to 1989 and the Department of Health from 1989 to 1992. Hooper has enjoyed a number of positions closely associated with the Latin American region, including Vice-President of Canning House (Hispanic and Luso-Brazilian Council), President of the Anglo-Latin American Foundation and President of the Friends of Colombia for Social Aid. Lady Hooper still sits today as a Conservative peer in the House of Lords.

Lord Geoffrey Howe of Aberavon CH QC PC is a former British Conservative Party politician. He was Margaret Thatcher's longest-standing Cabinet minister. Howe served as Thatcher's Shadow Chancellor of the Exchequer from 1975 to 1979. Thatcher appointed him Chancellor of the Exchequer in 1979, a post which he held until 1983. After the general election in June 1983, Howe was appointed Secretary of State for Foreign and Commonwealth Affairs. Howe held this position until July 1989 when he was replaced by John Major as part of a Cabinet reshuffle by Thatcher. He was appointed Leader of the House of Commons, Lord President of the Council and Deputy Prime Minister of the UK in July 1989. He held this position until November 1990 when he famously resigned from the Thatcher government. He was made a life peer in 1992 as Lord Howe of Aberavon of Tandridge, Surrey. Lord Howe still sits today as a Conservative peer in the House of Lords.

Sir Bernard Ingham is a former journalist and civil servant. After Thatcher came to power he was recruited by the Prime Minister as her Chief Press Secretary. Ingham was a staunch supporter of Thatcher, and was considered a formidable adversary by journalists during Thatcher's premiership. Ingham was also head of the Government Information Services from 1989 to 1990. He retired shortly after Thatcher's departure in 1990 and was knighted in that year's Resignation Honours List.

Lord Neil Kinnock of Bedwellty PC is a former British Labour Party politician. Kinnock was appointed Shadow Education Secretary by James Callaghan from 1979 to 1983. He was Leader of Opposition Labour Party from 1983 to 1992. During this time he was an outspoken critic of the Thatcher government and its policies. Kinnock also acted as MP to Islwyn from 1983 to 1995. He was European Commissioner for Transport from 1995 to 1999. He was appointed European Commissioner for Administrative Reform from 1999 to 2004, and he was also Vice-President of the European Commission from 1999 to 2004. He was made a life peer as Lord Kinnock of Bedwellty, Gwent, Wales, in 2005. Lord Kinnock still sits today as a Labour peer in the House of Lords.

Sir John Nott KCB is a former British Conservative Party politician. Nott joined the Shadow Cabinet in 1975 when he became the Conservative frontbench spokesman on Treasury and Economic Affairs between 1975 and 1976. This was closely followed by a similar position as spokesman for Trade between 1976 and 1979. Thatcher appointed him Privy Councillor in 1979. He was also appointed Secretary of State for Trade and Industry in 1979, a position he held until 1981. In January 1981, Nott was appointed Secretary of State for Defence and was subsequently a member of the Falklands War Cabinet. Having submitted his resignation to Thatcher in mid-1982, Nott agreed to remain in the position until the end of the year. He resigned in January 1983. Nott was knighted as a Knight Commander of the Order of the Bath in 1983.

Lord Cecil Parkinson of Carnforth PC is a former British Conservative Party politician. Parkinson was made a junior minister at the Department of Trade and Industry in the Thatcher government of 1979, and was later appointed as Chairman of the Conservative Party in 1981. Parkinson established a solid working and personal relationship with the Prime Minister during this time. He was appointed Paymaster General in 1981, a position which afforded him a seat in the Cabinet. Thatcher included him as a member of the Falklands War Cabinet in 1982. Parkinson worked on the Conservative Party's election campaign in 1983 alongside Geoffrey Howe. He was appointed as Secretary of State for Trade and Industry in June 1983. He held this position until October 1983 when he resigned. Parkinson was elected as

MP for Hertsmere in 1983, a position he held until 1992. After four years on the backbenches Parkinson returned as Secretary of State for Energy in 1987. He was appointed Secretary of State for Transport in 1989, and held this position until he resigned along with Thatcher in November 1990. He was made a life peer as Lord Parkinson of Carnforth, Lancashire, in 1992. Lord Parkinson still sits today as a Conservative peer in the House of Lords.

Lord Charles Powell of Bayswater KCMG OBE is a former diplomat, politician and businessman. Powell was appointed as Private Secretary to Margaret Thatcher in 1983 and subsequently became one of her most trusted foreign policy advisers. Powell remained in this position until 1990 when Thatcher left office. Long associated with the Conservative Party, he was made a life peer as Lord Powell of Bayswater, Canterbury, Kent, in 2000. Lord Powell still sits today as a Crossbench peer in the House of Lords.

Select Bibliography

Primary sources

Ronald Reagan Presidential Library, Simi Valley, California
Blair, Dennis C. Files
Clark, William P. Files
Crisis Management Center NSC Records
Culvahouse, Arthur B. Files
European and Soviet Affairs Directorate NSC Records
Executive Secretariat NSC Cable File Records 1981–5
Executive Secretariat NSC Country Files
Executive Secretariat NSC Head of State File Records 1981–9
Executive Secretariat NSC Meeting Files
Executive Secretariat NSC NSDD Files
Executive Secretariat NSC VIP Visit Files
Fontaine, Roger W. Files
Holladay, J. Douglas Files
Kojelis, Linas J. Files
Latin American Affairs Directorate NSC Records
Ledsky, Nelson C. Files
Lehman, Christopher M. Files
Lilac, Robert H. Files
Meese, Edwin Files
Menges, Constantine C. Files
North, Oliver L. Files
Office of the Counsel to the President Records
Rentschler, James M. Files
Sapia-Bosch, Alfonso Files
Sommer, Peter R. Files
Tillman, Jacqueline Files

Tyson, Charles P. Files
WHORM Subject Files 1981–9

The United Kingdom National Archives, Kew
CAB   Cabinet Office records
        CAB   128/76/30
        CAB   128/76/31
        CAB   128/78/13
        CAB   128/79/13
DEFE   Ministry of Defence records
        DEFE   11/890
        DEFE   13/1152
        DEFE   13/1281
        DEFE   25/414
        DEFE   25/416
        DEFE   25/417
        DEFE   71/198
FCO   Foreign and Commonwealth Office records
        FCO   7/2432
        FCO   7/3084
        FCO   7/3487
        FCO   7/3726
        FCO   7/3805
        FCO   46/2848
        FCO   46/2850
        FCO   46/2879
        FCO   58/1983
        FCO   99/318
        FCO   99/347
        FCO   99/350
        FCO   99/356
        FCO   99/358
        FCO   99/361
        FCO   99/561
        FCO   99/568
        FCO   99/623
        FCO   99/624
        FCO   99/625
        FCO   99/626
        FCO   99/631
        FCO   99/642

FO   Records created and inherited by the Foreign Office
        FO   973/101
        FO   973/188
        FO   973/231
        FO   973/262
OD   Records created and inherited by the Department of
        Technical Cooperation and successive Overseas Development
        Bodies
        OD   28/385
PREM   Prime Minister's Office records
        PREM   15/2089
        PREM   16/13
        PREM   19/331
        PREM   19/383
        PREM   19/624
        PREM   19/633
        PREM   19/652
        PREM   19/959
        PREM   19/979
        PREM   19/1048
        PREM   19/1049
        PREM   19/1151
        PREM   19/1152
        PREM   19/1153

The Churchill Archives Centre, Cambridge
THCR   The Papers of Baroness Thatcher
        THCR   1/10/18
        THCR   3/1/12 (1)
        THCR   3/1/18
        THCR   6/4/1/7

Published documents and records/electronic resources
Hansard, House of Commons/House of Lords Debates, www.hansard.
    millbanksystems.com (online documents).
HMSO, *Britain and the Falkland Islands*, London, 1993.
HMSO, *Falkland Islands Review: Report of a Committee of Privy
    Councillors* (Franks Report), 1983.
HMSO, *The Falklands Campaign: The Lessons*, Defence White Paper,
    1982.

House of Commons Parliamentary Papers (HCPP), www.parlipapers. chadwyck.co.uk (online documents).

The Margaret Thatcher Foundation, www.margaretthatcher.org (online documents).

The Public Papers of President Ronald W. Reagan, www.reagan.utexas. edu (online documents).

The Reagan Files, www.thereaganfiles.com (online documents).

The Richard Nixon Presidential Library Archives, www.nixon.library. gov (online documents).

The Ronald Reagan Oral History Project, www.millercenter.org/ president/reagan/oralhistory (online transcripts).

Newspapers
The Guardian
Le Monde
Los Angeles Times
New York Times
Washington Post

Diaries and memoirs
Baker, Kenneth, *The Turbulent Years: My Life in Politics*. London: Faber & Faber, 1993.

Binns, Jack R., *The United States in Honduras, 1980–1981: An Ambassador's Memoir*. Jefferson, NC: McFarland, 2000.

Brzezinski, Zbigniew, *Power and Principle: Memoirs of the National Security Advisor, 1977–1981*. New York: Farrar, Straus & Giroux, 1983.

Callaghan, James, *Time and Chance*. London: Politico's, 2006.

Carrington, Lord, *Reflect on Things Past: The Memoirs of Lord Carrington*. London: William Collins, 1988.

Carter, Jimmy, *Keeping Faith: Memoirs of a President*. New York: Bantam, 1982.

Carter, Jimmy, *White House Diary*. New York: Farrar, Straus & Giroux, 2010.

Deaver, Michael K., *A Different Drummer: My Thirty Years with Ronald Reagan*. New York: HarperTorch, 2001.

Gorbachev, Mikhail, *Memoirs*. New York: Doubleday, 1996.

Haig, Alexander M., Jr, *Caveat: Realism, Reagan, and Foreign Policy*. London: Weidenfeld & Nicolson, 1984.

Heath, Edward, *The Course of My Life: My Autobiography*. London: Hodder & Stoughton, 1998.

Henderson, Nicholas, *Mandarin: The Diaries of an Ambassador, 1969–1982*. London: Weidenfeld & Nicolson, 1994.

Heseltine, Michael, *Life in the Jungle: My Autobiography*. London: Hodder & Stoughton, 2000.

Howe, Geoffrey, *Conflict of Loyalty*. London: Macmillan, 1994.

Ingham, Bernard, *Kill the Messenger*. London: HarperCollins, 1991.

Kissinger, Henry, *Years of Upheaval*. London: Weidenfeld & Nicolson, 1982.

Luce, Richard, *Ringing the Changes: A Memoir*. Norwich: Michael Russell, 2007.

McFarlane, Robert C. and Zofia Smardz, *Special Trust*. New York: Cadell & Davies, 1994.

Meese, Edwin, III, *With Reagan: The Inside Story*. Washington, DC: Regnery, 1992.

Menges, Constantine C., *Inside the National Security Council: The True Story of the Making and Unmaking of Reagan's Foreign Policy*. New York: Simon & Schuster, 1988.

Nixon, Richard, *RN: The Memoirs of Richard Nixon*, revised edn. New York: Simon & Schuster, 2013.

Nott, John, *Here Today, Gone Tomorrow: Recollections of an Errant Politician*. London: Politico's, 2002.

Nott, John, *Haven't We Been Here Before? Afghanistan to the Falklands: A Personal Connection*. London: Discovered Authors, 2007.

Owen, David, *Time to Declare*. London: Michael Joseph, 1991.

Parkinson, Cecil, *Right at the Centre: An Autobiography*. London: Weidenfeld & Nicolson, 1992.

Pym, Francis, *The Politics of Consent*. London: Hamish Hamilton, 1984.

Reagan, Ronald, *An American Life*. New York: Simon & Schuster, 1990.

Reagan, Ronald, *The Reagan Diaries*, ed. Douglas Brinkley. New York: HarperCollins, 2007.

Renwick, Robin, *A Journey with Margaret Thatcher: Foreign Policy under the Iron Lady*. London: Biteback, 2013.

Ridley, Nicholas, *My Style of Government: The Thatcher Years*. London: Hutchinson, 1991.

Shultz, George P., *Turmoil and Triumph: My Years as Secretary of State*. New York: Charles Scribner's, 1993.

Speakes, Larry and Robert Pack, *Speaking Out: Inside the Reagan White House*. New York: Charles Scribner's, 1988.

Tebbit, Norman, *Upwardly Mobile*. London: Weidenfeld & Nicolson, 1988.

Thatcher, Margaret, *In Defence of Freedom: Speeches on Britain's Relations with the World, 1976–1986*. London: Aurum Press, 1986.

Thatcher, Margaret, *The Downing Street Years*. New York: HarperCollins, 1993.

Thatcher, Margaret, *The Path to Power*. London: HarperCollins, 1995.

Thatcher, Margaret, *Statecraft: Strategies for a Changing World*. London: HarperCollins, 2002.

Thatcher, Margaret, *Thatcher's War: The Iron Lady on the Falklands*. London: HarperCollins, 2012.

Vance, Cyrus, *Hard Choices: Critical Years in America's Foreign Policy*. New York: Simon & Schuster, 1983.

Weinberger, Caspar, *Fighting For Peace: Seven Critical Years in the Pentagon*. New York: Warner Books, 1990.

Weinberger, Caspar, with Gretchen Roberts, *In the Arena: A Memoir of the 20th Century*. Washington, DC: Regnery, 2001.

Whitelaw, William, *The Whitelaw Memoirs*. London: Headline Books, 1990.

Secondary sources

Books

Adkin, Mark, *Urgent Fury: The Battle for Grenada*. Lanham, MD: Lexington Books, 1989.

Aiken, Jonathan, *Margaret Thatcher: Power and Personality*. London: Bloomsbury, 2013.

Aldous, Richard, *Reagan and Thatcher: The Difficult Relationship*. London: Hutchinson, 2012.

Aldrich, Richard J., *GCHQ: The Uncensored Story of Britain's Most Secret Intelligence Agency*. London: HarperPress, 2010.

Anderson, Duncan, *The Falklands War 1982*. Oxford: Osprey, 2002.

Anderson, Martin, *Revolution: The Reagan Legacy*. Stanford, CA: Hoover Institution Press, 1990.

Ashton, Nigel J., *Kennedy, Macmillan and the Cold War: The Irony of Interdependence*. Basingstoke: Palgrave Macmillan, 2002.

Bagley, Bruce M. (ed.), *Contadora and the Diplomacy of Peace in Central America: vol. 1: The United States, Central America and Contadora*. Boulder, CO: Westview Press, 1987.

Bakan, Abigail B., David Cox and Colin Leys (eds), *Imperial Power and*

Regional Trade: The Caribbean Basin Initiative. Waterloo, Ontario: Wilfrid Laurier University Press, 1993.

Ball, Stuart and Anthony Seldon (eds),*The Heath Government, 1970–1974: A Reappraisal*, revised end. Abingdon: Routledge, 2013.

Banks, William C. and Peter Raven-Hansen, *National Security Law and the Power of the Purse*. New York: Oxford University Press, 1994.

Bartlett, C. J., *The 'Special Relationship': A Political History of Anglo-American Relations since 1945*. London: Longman, 1992.

Baylis, John, *Anglo-American Defence Relations, 1939–1984: The Special Relationship*. London: Macmillan, 1984.

Baylis, John (ed.), *Anglo-American Relations since 1939: The Enduring Alliance*. Manchester: Manchester University Press, 1997.

Beck, Robert J., *The Grenada Invasion: Politics, Law, and Foreign Policy Decisionmaking*. Boulder, CO: Westview Press, 1993.

Beckett, Andy, *Pinochet in Piccadilly: Britain and Chile's Hidden History*. London: Faber & Faber, 2002.

Bicheno, Hugh, *Razor's Edge: The Unofficial History of the Falklands War*. London: Phoenix House, 2007.

Bizzaro, Salvatore, *Historical Dictionary of Chile*, 3rd edn. Lanham, MD: Scarecrow Press, 2005.

Black, George, Milton Jamail and Norma Stoltz Chinchilla, *Garrison Guatemala*. London: Zed Books, 1984.

Boyce, D. George, *The Falklands War*. Basingstoke: Palgrave Macmillan, 2005.

Brody, Richard A., *Assessing the President: The Media, Elite Opinion, and Public Support*. Stanford, CA: Stanford University Press, 1991.

Bulmer-Thomas, Victor, *The Political Economy of Central America since 1920*. Cambridge: Cambridge University Press, 1987.

Bulmer-Thomas, Victor (ed.), *Britain and Latin America: A Changing Relationship*. Cambridge: Cambridge University Press, 1989.

Burk, Kathleen, *Old World, New World: The Story of Britain and America*, 2nd edn. London: Little, Brown, 2009.

Burns, Jimmy, *The Land that Lost its Heroes: How Argentina Lost the Falklands War*, 2nd edn. London: Bloomsbury, 2002.

Campbell, Duncan, *The Unsinkable Aircraft Carrier: American Military Power in Britain*, 2nd edn. London: Paladin Grafton Books, 1986.

Campbell, John, *Edward Heath: A Biography*. London: Pimlico, 1994.

Campbell, John, *Margaret Thatcher, vol. 2: The Iron Lady*. London: Jonathan Cape, 2003.

Carothers, Thomas, *In the Name of Democracy: US Policy toward*

Latin America in the Reagan Years. Berkeley, CA: University of California Press, 1991.

Childress, Diana, *Augusto Pinochet's Chile*. Minneapolis, MN: Twenty-First Century Books, 2009.

Chomsky, Noam, *Hegemony or Survival: America's Quest for Global Dominance*. New York: Penguin, 2003.

Cockburn, Alexander, *Corruptions of Empire: Life Studies and the Reagan Era*. London: Verso, 1987.

Cockburn, Alexander and Jeffrey St. Clair, *Whiteout: The CIA, Drugs and the Press*. London: Verso, 1998.

Cockburn, Leslie, *Out of Control: The Story of the Reagan Administration's Secret War in Nicaragua, the Illegal Arms Pipeline, and the Contra Drug Connection*. London: Bloomsbury, 1988.

Cole, Ronald H., *Operation Urgent Fury: Grenada*. CreateSpace Independent Publishing Platform, 2013.

Cooper, James, *Margaret Thatcher and Ronald Reagan: A Very Political Special Relationship*. Basingstoke: Palgrave Macmillan, 2012.

Coopey, Richard and Nicholas Woodward (eds), *Britain in the 1970s: The Troubled Economy*. London: UCL Press, 1996.

Cottam, Martha L., *Images and Intervention: US Policies in Latin America*. Pittsburgh, PA: University of Pittsburgh Press, 1994.

Crandall, Russell, *Gunboat Diplomacy: US Interventions in the Dominican Republic, Grenada, and Panama*. Lanham, MD: Rowman & Littlefield, 2006.

Crozier, Brian, *Free Agent: The Unseen War, 1941–1991*. Toronto: HarperCollins, 1993.

Curtis, Mark, *Web of Deceit: Britain's Real Role in the World*. London: Vintage, 2003.

Daadler, Ivo H. and I. M. Destler, *In the Shadow of the Oval Office: Profiles of the National Security Advisors and the Presidents they Served: From JFK to George W. Bush*. New York: Simon & Schuster, 2009.

Danchev, Alex, *On Specialness: Essays in Anglo-American Relations*. Basingstoke: Macmillan, 1998.

Desch, Michael C., *Power and Military Effectiveness: The Fallacy of Democratic Triumphalism*. Baltimore, MD: Johns Hopkins University Press, 2008.

Diederich, Bernard, *Somoza and the Legacy of US Involvement in Central America*. Princeton, NJ: Markus Wiener, 2007.

Diggins, John Patrick, *Ronald Reagan: Fate, Freedom, and the Making of History*. New York: W. W. Norton, 2007.

Dimbleby, David and David Reynolds, *An Ocean Apart: The Relationship between Britain and America in the Twentieth Century*. New York: Vintage Books, 1989.

Dobson, Alan P., *The Politics of the Anglo-American Economic Special Relationship, 1940–1987*. Brighton: Wheatsheaf, 1988.

Dobson, Alan P., *Anglo-American Relations in the Twentieth Century: Of Friendship, Conflict and the Rise and Decline of Superpowers*. London: Routledge, 1995.

Dockrill, Saki, *Britain's Retreat from East of Suez: The Choice between Europe and the World? 1945–1968*. London: Palgrave Macmillan, 2002.

Dodds, Klaus, *Pink Ice: Britain and the South Atlantic Empire*. London: I. B. Tauris, 2002.

Dorrill, Stephen, *The Silent Conspiracy: Inside the Intelligence Services in the 1990s*. London: Mandarin, 1993.

Draper, Theodore, *A Very Thin Line: The Iran–Contra Affairs*. New York: Simon & Schuster, 1991.

D'Souza, Dinesh, *Ronald Reagan: How an Ordinary Man became an Extraordinary Leader*. New York: Touchstone, 1999.

Dumbrell, John, *American Foreign Policy: Carter to Clinton*. Basingstoke: Macmillan, 1997.

Dumbrell, John, *A Special Relationship: Anglo-American Relations from the Cold War to Iraq*, 2nd edn. Basingstoke: Palgrave Macmillan, 2006.

Durán, Esperanza, *European Interests in Latin America*. London: Routledge & Kegan Paul, 1985.

Ebel, Roland H., Raymond Taras and James D. Cochrane, *Political Culture and Foreign Policy in Latin America: Case Studies from the Circum-Caribbean*, Albany, NY: State University of New York Press, 1991.

Evans, Eric J., *Thatcher and Thatcherism*, 2nd edn. London: Routledge, 2004.

Falcoff, Marc, *Small Countries, Large Issues: Studies in US–Latin American Asymmetries*. Washington, DC: American Enterprise Institute for Public Research, 1984.

Fawcett, Louise and Eduardo Posada-Carbó, *Britain and Latin America: Hope in a Time of Change?* London: Institute of Latin American Studies, 1996.

Ferguson, James, *Grenada: Revolution in Reverse*. London: Latin America Bureau, 1990.

Freedman, Lawrence D., *Britain and Nuclear Weapons*. Basingstoke: Macmillan, 1980.

Freedman, Lawrence D., *Britain and the Falklands War*. Oxford: Blackwell, 1988.

Freedman, Lawrence D., *The Official History of the Falklands Campaign, vol. II: War and Diplomacy*, revised edn. London: Routledge, 2007.

Freedman, Lawrence D. and Virginia Gamba-Stonehouse, *Signals of War: The Falklands Conflict of 1982*. Princeton, NJ: Princeton University Press, 1991.

Gardiner, Nile and Stephen Thompson, *Margaret Thatcher on Leadership: Lessons for American Conservatives Today*. Washington, DC: Regnery Publishing, 2013.

Geelhoed, Bruce E., *Eisenhower, Macmillan and Allied Unity 1957–1961*. Basingstoke: Palgrave Macmillan, 2003.

Gilmore, William C., *The Grenada Intervention: Analysis and Documentation*. London: Mansell Publishing, 1984.

Gordon, Wendell, *The United Nations at the Crossroads of Reform*. New York: M. E. Sharpe, 1994.

Grandin, Greg, *Empire's Workshop: Latin America, the United States and the Rise of the New Imperialism*. New York: Metropolitan Owl Books, 2007.

Grant, C. H., *The Making of Modern Belize: Politics, Society and British Colonialism in Central America*. Cambridge: Cambridge University Press, 1976.

Gutman, Roy, *Banana Diplomacy: The Making of American Policy in Nicaragua, 1981–1987*. New York: Simon & Schuster, 1988.

Hahn, Walter F. (ed.), *Central America and the Reagan Doctrine*, Lanham, MD: University Press of America, 1987.

Hamilton, Keith and Patrick Salmon (eds), *The Year of Europe: America, Europe and the Energy Crisis, 1972–74: Documents on British Policy Overseas, Series III, vol. 4*, 2nd edn. Abingdon: Routledge, 2012.

Harmer, Tanya, *Allende's Chile and the Inter-American Cold War*. Chapel Hill, NC: University of North Carolina Press, 2011.

Hastings, Max and Simon Jenkins, *The Battle for the Falklands*, 2nd edn. London: Pan Books, 1997.

Heppell, Timothy, *The Tories: From Winston Churchill to David Cameron*. London: Bloomsbury, 2014.

Hickson, Kevin, *The IMF Crisis of 1976 and British Politics*. London: I. B. Tauris, 2005.

Hitchens, Christopher, *Blood Class and Empire: The Enduring Anglo-American Relationship*, 2nd edn. London: Atlantic Books, 2006.

Horne, Alistair, *Kissinger's Year: 1973*. London: Weidenfeld & Nicolson, 2009.

Horton, Lynn, *Peasants in Arms: War and Peace in the Mountains of Nicaragua, 1979–1994*. Athens, OH: Ohio University Press, 1998.

Hynes, Catherine, *The Year that Never Was: Heath, the Nixon Administration and the Year of Europe*. Dublin: University College Dublin Press, 2009.

Inouye, Daniel K., Lee H. Hamilton, with Joel Brinkley and Stephen Engelberg (eds), *Report of the Congressional Committees Investigating the Iran–Contra Affair: With Minority Views*. New York: Random House, 1988.

Jenkins, Simon, *Thatcher and Sons: A Revolution in Three Acts*. London: Penguin, 2007.

Kagan, Robert, *A Twilight Struggle: American Power and Nicaragua, 1977–1990*. New York: Free Press, 1996.

Kavanagh, Dennis, *Thatcherism and British Politics: The End of Consensus?* Oxford: Oxford University Press, 1987.

Kempe, Frederick, *Divorcing the Dictator: America's Bungled Affair with Noriega*. London: I. B. Tauris, 1990.

Kinzer, Stephen, *Overthrow: America's Century of Regime Change from Hawaii to Iraq*. New York: Times Books, 2007.

Kornbluh, Peter, *Nicaragua: The Price of Intervention: Reagan's Wars Against the Sandinistas*. Washington, DC: Institute for Policy Studies, 1987.

Kornbluh, Peter, *The Pinochet File: A Declassified Dossier on Atrocity and Accountability*. New York: New Press, 2004.

Krieger, Joel, *Reagan, Thatcher and the Politics of Decline*. Cambridge: Polity Press, 1986.

Lagon, Mark P., *The Reagan Doctrine: Sources of American Conduct in the Cold War's Last Chapter*. Westport, CT: Praeger, 1994.

Langley, Lester D., *America and the Americas: The United States in the Western Hemisphere*, 2nd edn. Athens, GA: University of Georgia Press, 2010.

Larres, Klaus, *Churchill's Cold War: The Politics of Personal Diplomacy*. New Haven, CT: Yale University Press, 2002.

Latin America Bureau, *The Thatcher Years: Britain and Latin America*. Latin America Bureau, London, 1988.

Laver, Roberto C., *The Falklands/Malvinas Case: Breaking the Deadlock in the Anglo-Argentine Sovereignty Dispute*. The Hague: Martinus Nijhoff, 2001.

Lehman, John F., Jr, *Command of the Seas*. Annapolis, MD: Naval Institute Press, 1988.

LeoGrande, William M., *Our Own Backyard: The United States in*

Central America, 1977–1992. Chapel Hill, NC: University of North Carolina Press, 1998.

Leonard, Thomas M., *Central America and the United States: The Search for Stability*. Athens, GA: University of Georgia Press, 1991.

Liebmann, George W., *The Last American Diplomat: John D. Negroponte and the Changing Face of US Diplomacy*. London: I. B. Tauris, 2012.

Livingstone, Grace, *America's Backyard: The United States and Latin America from the Monroe Doctrine to the War on Terror*. London: Zed Books, 2009.

Louis, William Roger, *Ends of British Imperialism: The Scramble for Empire, Suez and Decolonization*. London: I. B. Tauris, 2006.

Lundestad, Geir, *The United States and Western Europe since 1945: From 'Empire' by Invitation to Transatlantic Drift*. Oxford: Oxford University Press, 2005.

Lynch, Edward A., *The Cold War's Last Battlefield: Reagan, the Soviets and Central America*. Albany, NY: State University of New York Press, 2011.

Lyons, John F., *America in the British Imagination, 1945 to the Present*. New York: Palgrave Macmillan, 2013.

Mares, David R. and Francisco Rojas Aravena, *The United States and Chile: Coming in from the Cold*. New York: Routledge, 2001.

Martin, Tony, with Dessima Williams (eds), *In Nobody's Backyard: The Grenada Revolution in its Own Words, vol. II: Facing the World*. Dover, MA: Majority Press, 1983.

Matlock, Jack F., Jr, *Reagan and Gorbachev: How the Cold War Ended*. New York: Random House, 2004.

McClintock, Michael, *The American Connection, vol. 1: State Terror and Popular Resistance in El Salvador*. London: Zed Books, 1985.

Mercer, Derrik, Geoff Mungham and Kevin Williams, *The Fog of War: The Media on the Battlefield*. London: Heinemann, 1987.

Mermin, Jonathan, *Debating War and Peace: Media Coverage of US Intervention in the Post-Vietnam Era*. Princeton, NJ: Princeton University Press, 1999.

Middlebrook, Martin, *The Falklands War 1982*. London: Penguin, 2001.

Miller, Rory, *Britain and Latin America in the Nineteenth and Twentieth Centuries*. London: Longman, 1993.

Mills, Thomas C., *Post-War Planning on the Periphery: Anglo-American Economic Diplomacy in South America, 1939–1945*. Edinburgh: Edinburgh University Press, 2012.

Moore, Charles, *Margaret Thatcher: The Authorized Biography, vol. 1: Not For Turning*. London: Penguin, 2014.

Morgan, Kenneth O., *Callaghan: A Life*, Oxford: Oxford University Press, 1997.

Morris, Edmund, *Dutch: A Memoir of Ronald Reagan*. New York: Modern Library, 1999.

Morris, Kenneth E., *Unfinished Revolution: Daniel Ortega and Nicaragua's Struggle for Liberation*. Chicago, IL: Lawrence Hill Books, 2010.

Niskanen, William A., *Reaganomics: An Insider's Account of the Policies and the People*, Oxford: Oxford University Press, 1988.

O'Shaughnessy, *Grenada: Revolution, Invasion and Aftermath*. London: Sphere Books, 1984.

O'Sullivan, John, *The President, the Pope, and the Prime Minister: Three Who Changed the World*. Washington, DC: Regnery Publishing, 2006.

Parsi, Trita, *Treacherous Alliance: The Secret Dealings of Israel, Iran, and the US*. New Haven, CT: Yale University Press, 2007.

Parsons, Michael, *The Falklands War*. Stroud: Sutton Publishing, 2000.

Pastor, Robert A., *Congress and the Politics of US Foreign Economic Policy*. Berkeley, CA: University of California Press, 1982.

Pastor, Robert A., *Condemned to Repetition: The United States and Nicaragua*. Princeton, NJ: Princeton University Press, 1987.

Payne, Anthony, Paul Sutton and Tony Thorndike, *Grenada: Revolution and Invasion*. London: Croom Helm, 1984.

Pickering, Jeffrey, *Britain's Withdrawal from East of Suez: The Politics of Retrenchment*. New York: St. Martin's Press, 1998.

Podmore, Will, *British Foreign Policy since 1870*. Bloomington, IN: Xlibris, 2008.

Prados, John, *Safe for Democracy: The Secret Wars of the CIA*. Chicago, IL: Ivan R. Dee, 2006.

Quainton, Anthony C. E., *'Five or One', Nicaragua and its Neighbors*. Miami, FL: Latin American and Caribbean Center, Florida International University, 1984.

Raines, Edgar F. and Richard Winship Stewart, *Operation Urgent Fury: The Invasion of Grenada, October 1983*. Washington, DC: US Government Printing Office, 2008.

Reeves, Richard, *President Nixon: Alone in the White House*. New York: Simon & Schuster, 2007.

Reynolds, David, *From World War to Cold War: Churchill, Roosevelt and the International History of the 1940s*. Oxford: Oxford University Press, 2007.

Richardson, Louise, *When Allies Differ: Anglo-American Relations during the Suez and Falklands Crises*. Basingstoke: Macmillan, 1996.

Robinson, William I. and Kent Norsworthy, *David and Goliath: Washington's War against Nicaragua*. London: Zed Books, 1987.

Ryan, David, *US–Sandinista Diplomatic Relations: Voice of Intolerance*. Basingstoke: Macmillan, 1995.

Sandford, Gregory and Richard Vigilante, *Grenada: The Untold Story*. Lanham, MD: Madison Books, 1984.

Schoultz, Lars, *Beneath the United States: A History of US Policy Toward Latin America*. Cambridge, MA: Harvard University Press, 2009.

Schweizer, Peter, *Reagan's War: The Epic Story of His Forty-Year Struggle and Final Triumph over Communism*. New York: Anchor Books, 2003.

Scoon, Paul, *Survival for Service: My Experiences as Governor General of Grenada*. Oxford: Macmillan-Caribbean, 2003.

Scott, James M., *Deciding to Intervene: The Reagan Doctrine and American Foreign Policy,*. Durham, NC: Duke University Press, 1996.

Seldon, Anthony and Daniel Collings, *Britain under Thatcher*. Harlow: Longman, 2000.

Shields, David Brandon, *Kennedy and Macmillan: Cold War Politics*. Lanham, MD: University Press of America, 2006.

Shoman, Assad, *Belize's Independence and Decolonization in Latin America: Guatemala, Britain, and the UN*. New York: Palgrave Macmillan, 2010.

Sigmund, Paul E., *The Overthrow of Allende and the Politics of Chile, 1964–1976*. Pittsburgh, PA: University of Pittsburgh Press, 1977.

Sklar, Holly, *Washington's War on Nicaragua*. Boston, MA: South End Press, 1988.

Smith, Geoffrey, *Reagan and Thatcher*. London: Bodley Head, 1990.

Smith, Hazel, *Nicaragua: Self-determination and Survival*. London: Pluto Press, 1993.

Smith, Hazel, *European Union Foreign Policy and Central America*. Basingstoke: Macmillan, 1995.

Smith, Joseph, *The United States and Latin America: A History of American Diplomacy, 1776–2000*. London: Routledge, 2005.

Stavridis, Stelios and Christopher Hill, *The Domestic Sources of Foreign Policy: West European Reactions to the Falklands Crisis*. Oxford: Berg, 1996.

Thatcher, Carol, *Below the Parapet: The Biography of Denis Thatcher*. Bath: Chivers Press, 1997.

Thornton, Richard C., *The Falklands Sting: Reagan, Thatcher, and Argentina's Bomb*. London: Brassey's, 1998.

Thornton, Richard C., *The Reagan Revolution II: Rebuilding the Western Alliance*. Oxford: Trafford Publishing, 2004.

Tower, John, Edmund Muskie and Brent Scowcroft, *The Tower Commission Report: The Full Text of the President's Special Review Board*. New York: Bantam, 1987.

Valdés, Juan Gabriel, *Pinochet's Economists: The Chicago School in Chile*. Cambridge: Cambridge University Press, 1995.

Walker, Thomas W., *Reagan versus the Sandinistas: The Undeclared War on Nicaragua*. Boulder, CO: Westview Press, 1987.

Walker, Thomas W. and Christine J. Wade, *Nicaragua: Living in the Shadow of the Eagle*. Boulder, CO: Westview Press, 2011.

Walldorf, C. William, Jr, *Just Politics: Human Rights and the Foreign Policy of Great Powers*. New York: Cornell University Press, 2008.

Wallison, Peter J., *Ronald Reagan: The Power of Conviction and the Success of his Presidency*. Boulder, CO: Westview Press, 2004.

Wapshott, Nicholas, *Ronald Reagan and Margaret Thatcher: A Political Marriage*. New York: Sentinel, 2007.

Wapshott, Nicholas and George Brock, *Thatcher*. London: Futura, 1983.

Watt, Donald Cameron, *Succeeding John Bull: America in Britain's Place, 1900–1975*. Cambridge: Cambridge University Press, 1984.

Woodward, Bob, *Veil: The Secret Wars of the CIA 1981–1987*. London: Simon & Schuster, 1987.

Yoshitani, Gail E. S., *Reagan on War: A Reappraisal of the Weinberger Doctrine, 1980–1984*. College Station, TX: Texas A&M University Press, 2011.

Young, Hugo, *One of Us*. London: Macmillan, 1989.

Ziegler, Philip, *Edward Heath: The Authorised Biography*. London: HarperPress, 2010.

Zimmermann, Matilde, *Sandinista: Carlos Fonseca and the Nicaraguan Revolution*. Durham, NC: Duke University Press, 2004.

Articles and chapters

Atkinson, David, 'Trade, aid and investment since 1950', in Victor Bulmer-Thomas (ed.), *Britain and Latin America: A Changing Relationship*. Cambridge: Cambridge University Press, 1989, pp. 103–20.

Barnes, Jon, 'Birds of a feather: Britain and Chile', in Latin America Bureau, *The Thatcher Years: Britain and Latin America*. London: Latin America Bureau, 1988, pp. 54–66.

Blasier, Cole, 'Security: the extracontinental dimension', in Kevin J. Middlebrook and Carlos Rico (eds), *The United States and Latin America in the 1980s*. Pittsburgh, PA: University of Pittsburgh Press, 1988, pp. 523–64.

Bluth, Christoph, 'The British resort to force in the Falklands/Malvinas conflict 1982: international law and war theory', *Journal of Peace Research*, 24(1) (March 1987): 5–20.

Boyle, Francis A., Abram Chayes, Isaak Dore, Richard Falk, Martin Feinrider, C. Clyde Ferguson, Jr, J. David Fine, Keith Nunes and Burns Weston, 'International lawlessness in Grenada', *American Journal of International Law*, 78(1) (January 1984): 172–5.

Bratton, Patrick and Wallace Thies, 'When governments collide in the South Atlantic: Britain coerces Argentina during the Falklands War', *Comparative Strategy*, 30(1) (2011): 1–27.

Burk, Kathleen, 'Old world, new world: Great Britain and America from the beginning', in John Dumbrell and Axel R. Schäfer (eds), *America's 'Special Relationships': Foreign and Domestic Aspects of the Politics of Alliance*. Abingdon: Routledge, 2009, pp. 24–44.

Connell-Smith, Gordon, 'The OAS and the Falklands conflict', *World Today*, 38(9) (September 1982): 340–7.

Connell-Smith, Gordon, 'The Grenada invasion in historical perspective: from Monroe to Reagan', *Third World Quarterly*, 6(2) (April 1984): 432–45.

Cuthbert, Marlene, 'Ideological differences in press coverage of the Grenada crisis', in Stuart H. Surlin and Walter C. Soderlund (eds), *Mass Media and the Caribbean*. New York: Gordon & Breach, 1990, pp. 331–50.

Duncan, W. Raymond, 'Soviet interests in Latin America: new opportunities and old constraints', *Journal of Interamerican Studies and World Affairs*, 26(2) (May 1984): 163–98.

Durán, Esperanza, 'The Contadora approach to peace in Central America', *World Today*, 40(8/9) (August/September 1984): 347–54.

Ferguson, James, James Painter and Jenny Pearce, 'Under attack: Central America and the Caribbean', in Latin America Bureau, *The Thatcher Years: Britain and Latin America*. London: Latin America Bureau, 1988, pp. 26–53.

Freedman, Lawrence D., 'The impact of the Falklands conflict on international affairs', in Stephen Badsey, Rob Havers and Mark Grove (eds), *The Falklands Conflict Twenty Years On: Lessons for the Future*. Abingdon: Frank Cass, 2005, pp. 9–22.

Freedman, Lawrence D., 'The special relationship, then and now', *Foreign Affairs*, 85(3): (May/June 2006): 61–73.

Freedman, Lawrence D., 'The Falklands/Malvinas conflict', in Andrew Dorman and Greg Kennedy (eds), *War and Diplomacy: From World War I to the War on Terrorism*. Dulles, VA: Potomac Books, 2008, pp. 131–47.

Gompert, David C., 'American diplomacy and the Haig mission: an insider's perspective', in Alberto R. Coll and Anthony C. Arend (eds), *The Falklands War: Lessons for Strategy, Diplomacy, and International Law*. London: George Allen & Unwin, 1985, pp. 106–17.

Grabendorff, Wolf, 'European Community relations with Latin America', *Journal of Interamerican Studies and World Affairs*, 29(4) (Winter 1987/8): 69–87.

Graham, Robert, 'British policy towards Latin America', in Victor Bulmer-Thomas (ed.), *Britain and Latin America: A Changing Relationship*. Cambridge: Cambridge University Press, 1989, pp. 52–67.

Hendershot, Robert M., '"Affection is the cement which binds us": understanding the cultural sinews of the Anglo-American special relationship', in Alan P. Dobson and Steve Marsh (eds), *Anglo-American Relations: Contemporary Perspectives*. Abingdon: Routledge, 2013, pp. 52–81.

Humphreys, R. A., 'The Anglo-Guatemalan dispute', *International Affairs*, 24(3) (July 1948): 387–404.

Jonas, Susanne, 'Democratization through peace: the difficult case of Guatemala', *Journal of Interamerican Studies and World Affairs*, 42(4) (Special Issue: Globalization and Democratization in Guatemala) (Winter 2000): v–38.

Joyner, Christopher C., 'Reflections on the lawfulness of invasion', *American Journal of International Law*, 78(1) (January 1984): 131–44.

Kinney, Douglas, 'Anglo-Argentine diplomacy and the Falklands crisis', in Alberto R. Coll and Anthony C. Arend (eds), *The Falklands War: Lessons for Strategy, Diplomacy, and International Law*. London: George Allen & Unwin, 1985, pp. 81–105.

Kirton, Claremont D., 'Grenada and the IMF: the PRG's Extended Fund Facility program, 1983', *Latin American Perspectives*, 16(3) (Summer 1989): 121–44.

Lehman, John F., Jr, 'The Falklands War: reflections on the "Special Relationship"', *RUSI Journal*, 157(6) (December 2012): 80–5.

Lewis Feldman, David, 'The United States role in the Malvinas crisis, 1982: misguidance and misperception in Argentina's decision to go to war', *Journal of Interamerican Studies and World Affairs*, 27(2) (Summer 1985): 1–22.

Marsh, Steve, 'The Anglo-American defence relationship', in Alan P. Dobson and Steve Marsh (eds), *Anglo-American Relations: Contemporary Perspectives*. Abingdon: Routledge, 2013, pp. 179–206.

Martin, Lisa L., 'Institutions and cooperation: sanctions during the Falkland Islands conflict', *International Security*, 16(1) (Spring 1992): 143–78.

Menon, P. K., 'The Anglo-Guatemalan territorial dispute over the colony of Belize (British Honduras)', *Journal of Latin American Studies*, 11(2) (November 1979): 343–71.

Middlebrook, Kevin J. and Carlos Rico, 'The United States and Latin America in the 1980s: change, complexity, and contending perspectives', in Kevin J. Middlebrook and Carlos Rico (eds), *The United States and Latin America in the 1980s*. Pittsburgh, PA: University of Pittsburgh Press, 1988, pp. 3–58.

Norton Moore, John, 'The Inter-American system snarls in Falklands War', *American Journal of International Law*, 76(4) (October 1982): 830–1.

Norton Moore, John, 'Grenada and the international double standard', *American Journal of International Law*, 78(1) (January 1984): 145–68.

Parsons, Anthony, 'The Falklands crisis in the United Nations, 31 March–14 June 1982', *International Affairs*, 59(2) (Spring 1983): 169–78.

Reynolds, David, 'A "special relationship?" America, Britain and the international order since the Second World War', *International Affairs*, 62(1) (Winter 1985/6): 1–20.

Reynolds, David, 'Rethinking Anglo-American relations', *International Affairs*, 65(1) (Winter 1988/9): 89–111.

Roett, Riordan, 'The debt crisis and economic development in Latin America', in Jonathan Hartlyn, Lars Schoultz and Augusto Varas (eds), *The United States and Latin America in the 1990s: Beyond the Cold War*. Chapel Hill, NC: University of North Carolina Press, 1992, pp. 131–51.

Rogers, William D., 'The "unspecial relationship" in Latin America', in

William Roger Louis and Hedley Bull (eds), *The 'Special Relationship': Anglo-American Relations since 1945*. Oxford: Clarendon Press, 1989, pp. 341–54.

Rubenberg, Cheryl A., 'US policy toward Nicaragua and Iran and the Iran–Contra affair: reflections on the continuity of American foreign policy', *Third World Quarterly*, 10(4) (October 1988): 1467–504.

Rubner, Michael, 'The Reagan administration, the 1973 War Powers Resolution, and the invasion of Grenada', *Political Science Quarterly*, 100(4) (Winter 1985/6): 627–47.

Scott, James M., 'Interbranch rivalry and the Reagan Doctrine in Nicaragua', *Political Science Quarterly*, 112(2) (Summer 1997): 237–60.

Shackleton, Lord Edward, 'The Falkland Islands and their history', *Geographical Journal*, 249(1) (March 1983): 1–4.

Thomas, David, 'The United States factor in British relations with Latin America', in Victor Bulmer-Thomas (ed.), *Britain and Latin America: A Changing Relationship*. Cambridge: Cambridge University Press, 1989, pp. 68–82.

Treharne, Sally-Ann, 'The Reagan presidency in retrospect: an assessment of Reagan's legacy', in Michael Patrick Cullinane and Clare Frances Elliott (eds), *Perspectives on Presidential Leadership: An International View of the White House*. New York: Routledge, 2014, pp. 164–78.

Waddell, D. A. G., 'Developments in the Belize question 1946–1960', *American Journal of International Law*, 55(2) (April 1961): 459–69.

Waters, Maurice, 'The invasion of Grenada, 1983 and the collapse of legal norms', *Journal of Peace Research*, 23(3) (September 1986): 229–46.

Watt, David, 'Perceptions of the United States in Europe, 1945–83', in Lawrence D. Freedman (ed.), *The Troubled Alliance: Atlantic Relations in the 1980s*. New York: St. Martin's Press, 1983, pp. 28–43.

Wilkinson, Michael D., 'The Chile Solidarity Campaign and British government policy towards Chile, 1973–1990', *European Review of Latin American and Caribbean Studies (Revista Europea de Estudios Latinoamericanos y del Caribe)*, No. 52 (June 1992), pp. 57–74.

Williams, Gary, 'The tail that wagged the dog: the Organisation of Eastern Caribbean States' role in the 1983 intervention in Grenada', *European Review of Latin American and Caribbean Studies (Revista*

Europea de Estudios Latinoamericanos y del Caribe), No. 61 (December 1996): 95–115.

Williams, Gary, 'Prelude to an intervention: Grenada 1983', *Journal of Latin American Studies*, 29(1) (February 1997): 131–69.

Williams, Gary, 'Brief encounter: Grenadian Prime Minister Maurice Bishop's visit to Washington', *Journal of Latin American Studies*, 34(3) (August 2002): 659–85

Winegard, Timothy C., 'Canadian diplomacy and the 1982 Falklands War', *International History Review*, 35(1) (2013): 162–83.

Index

Page numbers followed by 'n' indicate chapter notes. Page numbers followed by *biog* refer to the Appendix, which includes interviewees' subsequent honours.

EU representative:
Easy Access System Europe
Mustamäe tee 50, 10621 Tallinn, Estonia
Gpsr.requests@easproject.com